'I've never been to Jamaica, but there's no one I'd rather send on my behalf than Chris Salewicz. His combination of awesome erudition, self-deprecating dry wit and enviable powers of evocation and description render this book strickly irie all the way'
    Charles Shaar Murray

'Much more than a travelogue, or a musical history, *Rude Boy* is a thrilling and highly personal journey to the very heart of the most vibrantly creative and anarchistic island on earth. Nobody knows more about Jamaica and its culture than Chris Salewicz and no one has ever written about it with such sparkling *élan*'
    Mick Brown, *Daily Telegraph*

'Jamaica – a paradise, or a pair of dice? This book has the answer: an essential insight into one island that has culturally colonized the world. Crucial!'
    Don Letts

'A personal odyssey which splendidly captures the intoxicating flavours and unruly spirit of Jamaica. From Rasta reasonings to tourist rum bars, from sweltering sound systems to enchanted landscapes, Chris Salewicz stays unerringly on the island's vital pulse'
    Neil Spencer, *Observer*

Dearest Ch

Happy Chri,
lots of love, Maeve xxx

By the same author

The Pretenders
Paul McCartney: the Biography
Billy Bragg: Midnights in Moscow
Bob Marley: Songs of Freedom
Jimi Hendrix: the Ultimate Experience
Punk: the Illustrated History of a Music Revolution
Oliver Stone: the Making of His Movies
George Lucas: the Making of His Movies
Firefly: Noël Coward in Jamaica

RUDE BOY

Once Upon a Time in Jamaica

CHRIS SALEWICZ

VICTOR GOLLANCZ
LONDON

A Gollancz Paperback Original

First published in Great Britain in 2000 by Victor Gollancz
An imprint of The Orion Publishing Group
Orion House, 5 Upper St Martin's Lane, London WC2H 9EA

Permission to reproduce lyrics from Luciano's 'How Can You'
is gratefully acknowledged: © XtM Sounds
All photographs and illustrations © Adrian Boot

A CIP catalogue record for this book is available
from the British Library

ISBN 0 575 06522 2

Typeset in Great Britain by Selwood Systems, Midsomer Norton
Printed by Butler & Tanner Ltd, Frome and London

Contents

Acknowledgements

The first story I ever wrote was when I was nine years old: it was a pirate story, set in Jamaica. I loved the island before I had even been there: as it has for so many people, Jamaica – the Rude Boy of the title – has clearly long held a place in my life that would appear to be utterly disproportionate to its size. In lesser or greater ways, all the following have helped in the writing of this book:

Abede, Julian Alexander, Bagga, Jon and Ziggi Baker, Buju Banton, Steve Barrow, Beenie Man, Chris Blackwell, Vas Blackwood, Anthony B, Brian Blevins, John Bold, Mrs Cedella Booker, Adrian Boot, Graham Boynton, David Boxer, Carl Bradshaw, Mick Brown, Mrs Brown, Burning Spear, Fattis Burrell, Buru, Capleton, Carlene the Dancehall Queen, Lucinda Cook, Caroline Coon, Carolyn Cooper, Karen Cova, Valerie Cowan, Kwesi Dickson, Dipstick, Rick Elgood, Pamela Esterson, Marianne Faithfull, Suzanne Fenn, Willie Fielding, Oliver Foot, Neville Garrick, Dan Genetti, the Gladiators, Vivien Goldman, Granny Ivy, Greggie, Cecil Gutzmore, Martin Hayman, Topper Headon, the Heptones, Perry Henzell, Toots Hibbert, Joseph Hill, Inner Circle, Diane Jobson, Dickie Jobson, Wayne Jobson, Mick Jones, Guy Kennaway, Don Letts, Luciano, John Lydon, Versa Manos, Bob Marley, Rita Marley, Cedella Marley, Ziggy Marley, Mashie, Gaylene Martin, Janis Marsh, Denise Mills, Suzette Newman, Lee 'Scratch' Perry, Mike Petty, Mortimer Planner, James Plummer, Ian Preece, Humphrey Price, John Pringle, Simon

Puxley, Penny Reel, Jumbo Van Rennen, David Rodigan, Alex Manos Salewicz, Cole Salewicz, Paul Simonon, Sizzla, Cathy Snipper, Neil Spencer, Roger Steffens, the staff of Strawberry Hill, Butch Stewart, Jah Stone, Joe Strummer, Jonathan Stuart, Peter Tosh, Ingrid von Essen, Bunny Wailer, Timothy White, Tom Wilkinson, Richard Williams, Bobby Wilmott, Stephen Wood, Trevor Wyatt, Tapper Zukie.

Please don't take it personally if you feel your name has been accidentally omitted from this list: you are not alone – as none of us are.

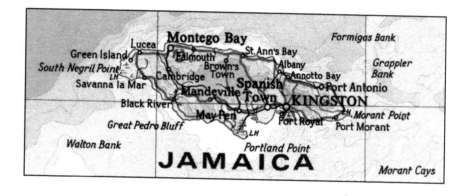

For my father Mieczyslaw Salewicz,
April 2 1909 – May 11 1997

12 *August 1995*

When we land four hours late at Kingston's Norman Manley airport, I am exhausted after the flight from London via Miami. I am excited too, and anxious: will Carl Bradshaw, the film producer and actor, be at the airport to meet me? Bradshaw ran for Jamaica in the 1970 Olympics, but is famous on the island for his part in Perry Henzell's 1972 film classic *The Harder They Come* as the badman Jose, by which name he's universally known on the streets of Jamaica.

In my overhead locker are a brand-new Apple Mac Power-book and printer, my proud new equipment. In 1989 I had arrived in JA with a similarly new video-8 camera and been obliged to deposit $US300 to ensure I didn't sell it while on the island (money I would otherwise have spent in Jamaica, but I suppose that's another matter). If Bradshaw isn't there I'm not sure whether I have the energy to deal with the officious exchanges that will take place.

But Carl Bradshaw is there, at the end of the long, scruffy corridor that leads to immigration, looking cool and exuding good vibes in a lightweight grey and silver check suit. The whites of his eyes are almost bright red.

'Give me your passport and arrivals card,' he says.

Already there are long lines at immigration. A senior immigration official, a tall man crisp in his white shirt and pressed black pants, stands nearby. Bradshaw, whom he evidently recognizes, speaks in his ear. After a minute Bradshaw follows the man into his office; emerging with my documents, the official goes over to an immigration booth and stamps my passport.

Stepping past the rest of the plane's passengers who are still waiting to be admitted to Jamaica, I get a glowing special-treatment buzz, and for a moment I feel guilty. My pair of bags, the battered maroon Pierre Cardin and the solid vinyl case I'd bought at an Arab shop in London's Queensway two days before, believing that its canary-yellow colour would mean I would never pick up the wrong bag, are already rattling around the rickety carousel. In my jet-lagged haze I've picked a baggage cart that has no supporting struts underneath, which seems very Zen Jamaican. Bradshaw grabs another one and dumps my luggage on it.

Then we head for customs: two officials stand at the right of four platformed booths. 'Hey, rude boy,' Bradshaw collectively greets them, his familiarity indicating status. They clearly recognize him.

Then it begins.

Is the computer used?

Yes.

How long have I had it?

I just got it.

So it's new, not used.

Just look at the fingerprint marks on the keyboard, Bradshaw blusters.

The one on his left says he can't see any.

'Anyway, it doesn't matter: is the tools of his trade we have here. Can't mek a man pay for tools of his trade.'

Receipts are produced, serial numbers checked. I produce a letter from the people with whom I have a contract to work in Jamaica, promising I will take the computer out of the country again. The official on the left disappears with it.

'Mon here to write new film to put JA on the map – you can all have parts in it, with Grace Jones, Naomi Campbell,' Bradshaw promises shamelessly.

'I wrote a book here last year about Bob Marley, and your prime minister held it aloft and said it was a tribute to Jamaica,' I say, to no great effect, and feel embarrassed.

The other official comes back. Laboriously he notes down the serial numbers on the computer and printer. 'OK, you can go through,' he says.

We pack up the equipment.

'Respect,' says Bradshaw.

'Respect,' say I, a little self-consciously.

As we exit the customs hall I am obliged to transfer my bags from the cart to a porter's trolley for the very short walk to the car park; the result of a local official effort at ensuring employment that all the same never fails to baffle first-time visitors to the island.

We step past a trio of TV sets on which a West Indies cricket match is avidly being watched by massed ranks of Jamaicans sitting by the arrivals exit.

And then we are outside the terminal building, encountering anarchy on a scale that reminds me of Lagos airport. (Although here at least the customs officials aren't running after us demanding 'dash' because they've let me through without too much hassle – as happened on my only visit to the Nigerian city.) Men leap in front of the porter's trolley demanding to put the luggage in their cabs. Bradshaw is assaulted with demands for money. A white Toyota Corolla, that archetypal saloon car of the Third World, backs towards us, nearly knocking over the porter. His eyes flashing bright red, his balding short locks twisted into what look like fuses for gunpowder kegs, Bradshaw looks like a pirate. For me this impression is enhanced by the knowledge that the cracked concrete on which he is standing is the approximate site of the former Port Royal, the headquarters of the buccaneer baron Henry Morgan. Bradshaw snaps instructions, and the luggage is hefted up and hoisted into the boot of the Corolla.

Bradshaw ushers me into the shotgun seat and gets behind the wheel. Paul, his baseball-capped son, jumps in the back.

Bradshaw starts the engine and drives off. As he does so, we pass a giant billboard on which an enormous image of Bob Marley represents the Jamaica Tourist Board. It is designed so

3

that Bob's smiling eyes appear to be gazing into your own from whatever angle you look at it.

So naturally he appears to catch my eye. Despite the clear contrivance of the image, his universal good vibes have their effect. Almost immediately everything feels different, and my stress appears to dissipate utterly.

Hello, Jamaica, good to be back. Thank you for having me again.

February 1978

I first came to Jamaica in February 1978, on the same reggae fanatics' pilgrimage as John 'Johnny Rotten' Lydon and the Rastafarian film director Don Letts, who were engaged in a similar rite of passage. Lydon had been despatched to Jamaica by Virgin Records boss Richard Branson with a purpose that was double-edged: to hide him away from the media spotlight after the break-up of the Sex Pistols the previous month; and to advise on which Jamaican acts Branson should sign up for Virgin's new Front Line reggae label. For months before my instinct had told me that I would shortly be going to Jamaica – though at the time there was no concrete reason to justify such a feeling. When Lech Kowalski, an American film director with whom I had been working on the punk documentary *DOA*, suddenly suggested I travel down to the island to recce the possibilities of shooting Lydon's visit there, I jumped at the offer. Although I quickly saw there was no chance at all of doing any filming, I stayed on to write about my experiences for the *New Musical Express*, for which I was then working.

Later I fell out with Lydon at a shoot for a Big Audio Dynamite video in which he had a cameo part: he smashed the side of my head with a Red Stripe can for daring to disagree with him (I had forgotten the rules for dealing with petulant pop stars). But I remained good friends with Letts, and he was part of the team I was now, in 1995, working with in Jamaica.

That first time in Jamaica had been a profound experience. As well as Rotten and Don Letts, the photographers Dennis Morris and Kate Simon were there, together with Vivien Goldman, another writer for the music press. All Kingston's top rankings would come by the first-floor annexe of the Sheraton where Richard Branson had booked some suites. With Lee 'Scratch' Perry producing, Rotten re-recorded the Pistols' 'Anarchy In The UK' and 'Holidays In The Sun': the resulting reggae versions of the songs were not a patch on the originals, however. 'They were getting paid, and it sounded like it,' said Letts at the time.

Most mornings the assembled collective would pay a visit to the great deejay U Roy, whose music and chalice were of roughly equivalent attraction. One night at the Zinc Fence Club, early in the evening at a sound system he had organized, U Roy passed Rotten and Letts a pipe of lamb's-breath herb. The next thing they knew, U Roy was knocking them on the shoulder to wake them, telling them it was time to leave. Tapper Zukie took them down to Trench Town. What's all this with guns? they asked him. And, as though to prove a point, Tapper's brethren all pulled out their revolvers and automatics.

That trip in 1978 marked a major turning point in my life. As soon as I arrived there, I fell in love with Jamaica. Thanks to the palpable energy in that era of positive change that was punk, I'd just embarked on a new life course in which Jamaica had already played a part. In the UK punk was a chapter marker for a cultural shift that ushered in the last quarter of the twentieth century; and its fusion with reggae was integral to this, epitomized for me by two specific tunes: Bob Marley's 'Punky Reggae Party' and 'Two Sevens Clash', a song by Culture that celebrated the numerological shift to a higher level said to take place with the advent of 1977. Jamaica healed and restored me and continued this internal sea-change of attitude. '*Positive*, man,' Lee 'Scratch' Perry, the Picasso of sound, would laughingly bray at me at his Black Ark recording studio; I would listen, and take it on board.

Jamaica in early 1978 was like nothing else I had ever experienced: sunshine, sultriness, shots at any time of day or night, and above all a sense of universal profundity that slid into me the moment I stepped off the plane to the airport tarmac.

Two months after I arrived there, Bob Marley was to head the legendary One Love Peace Concert, on 22 April 1978, in Kingston under the auspices of the Twelve Tribes of Israel, the branch of Rastafari of which Bob was a member. At north London's Keskidee Centre, at a video shoot for his tune 'Is This Love' (one of the children in the audience was a very young Naomi Campbell), the Tuff Gong, as Bob Marley was nicknamed, had been approached by Claudie Massop, Bucky Marshall and Tony Welch, three Kingstonians who did not let their positions as rankin' gunmen interfere with their shared insight that the undeclared civil war in Jamaica was seriously out of hand. During his performance of the song 'Jammin'' at the open-air event, Bob held aloft and joined together the reluctant hands of Prime Minister Michael Manley of the People's National Party and the opposition leader Edward Seaga (Jamaica Labour Party), two sworn enemies, thereby stage-managing one of the great symbolic moments of contemporary Jamaican life.

Riven by its civil war inspired by the CIA and the Cuban secret service, Jamaica was undergoing an armed struggle as deadly as anything in the nearby countries of El Salvador or Nicaragua or the more distant Northern Ireland. A consensus of opinion, incidentally, holds that there is a Jamaica–Ireland connection, both actual and metaphorical: Ireland provided a sizable amount of the indentured labour that was strapped into service alongside the African slaves; both are islands once ruled entirely by the British; both have poetry and a fondness for mysticism in their nation's souls; both are similarly eccentric and absurd, in a manner of which Samuel Beckett would have been proud.

But the political conditions that exist in Jamaica are hardly the same as those of the United States or western Europe; they are more akin to those of a banana republic. It often seems as though some Jamaicans have utterly misunderstood the dividing line between reality and art, allowing it to become blurred and indistinct – a direct consequence, you may feel, of their enthusiasm for spaghetti westerns.

One of the most specific and immediate problems I encountered on that first visit to Jamaica was that I could hardly understand anything anyone was saying to me. In the general cool stakes, this is not very hip, but everyone eventually admits to having had the same experience. (It is especially disconcerting being unable to understand others speaking in a language that is ostensibly one's own – as might be appreciated by many English speakers who have spent a night out in Glasgow, for example.) Many words in Jamaican speech mutate with a poetic, innocent beauty that to me renders their meaning with an even greater exactness: for example, I love the way that old people can be described as 'ageable', or good-hearted individuals are said to be 'heartical'. Contemporary street terms like 'bashment', which basically means a great night out incorporating dancing, music and general sexy hedonism, are simply fabulous words for any lover of language.

On that trip I encountered for the first time new spins on English words in which the wit and invention of their development provides a wonderfully explicit philosophical high: the verb 'overstand', for example, as a development on the need to 'understand' a matter – clearly, you are unable to understand a matter fully unless you can thoroughly overstand it. Many such words have entered the Jamaican vocabulary through believers in the Rastafarian faith, which encourages the semantical twists that occur during lengthy, frequently ganja-inspired 'reasonings' – another splendid, self-explanatory term whose usage is particular to Jamaica.

7

Because of the different intonations placed on syllables, moreover, words I knew as an everyday part of my English vocabulary suddenly meant nothing to me at all: when Robbie Shakespeare asked me for a *cass*ette, instead of for a cass*ette*, he had to repeat the word several times before I could take in what he meant.

The ubiquitous Jamaican mutation of the basic 'th' sound, in which the 'h' is dropped (hence in the written form the word 'the' is frequently rendered as 'de'), can also lead from time to time to considerable, quite surreal confusion. 'Where exactly in Florida is it that your relatives live?' I ask a friend. 'Dem a' Fort Lauderdale,' she muses. Then she thinks again for a moment and changes her mind: 'Fourt' Lauderdale? No, Fift' Lauderdale.' 'Fort Lauderdale,' I correct her, initially a little baffled. 'Fourt'? No, no: it definitely a Fift' Lauderdale dem a live at.'

In the seminal text about the Jamaican language, Professor Frederic G. Cassidy's *Jamaica Talk*, a simple explanation is proffered for this 'th' problem:

speakers of West African languages trying to learn English in Jamaica already had most of the sounds in their possession, but lacked our *th* sounds, often *v*, and though many had *r* where some had *l* they seldom used both contrasting sounds together. Jamaican folk speech still has *dis ting*, *bery* and *bickle* for *very* and *victuals*, and numerous interchanges of *l* and *r*. [Is this one of the reasons the Japanese seem to feel so at home here?] The difficulty with the *th*'s may have been increased by the fact that many Welsh and Irish speakers were about who themselves stumbled with these English sounds and cannot have furnished perfect models.

Somewhere down the line I found that I had come to accept and enjoy English written in patois. And at the same time a shock came over me when I realized that before this acceptance I had secretly filed it mentally away as childish, quaint and naive. Finally, however, I had felt the force and immense power of what is essentially literary dub, the language of Afro-Saxon. And, like audio dub, much of the meaning is in the spaces in between. Remember the ethereal nature of dub music: reduce something to almost nothing, and you have almost something. Compared with other countries, Jamaica is such a 'version' – a 'Version Galore', to steal the title of an early U Roy LP.

After spending three or so weeks in Kingston on that first trip I had taken, for sixteen US dollars, a twenty-minute light plane trip from Tinsom Pen airport in downtown Kingston over the mountains to Port Antonio's tiny Ken Jones airport, quite distant from the town. From there I travelled to the other side of Port Antonio to the small, rather rough hamlet of Drapers, to the home of a friend of the photographer Adrian Boot, who had once taught at Titchfield the local secondary school.

Difficult to get to, its potholed roads filled with pothead drivers, this part of Portland has always had far fewer people vacationing in it than you might expect for such a paradise, even one a little run down at the edges – though that is part of its considerable charm. In 1978, the area's sensual elegance was in serious decline. Even the palm trees seemed to have surrendered to the prevailing anarchy. A virus had eaten the tops off many of the palms on the island, leaving large stretches of countryside a forest of stumps. Jamaica's political gun battles, moreover, had led to the island being placed on the US State Department's 'not recommended' list. So the fat wallets of American tourists were a rarity.

At Drapers I found myself perched on top of a hill, writing my articles for the *NME*, wondering whether the cracked, leaf-strewn swimming pool would ever be fixed and filled. Within two years, like a metaphor for the bad times the island was undergoing, its owner (who had become a very good friend) was attacked in a vendetta by two men sent with machetes by a former lover. She and her boyfriend retreated through the rooms of the railroad-style bungalow as the would-be killers systematically slashed their way through the slats of the building with their cutlasses. My friends were saved when a neighbour heard the racket and blew several times on a whistle – the hitmen ran off, evidently believing that this signalled the arrival of the police. Later it occurred to me that this would have been worth bearing in mind.

24 August 1995. It is the night before the new moon, a little after eleven o'clock in the evening. The darkest night of the month.

I am lying in bed, dropping off to sleep. Through the gaps between the shutters' slats a balmy, salty breeze blows off the Caribbean, ten yards on the other side of the white beach outside my bedroom.

I hear the sound of someone – Peter, I think, my friend and the co-owner of this house – mentioning my name. I am half conscious, lying there, drifting off to sleep.

Then I hear a knocking on my door. 'Chris, Chris.' It is a man's voice.

I get up. As I pull the door towards me, it is pushed open. I back away.

A man stands there with a gun. He holds it in his left hand, pointing downwards. He lets me see it. He seems lithe and springy, about six foot tall, certain of himself, almost likably so. These days it's always good to meet someone who knows what they are doing.

I back off even more, another two or three steps.

'Come on, Chris: come out now.'

He is very casual. How does he know my name? Do I know him? I look at his face, expecting to recognize him in a moment, and then I will realize it is all one big joke.

Then it flashes through my mind that if this is the real thing, then I should not be looking at his face. In Jamaica legend has it that gunmen holding you up kill you if you see their face. So I turn away. I stand there silently looking away, towards the window.

Nothing is happening. I'm standing there frozen, my arms extending outwards slightly from my sides.

The guy all of a sudden appears angry, or freaked. He points the muzzle of the gun at me. I'm no expert on guns, but I can tell that it is not a revolver, but what I understand to be an automatic. Silver-grey in colour, it looks almost petite. Until he steps forward and strikes me several times around the forehead with it. Quite lightly, though hard enough to leave bruises.

'Come on,' he says again.

March 1978

How I found Jamaica in 1978 went something like this...

'Welcome to Rema. Peace, Love and Unity,' reads the paint-pot graffiti down by Seventh Street in Trench Town. Over on the other side of the Calamite Road, the no-man's land separating the PNP Concrete Jungle from the adjacent JLP's Rema, there's another message of ideological hope: 'Enter Socialist Town. We Love Cuba.'

Pointing out the fifteen-feet-high barbed-wire fence around the fortresslike police station that squats intimidatingly just inside the JLP side of the dividing line, the semi-name reggae star who's accompanying me ignores the bulldozers that are pushing straight through row after row of slum bungalows and, squinting his eyes against the one-o'clock sun, heads straight across these demolition sites for the home of Tapper Zukie.

Everywhere there are deep holes in the earth, as though this is a burial ground for a community. Walking silently two or three paces behind us is a man who was with the musician when we met ten minutes ago in Randy's Record Store on North Parade; he sports full urban guerrilla chic: shades, black beret pulled down low over the forehead, dark T-shirt and pants. The deep machete welt that runs from his left temple across his left eye, tapering neatly into almost the very centre of his chin, suggests something beyond the politics of style.

The reggae musician turns to him. No doubt for my benefit, he points to one of the holes in the ground. 'Like t'ese t'ings. T'ese 'oles. Save me lotsa bullets. Just push a man down. Cover 'im up. No one remembers 'ole, let alone 'im.'

'Do you ever carry a gun?' I ask the musician.

'Sometime you 'aveta,' he nods, with inscrutable herb cool, and crosses the road deeper into Rema.

The cauldron of Trench Town has always held one of the great cultural truths about Jamaica (and other impoverished Third World countries). Those who have nothing, and therefore nothing to lose, are not afraid to express their talents. Such people seem to have a pride and confidence in their natural abilities – a pride and confidence that Western educational and employment systems seem to conspire against. The pace of life in Jamaica is also more in keeping with the rhythms of nature: rising with the sun, people are active from early morning until the sun goes down. Such a harnessing of man's soul to the day's natural process seems to allow the creative forces a greater freedom to emerge.

It is said that during the 1965 Watts riot in Los Angeles half the European correspondents who went out to the West Coast to cover the burning and looting drove out to south central LA in their rental car and went straight through Watts and out the other side, still looking for 'the ghetto'. Looking at the palm trees and sunshine of Trench Town I can see how that could come about. Trench Town is very literally in downtown Kingston: you can't get any further downtown without wading into the ocean.

As soon as any *yout'* born there is able to stand up and take a look around, he can see that he'll need to be an extremely upwardly mobile individual to escape. All he needs do is glance up at the hills where he can see the middle-class homes looking down on him, like sugar planters' great houses, and he can tell it's literally going to be a steep climb all the way.

Once, however, this was prime real estate, desirable middle-class housing that had been built on the grounds of a former sugar plantation, owned by the Lindos, one of the twenty-one families that are said to rule Jamaica. You can still see the decayed shell of the Ambassador Theatre, where once Louis

Armstrong performed. A nearby abandoned building was once a Women's Institute: it still bears a cornerstone laid in 1947 by the wife of Sir Hugh Foot, who was then governor-general. After World War II, shanty towns grew up in the immediate environs, around the former Kingston refuse dump, where newly arrived country folk and displaced city dwellers would scavenge. This led to the migration of the middle classes. After the 1951 hurricane destroyed the squatters' camps, a housing scheme was built where they had once stood. Trench Town, which was named after a Mr Trench, the most prominent of the builders on the project, was considered desirable accommodation for the slum and shantytown dwellers. The 'government yards' which were constructed comprised solid one- and two-storey concrete units, erected around a central courtyard which held communal cooking facilities and a standpipe for water. Few were so ungrateful as to complain that Jamaica's colonial masters had seen fit to build Trench Town without any form of sewerage system.

Alton Ellis, later to become one of Jamaica's greatest singers, moved to the area as soon as the first stage of building the government yards had been completed. Work began at Fifth Street and progressed to Seventh Street before the overgrown area known as the Dungle was cleared to make way for the construction of the first four streets. Ellis told me that, long before the songs and mythology of Bob Marley had given the area global recognition, Trench Town quickly became renowned as a haven for outlaw rejects. At the same time he remembered it as a 'peaceful, loving place'. Each apartment within the individual complexes had two bedrooms; in the communal yard would be four toilets and bathrooms; by each gate a mango or pawpaw tree was planted. 'But even though the place was nice, the poverty still existed. The poverty was so strong that you know what that lead to.'

In fact I've seen far worse, far more intimidating slums on the outskirts of African, Asian and Latin American cities. Forty or so years ago the deprived areas of Leeds, Liverpool and

Glasgow were far more extreme than anything I see here. Is that an illusion caused by the constant sunshine? Probably. The slum dwellers of those British cities could at least fall back on a social-security system that is nonexistent in Jamaica: you don't work, you don't have money – it's as simple as that. And in Trench Town the rays of the sun interact with the exhaust fumes to create the smog that always hangs over this lowest point of the city, the most polluted air on the island.

This low-rise housing project is painted an eco-friendly watery green. Even the colour of the outside of the police station is green, a couple of shades darker than the surrounding homes.

Tapper Zukie's place, however, is not painted green. He has one of the two central rooms that lead off the front verandah which serves as the general living room of a four-room twenty-five-year-old bungalow. Not only will it miss out on its coat of paint, he thinks, but it may even get bulldozed down.

Tapper resides in the JLP Rema half of Trench Town and there is a history of whichever side is in power mowing down – or, in the dialect of the island, mashing up – the homes of the opposition. Trench Town is seen by the rest of the country as a microcosm of what's going on in Jamaica. 'Wha' 'appen in Jamaica,' says Tapper, 'begin in Trench Town. All Jamaica check Trench Town. When we start war, all Jamaica fight.'

Trench Town at the moment is not fighting, though that situation is always liable to sudden change. For the time being, there is the Peace. The Peace is presently being celebrated on at least half a dozen 45s in the local top twenty – in a country where the literacy rate is only 60 per cent, songs are used for propaganda and political debate. Junior Murvin, for example, has 'Crossover' while on new manager Mrs Pottinger's High Note label, Culture have 'Peace Truce'.

The Peace, according to Tapper Zukie, 'just 'appen. Two individual rankings from each side come together. Decide to stop mashing things up. Then talk and reason with the youth.' ('The youth' is one of Jamaica's several contemporary cultural archetypes. See also: roots, culture, the system, even – briefly – the Peace.)

'Wha' 'appen in Jamaica begin in Trench Town,' Tapper claims again. Certainly the rate of armed crime in Jamaica is absurdly high and it was in Trench Town that the phenomenon of the armed political gunman first got under way.

Although perhaps that is overstating it. After the British left in 1962, the left-wing PNP and centre-right JLP each swung into independence with their own teams of gunmen. It was not until 1967 that the reality of a near-anarchic state, one in which both police and party hitmen were taking on the roles of overmighty medieval English barons, presented itself in very specific terms.

That year the police were sent to Marcus Garvey Drive to clear out the shantytowns. The shantytown dwellers responded by lobbing Molotov cocktails, an incident recorded in Desmond Dekker's huge international hit '007'.

Within a few years violence that had originally been political in inspiration had made the crossover to out-and-out hooliganism. Now hold-ups and general crimes of violence fill the papers. Rape is big, especially in the tourist areas like Montego Bay, where the US and Canadian holidaymakers have been arriving in reduced numbers for some years now. You must learn to expect to hear gunshots.

This ostensibly was the reason for the introduction of the Gun Court internment camp. Just possess one single part of such a weapon and you're in for indefinite detention. Of course, you are much more likely to end up inside the camp when the party you're supporting is out of office. The ganja laws are also said to be used for political repression.

According to Michael Thomas, the author of the excellent book *Babylon on a Thin Wire*, many of the guns are brought into Jamaica on light planes that fly down from Florida to land in the hills and load up with ganja, next to bauxite and tourism the country's most valuable dollar earner. On the way there and back they would cross Cuba. Someone who claimed to know about such 'runnings' told me that as you flew over Cuba on the return flight, a MiG would nose up alongside; but when you followed the known procedure by opening the door and showing the Cuban pilot the bales of prime weed, he would give you a thumbs-up and veer away, satisfied with his part in the continuing moral decline of the USA.

Trench Town guns allegedly come from another source, however. 'If we 'ave any gun,' says Tapper Zukie, 'we 'ave to go and find it for ourselves. Best to take it from a policeman. That where plenty man get their gun.' Although he adds, self-protectively, 'I don't carry a gun. My mouth is my gun.'

So what you have is a situation not unlike that which might have ruled in Dodge City or Tombstone a century ago. You might be this really *terrible* ranking gunman, a very cool character with maybe twenty or thirty hits to your credit. And you just keep coming up against these yout' out to make a rep for themselves. You just *have* to blow them away. Until the really hot one comes strutting into your yard and blows *you* away.

But does this not focus the spotlight on the very transitoriness of life itself in Jamaica? It is a country of such extremes, of such amplification of every emotion. With so many cultural variables: for example, in any rum-bar argument it is always worth considering that the blustery philosophical diatribe with which your ear is being bent is fuelled by the 150 degree 'overproof' white rum that is the staple alcoholic beverage of the island, along with Red Stripe beer. Your drinking companion's nervous system may well also be genuflecting to the effects of several spliffs of some of the world's strongest marijuana. This means that his sense of machismo is hyper-sensitive. So you better watch your step because otherwise you may find him strutting there in front of you, very roosterlike indeed, waving up by your Adam's apple the razor-sharp end of his made-in-Sheffield machete, which he has just gone outside and unstrapped from the side of his Suzuki.

All this is especially confusing because half the time the appearance and attitudes of Jamaica are those of England with sunshine. What with county names like Cornwall and Westmoreland, and roads laid out like leafy, winding English lanes (along which you motor your right-hand-drive, rusting, corroded 1964 Morris Oxford on the left-hand side of the road), and with red Royal Mail boxes still not removed, there are times when, observing the roadside cricket – and forgetting about the palm trees – you could easily be in some Cotswolds backwater.

Not where Tapper Zukie lives, though. Tapper is at present waiting for some more money from Kingston's local government. Just half a block from where he lives, across his rubble-strewn, cockroach-infested back yard, he's been working for months now on transforming a derelict building into a youth club: 'In the future mi club gwan turn out a lot o' very good musician and t'ing.'

The trouble is, for the meantime the money seems to have dried up. Could this have anything to do with Tapper residing, and the club's being situated, in JLP Rema? Tapper Zukie certainly thinks so. He says siding with the Jamaica Labour Party earns him the tag of 'capitalist', as opposed to the 'socialist' he would have become as a People's National Party supporter. 'But if the government don't decide to re-fix it,' his high, slightly monotonous voice declares, 'we do it ourselves and run it ourself. As a youth club. To learn the yout' the culture and t'ing. Learn 'em music.'

Tapper Zukie's records have always sold well in Britain and New York, where he enjoys something of a cult reputation, but hardly at all in Jamaica, where to the record-buying public he remains something of an unknown. This is related to his having cut 1973's reputation-forging first LP *Man Ah Warrior* (later reissued by Patti Smith and Lenny Kaye on their Mer label) not in Jamaica but in England, where the Ethnic/Fight label owner Larry Lawrence, knowing of the toaster's reputation from his deejay residency with the Virgo sound system, took him into the studio to lay down his first ever recorded tracks. His 'Klik MPLA' 45 was the largest-selling UK deejay hit of 1976, with the LP of the same name also a bestseller. Even now, with his aptly titled Virgin release 'Peace in the Ghetto' immediately in the UK reggae chart, Tapper still has no guarantee of improving his JA status. He may be better known in Africa – in Nigeria, for example, where Virgin offload a minimum of 200,000 copies of each of their reggae releases.

Talking to Tapper Zukie, I am given a sense of the extent to which the power of the PNP and JLP remains of paramount importance in the Jamaican ghettoes.

'The youth don't really too love it,' says Tapper Zukie, squatting on the drab floorboards of the front porch and glancing up at a sickening growth on the neck of one of his teenage neighbours. 'But because of the way the system is set up, some man say if you are not with them, then you must be against them. If you no fight them, them fight *you*.

'I know within mi'self I a true born Rasta,' he avows. 'God knows who I deal with. It's the politicians that create war amongst us. The politicians want to control, y'know. Want to use you. Divide the people. One side come and then the other side to keep the separation and each put up a new t'ief, a new slave master, while we the poor people do all the work and rich people sit at 'ome and collect money.

'All of them a-runnin' a rat race.'

Even so, the Peace, brought about by a meeting between Kingston's rankin' gunmen, is at least offering a semblance of solidarity. 'Seven weeks ago I couldn't drive around Rema with you. We'd 'ave to drive through with machine guns: kill or be killed. Right now we the youth is at peace. The government don't like that.

'Right now,' he continues, 'the policemen would like the war to start again. Because they are not policemen – they are thieves. These people brutalize you. Police perform a robbery and come and shoot up all innocent youth and child.

'The *police* –' he utters the word with undisguised contempt – 'are supposed to be behind plenty of the killing that is going on in Jamaica. They start to kill off the youth. But the masses start to go against the police.'

From all sides, from all colours, residents of Jamaica speak despairingly of and provide horror stories about the police force. They are alleged to be a corrupt, easily bribable, near-private army. In tandem with the military, with whom they operate the ever-threatening roadblocks, the police provide a constant, nagging fear. 'Army work with the police,' says Tapper. 'Youth no longer afraid of police. So the army come and the soldiers are worse than the police. The police don't know 'oo I am. But they terrorize me. They even take me off the street and lock me up for a few days.'

The police hate reggae music, it is claimed, somewhat simplistically, by those who play it. 'The police all like soul music,' I am told by the drummer Horsemouth Wallace. The lamentable musical headstate of the jumped-up aspiring bourgeoisie is seen as the main reason for computerized US disco-soul's having the audacity to vie with reggae for Jamaican ear-time.

'Them entitled not to like reggae,' Tapper decides. 'Man must expect it for they not love poor people. When God come, they know not God. Them crucify Jesus Christ. They don't love themselves. But the rich man not going to 'ave much more glory. This t'ing can't go on for ever.'

And Tapper Zukie echoes the opinions of Michael Holding, the Jamaican cricketer I had found myself next to on my way to the island. He was returning to play for the West Indies in the forthcoming test series. 'Manley is sincere. He believes in what he's doing,' he told me. 'I just don't trust his ministers at all. I believe they've all got their numbered bank accounts outside the country. They're all getting ready to leave.'

'As far as I see,' Tapper Zukie says, 'the ministers is all wanting to get richer. Drive a big car with the windows up and with a big-bottomed girl next to them and give lots of orders while we, the poor people, just work. When they passing the ghetto, they make up a face. Where them really set you up is in modern slavery.

'You 'ave a policeman come shoot a man in front of his children. Now today you 'ave man say: "Mi, as a youth, see a policeman shoot mi father in front of mi. When mi get big mi 'aveta shoot ten policemen for mi father." Them set up the youth that way. So it's like them build them 'eaven 'ere and still then live in fear.

'This peace . . . probably go on for ever. Probably end tomorrow . . . Because the blood don't run yet. And we know the blood 'ave to run: the blood of hope. Babylon still fight against the people. Babylon must go down. 'Eathen blood still 'ave to run.'

As prime minister from 1972 to 1980, Michael Manley took Jamaica some way towards a socialism that owed a large debt, spiritually and materially, to Fidel Castro's Cuba, ninety miles to the north. Just as my Trench Town guide's guerrilla chic owed a large debt to Che Guevara.

Besides, exemplifying that spartan work ethic that one always associates with Castro's personally striding forth with a machete into the sugar-cane plantation, Cuba, in addition to actually financing at least one secondary school in Kingston, has just donated a physical-education teacher-training college to Jamaica. The yout' can see who cares for its welfare.

Even though we know by now that such Jamaican terms of paranoid abuse as 'CIA spy' and 'Mafia member' should not necessarily be taken literally, it's still reasonable to assume that the wielders of such insults are right at least some of the time.

And the United States is highly disturbed by the possibility of another communist state peering insolently up into capitalism's soft white underbelly. Glancing about the breakfast room of my hotel in 1978 I noticed a large number of young men with US accents, dedicated to preserving A Certain Way of Life. In fact, a true paranoid wouldn't have been surprised to also come across some Sicilian chappies in the flesh. After all, not only were their right-wing CIA pals/allies down here, but maybe the Mafia enjoyed having somewhere just an hour's flight from Miami where they could take a vacation, smoke the finest cigars outside of Havana, pick up a suntan and get laid.

And maybe, with Jamaica crying out for foreign exchange, some loose change from their stateside operations could be laundered a little down here.

It reminded me of the manner in which the Syndicate was alleged to have involved itself in the affairs of some US soul record labels. And I couldn't help noticing that some of the record labels down here could benefit from a little expertise.

Years later I learned that not long after Castro had taken over Cuba, the owner of one of Jamaica's most prestigious hotels was contacted by Meyer Lansky, mob bookkeeper, and offered $300,000 to influence the Jamaican government to legalize casino-scale gambling on the island.

Jamaica is certainly one of the most beautiful countries in the world: lushly green, fertile land endowed with a flora that can provide you with your daily veg just by going and picking it off a tree.

It would almost seem that the island's Jah-provided natural attributes compensate, at least in part, for the perennial JA musician's lament of how he has been ripped off. Junior Murvin, who with 'Scratch' Perry wrote and recorded 'Police and Thieves', the enormous Jamaican and English hit of 1976, shares many of his musical brethren's sense that their being ripped off is an inevitable part of their apprenticeship as recording artists.

I call on Junior Murvin (or 'Mervin', as his surname is spelled on his Jamaican releases on Lee 'Scratch' Perry's Black Ark label) shortly after nine one morning at his home in Port Antonio, on the north side of the island, with a population of some 12,000 and one of the world's most breathtakingly beautiful natural harbours. The temperature is already up in the mid-80s. I find the man sitting on a couch in the living room of his bungalow just a couple of streets back from the seafront. A well-built, mustachioed figure in his late twenties, he is wearing just a pair of chocolate-brown pants, reading from the book of Genesis and half watching a cookery programme on television. Gilbert O'Sullivan is singing on the radio.

In the late 1960s Derek Harriott recorded Junior's songs 'Solomon' and 'Ting Tang Festival', and in the early 1970s he was managed by and recorded for the well-known Jamaican music figures Mr and Mrs Pottinger. Junior claims he never received any royalties for either venture, and also did not pick up any money when he worked as Junior Soul for Joe Gibbs. 'You 'ave some of them 'ave money and some 'ave none,' he observes, holding his copy of the Bible in his right hand. 'Some 'ave a lickle heart and give you a lickle mercy. In foreign land dem scrape more money for the artist. In Jamaica he just can't live. Dem is a terrible set of people.

'But *now* I get a big name. Don't worry about them lickle things like money. What is to be is to be. When the time come can't stop it 'appen. Evert'ing ripe now for reggae. It just the smugglers and hustlers and scufflers who mash it all up. Them small producers causing a *lot* of confusion. I rate them terrible.

'Sure, lots of bad t'ings 'appen. But –' he smiles amiably yet again. 'Could 'appen lot worse t'ing to you. Could wind up dead instead.'

Yet Junior Murvin is not entirely content with his lot. He feels that his talent is being underexposed abroad and that his royalty payments from past work are not what they should be. However, Murvin's supremely evocative peace-celebrating single 'Crossover' is high in the Jamaican charts.

'Evert'ing goin' good now,' he grins. 'Gonna blast through like an iron bar. Sell a million. I like work hard's why I like to work with Lee Perry, because he's so hard-working. Just go on and on until he gets it right. Got spirit. *Strength.*'

Junior maintains that his songs of social comment and protest are both easy and speedy to write. 'It just come flowing, y'know.' He passes over a notepad in which he's been working up lyrics for a song he intends to call 'International Confusion': 'Some see the light/While some is blind to it/It is an international confusion.' He will continue working on it until he goes up to Black Ark to lay it down. 'Perry will put some more t'ings to it. What he usually does,' he says, explaining Scratch's frequent songwriting credits on Murvin's songs, 'is after I've finished writing he adds some lickle t'ings to it.'

Junior is delighted with the Clash's version of 'Police And Thieves' on their first album. He would like, he says, to work onstage with them: 'You can write that down. Dem ol' people can't take the truth. Punk people my kind of people. Dem not make trouble. Just enjoy themselves.'

As his vocal style attests, it was Curtis Mayfield who was Junior's main vocal inspiration. 'Curtis is the first one to sing about roots, to open your eyes. 'Im go deep, *deep*,' he stresses. 'Name LP *Roots*. Sing messages to unite people. Long time I fight for peace with mi record. Lots of people in Jamaica not understand what I mean. Message *deep*. *Terrible* message to unite people together. Peace and justice for black and white. *Yeah!*' He laughs. 'Murvin sings *deep*. A serious t'ing. Man can't sing o' foolishness no more.'

If it's the real roots of Jamaica that you're searching for, you're more likely to find them in a place like Port Antonio than in Kingston. Maybe, as Tapper Zukie claims, all Jamaica does look to Trench Town to check what's going down, but if it's the true soul, the true spirit, the true feel of the island you're searching out, then it's essential to get out of the capital. Come to that, it's essential to clear out of the coastal plains altogether.

It was to the hills that the proud, warlike runaway slaves known as the Maroons fled from their slave-drivers. It is in the hills that you will come across men – the purest Rastas often – hacking away the undergrowth to cultivate their own small-holdings. If you are very privileged and travel into the most inaccessible and secret places, you might even sight some of the ganja fields that are tucked away up there.

It is *heavy* when a man goes into the hills (such words as 'heavy' and 'deep' and 'cool' have not been devalued here by constant cynical media exploitation). It is a very serious thing. Winston Rodney was not just looking for a cute album title when he named the second Burning Spear Island album *Man in the Hills*.

A man discovering the hills, with all their psychic associations, and learning to dwell within them is something akin to an occultist's deliberately removing himself from society to dwell for a time as an ascetic recluse, the better to open up his head-space. The relationship a Rastaman will build up with these lands begins to take on a near-sexual – no, near-Tantric – quality. No Western nonsense about communing with muses here: this is the spirits providing direct fuel-injection of their forces into his soul until it and that of Jamaica have become as one.

Bunny Wailer presently lives up in the hills above Haining in Portland, rising each morning at sun-up and disappearing for the whole of the day to return perhaps at sunset to his wife and kids, who've passed the day with a few pipebowls of herb, flicking the switches between Jamaican TV and the two channels of TV Cubana you can pick up if you live high enough up on the north side of the island.

Despite the chic khaki tracksuit he sports when I see him at the Kingston Sheraton, Bunny is feeling most uncomfortable. He's come for a meeting with the Island boss Chris Blackwell, but arrived ten minutes after Blackwell had to leave for the airport. Bunny dislikes the hustling brashness of the capital – the reason why he moved out to Haining eighteen months ago. 'The hills,' he sighs. 'The hills: all truth is in the hills.' He invites me to come and see him there.

I do.

Bunny's out.

In the hills.

Of course it is not possible for all Rastafarians to live outside Kingston and spend their days wandering the mountain slopes. But although a goodly percentage of the Rastas you come across in Kingston are close in spirit to weekend hippies and, while weaving oral spells of righteousness, are just as likely to rip you off, there are still many good and true Rastas there – abstaining from meat, alcohol, salt and anything containing chemical impurities.

At some point in their lives, these men have undergone something akin to a religious conversion: maybe they've gone out and wandered the hills or maybe, one day, the soul soaring free on the mantra-like, near-anaesthetic combination of pro-digious quantities of both reggae and ganja, and all those years of Bible-knowledge classes and psychic presences, have suddenly crashed into clarity as the cosmic pattern of the Jamaica Experience fitted into place ... *Hail, Rastafari!*

These are the men closest in spirit to the Rastafarians of the 1940s and 1950s, whose place in the community was akin to that of, say, a priest or a rabbi; who were seen as mystical men of knowledge and as teachers – a long way from the manner in which Rastas are regarded by those middle in age and class on the island today, which is approximately the same way the *News of the World* perceives punks. Lately every other yout' you see in the streets seems to be sporting a red, green and gold tam into which his locks have been tucked. Every Jamaican has an opinion on the Rastas.

A reasonably balanced viewpoint comes from Heptone Barry Llewellyn. 'Listen,' he says, 'if there's going to be a change in the situation, we gotta take it from *truth*. And that's what Rasta preaches: truth and rights and equality. So Rasta germinates the plant of t'ese t'ings in every young Jamaican. 'E's even going to school and 'e's saying, "'Ail Rastafari!"'

'It is truth and rights that Rasta fight for. Much of it is religion from the Bible, but also so much it is a realistic way of living. Rasta can be *any* man. Rasta don't have to know no difference between black and white as long as he knows truth and rights.

'The Twelve Tribes of Israel,' Llewellyn continues, attempt-ing to throw some light on one of the most important, yet also

27

most esoteric, schools of Rasta thought, 'is just a different version of Rasta. The twelve tribes of Israel just represent the sign they were born under. Is just the signs of the zodiac under which every man mu' 'ave 'is own tendency. In other words, you know that if you are an Aries so you must 'ave certain strengths but also certain weaknesses that can make you upset by other men's tendencies. But instead of hating someone because 'e 'urt you by these tendencies, you must just *love* him instead.

'Once again, as far as I am concerned, anyone can be a member of the Twelve Tribes. It's just like a society that's formed within a religion.'

All this business of Haile Selassie, Conquering Lion of Judah, and the joyful prospect of the voyage to Ethiopia on the Black Star liner is to many outsiders the most unpalatable aspect of Rastafarianism. The religion does, after all, contain within its amalgam of Zen and biblical truths a philosophy with which every reasonable human being must surely agree. Part of the Zen aspect of Rastafarianism is a nebulous, shadowy area into which it is impossible to penetrate with the intellect alone. After all, if someone is driven to find out about a philosophy, it is sometimes best that certain obstacles should be placed in his or her way.

If you are one of the dog-soldier Jesus-freaklike variety of Rasta intent on spouting forth endless raps to all who come within earshot, then almost certainly you do expect your salvation to manifest itself in quite extreme physical terms in the shape of the Black Star liner sailing into Kingston harbour to take you finally to your homeland. If you are not part of these innumerable legions of spiritual shock troops, however, and are perhaps a more highly evolved Rasta soul, it is more likely that you look upon such notions as holding a purely symbolic value.

Lee 'Scratch' Perry, for example, almost certainly has no desire to settle permanently in Africa. After all, the record engineer and producer is probably the vital chemistry man for all the reggae music and reggae thought that doesn't come out of the mainstream commercial Kingston studios, and he regards Jamaica itself as a truly God-blessed land.

Born a Piscean in 1939, he learned his craft as a camp follower of Clement 'Sir Coxsone' Dodd's Downbeat Sound System in the late 1950s to the mid-1960s. When Dodd began to cut his own Studio One records, Perry, along with the famous keyboards player Jackie Mittoo, operated the production side of the label. After parting from Coxsone in 1965, Scratch also worked with Joe Gibbs and Byron Lee. In 1968 he recorded himself singing the innovative 'People Funny Boy', one of the first records to use a new rhythm that became known as reggae. By 1970 he was working with Bob Marley, Peter Tosh and Bunny Livingston – the Wailers – for whom he produced singles and two albums, *Soul Rebel* and *Soul Revolution*, later reissued as *African Herbsman* and *Rasta Revolution*, and arguably far finer records than were put out by any subsequent Wailers line-up. Yet Scratch is said to have had a large uncredited hand in the making of every Island Wailers LP with the exceptions of *Exodus* and *Kaya*.

As the Upsetter, Lee Perry has preferred to make instrumental music in the form of LPs like *Africa's Blood* and deejay instrumental sets like *Double Seven*. Throughout the 1970s Scratch produced other artists – Junior Byles, U Roy, Dennis Alcapone, Jah Lion, even Susan Cadogan's 1975 British hit 'Hurts So Good' – and when I meet him in 1978 he has recently been producing his most prolific and (many would say) finest work with artists like Max Romeo (*War in a Babylon*), Prince Jazzbo (*Natty Pass Through Rome*) and Junior Murvin. He has also worked with white artists as diverse as Paul McCartney and the Clash.

The first time I call on Lee Perry, just after one o'clock on a humid afternoon, I find him in the kitchen of his bungalow in the Washington Gardens suburb of Kingston. As a crew of Scratch supporters, including George Faith and the Congoes, huddle around the table rolling perfect sno-cone spliffs from a maybe half-pound pile of ganja on the table, the English session singer Candy Mackenzie is reading aloud from Revelations in the New English Bible. The slight, wiry Scratch paces the kitchen, a bottle of Dragon Stout in one hand and the statutory giant spliff in the other, declaiming on the meanings contained within the verses.

Scratch carries an extraordinary aura about him. His dark eyes flash forth laser beams of righteousness that seem to provide a direct connection to the core of his soul. He prances, slapping both hands on the table to emphasize the points he is making – which relates Mussolini's end to predictions within Revelations. He delights in verbal banter, with metaphysical, often Rasta-related jokes a speciality.

'Where is truth?' He suddenly whips round on me.

'Umm ... Everywhere?' I suggest, half aware that some biblical quote is perhaps here called for.

'Is it in all good food that you eat? Yes?'

'Mmm ... yes,' cautiously agrees the journalist, half expecting a deflating punchline.

'So when you shit that food out, the truth is in there, too?' His features, which resemble one of those lined, dignified photographic portraits of Native American chiefs, twist into a delighted grin of pure bliss.

'Well, possibly, yes.' I nod, sensing that, although clearly still hardly even a novice, I should maybe follow the lateral logic I am absorbing from the herb-assisted wisdom all about me. 'Because if the shit is pure, then it may be used as fertilizer for making plants pure.'

'I-rie, I-rie!' Scratch chuckles, nodding and slapping the thighs of his scarlet tracksuit. Like an English neighbourhood butcher or baker might do, Lee Perry lives next to the shop: his Black Ark studio is housed in a building in his back yard. Perhaps it is this accessibility to his work that has made him one of the most influential and arguably most talented producers of reggae ever.

Although the rate for his services is something in the region of twenty Jamaican US dollars an hour, Scratch himself has of course unlimited studio time. An ardent follower of the Rasta belief that physical fitness ensures clarity of mind, he rises early and exercises rigorously, then puts in a few hours of knob-twiddling before anyone turns up to be recorded. His studio is only a four-track, with the sounds mastered on a Teac tape recorder, but then Scratch, who is renowned as a painstaking perfectionist, can work wonders: he is depicted on a mural just inside the door as *Lee Perry: the Mad Scientist*.

At that time, Scratch was working on the follow-up to his *Superape* LP – to be entitled, of course, *Return of Superape* – as well as recording an album with the diminutive, self-effacing melodica and keyboards maestro Augustus Pablo, recorder of the classic 45 'King Tubby Meets Rockers Uptown', amongst many, many others.

Two more brief visits to 5a Cardiff Crescent, Washington Gardens, and then I arrive there at 11.30 one Thursday morning for a formal interview session with Scratch.

A spliff smoulders in the ashtray. Scratch is wearing a splendid fawn cap, a white T-shirt and maroon swimming trunks, and is standing barefoot in the console room, almost imperceptibly shifting and switching knobs as he gives the distinctive Scratch treatment to Quake-In Vibrations, 'some young guys mekkin a try'.

The console room is decorated in the Rasta colours of the Ethiopian flag – red and green on the walls with a gold carpet. The word 'PEACE' cut in the red and green cloth covering the mixing desk gives an altarlike quality.

On the walls are assorted publicity stills of artists with whom Scratch has worked. Someone has written the word 'Judas' across the picture of Max Romeo. There's an Adrian Boot shot of the Clash in Belfast, a selection of Bruce Lee stills from *Enter the Dragon* and an aerosol can of Cooper's Roach Spray.

At Black Ark you feel the reason so much dreck emerges from UK and US studios is that they're so hermetically sealed.

Unlike Scratch's place, they have managed to isolate themselves utterly from all the life-forces about them. Anyway, finishing his work with Quake-In Vibrations, who are a five-piece group down from the country to record their first ever tracks, Scratch pauses to refresh himself with a bottle of Dragon Stout before settling down to give me 'a reasoning'.

Except that it is not quite as simple as that. There are others in the room: the Jamaica Broadcasting Corporation's morning deejay John Wakelin ('one of mi best bredren'), Candy MacKenzie, Cedric of the Congoes and several unnamed faces. It is time, Scratch has decided, that *he* should interview *me*. He must discover my aim and my purpose.

Certain of the people assembled, you see, have been most disturbed by what other writers have written. It goes further than Scratch's simply being irritated by their 'damn fool questions' about details of his life. He claims that some work written about him has a condescending tone that those present find especially distasteful. John Wakelin in particular is disturbed about what he considers to be superficial, derogatory reports he has read of the Rastafarian and elder Ras Michael, a man who deserves the utmost respect. 'Certain foreign correspondents come here and perpetuate this action and after a while we lock the door,' says John.

Scratch turns to him. 'Why some of them have to criticize it,' he sighs, 'is because they don't understand it. To understand it you have to overstand it.'

'It ain't a passin' fad,' John tells me, 'and man have to go into it and see what it is all about.'

A lot of printed word myths about Jamaica have been created, I say, in which the country seems to be populated by a race of cartoon characters.

'Because they don't know where to look,' nods Scratch, almost to himself. 'Because the place to look for this thing is *beyond* the scene.'

'And it's a different premise,' John Wakelin's soft voice tells me, 'that operates in different parts of the world. Down here

people don't always want you to come and write about them.'
The disc jockey is suspicious of the manner in which reggae is
treated by US and UK radio networks. 'The point at issue
here,' he continues, 'is that the very elements in reggae music
denouncing the very *heart* of the system on which much of the
capitalist world is built is perhaps an integral reason of the radio
hold-down. But even the press finds it hard to touch that
reason. Because true reggae music is pure protest music.'

With almost religious fervour and with passionate warmth
in his voice, Scratch interrupts. 'I and I – ' he paces the floor
waving a finger – is to warn them that the bomb going to blow
up on them that makes it! I and I is here to warn them that if
they use it then them *dead* by it, too.

'So our part is to make sure that reggae music take the
message across to the warriors in the war zone whom you can't
reach by the telephone. If it gets to him on a gramophone him
must hear it. And this *am* the message of reggae music! *We* turn
the world around *now*! We talk – man listen. See me! Because
the word is it, y'know. The army of Jah Rastafari set sail on a
ship on a mission that can never fail. With all his militant
soldier, armed to the teeth, the word of Jah Rastafari has come
to kill the wicked.

'*Equal rights and justice!* We take reggae and bring it forth to
earth. We no deal with the whiteman philosophy. We go deal
with His Majesty. Too long,' he continues, 'we have had to kill
a brother for his money. *Don't sell your soul for silver and gold!*
Dig me, man, Babylon is a con trick and mi going to lick it
with a brick.'

You really think Babylon's system of false values may only
be licked with a brick, that it may only be overturned by
physical violence?

'Of course! You take a brick and wrap it in a cloth and soak
it and wet it and you lick a Babylon with a raas claat. Because
then we will make a system that shows men how to live as
men.'

Even if our different cultures have ensured that I'm not

always able to understand every word you utter, I can only agree wholeheartedly with the truth of what you say. So in that case, and bearing in mind the revolutionary zeal of reggae musicians, why do the Jamaican record producers – not including yourself in this, naturally – appear to be able to dictate such outrageously unfair terms to reggae musicians? It does seem difficult to find a single record company in Jamaica that doesn't appear to have some gangster involvement...

'Well, this is not all gangsters, y'know. Not just gangsters. But why you want to make it record companies alone? *Everything else* run by gangster. Bad happen in evert'ing. Not happen bad alone in reggae music. Reggae music is just cleaner than most things that go on. You must look for what go on upstairs. Them that bring forth the production are the producers. Who produce the *money*? Who produce the *hate*? Who produce the *love*? Jah produce the love so who produce the hate? Producers of sin, producers of righteousness. Every man produce: some produce good, some produce evil. Just am A System.'

Despite the severe reservations of John Wakelin, Scratch himself has no desire to 'lock the door' if people want to journey down to JA to record what is happening there.

'They *have* to come to write about this ... Now we are in Revelations and Revelations reveal all things that are to reveal. They need something else to write about so they have to come down here in the valley of Jehosaphat to write their things.

'After all –' he speaks quietly, as though taking me fully into his confidence – 'Jamaica isn't just a name, y'know.' Then, quickly: 'What is the name of here?'

'Jamaica.'

'Yes.' He nods solemnly, as though summoning all his spiritual powers. '*Jah-make-'er.* Jah-make-'er. You should find out and try to check why it 'ave that name. I *knew* you would be coming here to Jamaica to write because you want to write about something new. Because,' his voice grows louder, 'the old-time writing is over. *Great* men will be coming here – like from way down in Genesis. Because we are closing Revelations now and are going to start again. That's why *you*'re here and reggae music carry it at this time.'

My appearing in Jamaica to write about a music I love dearly is beginning to take on the connotations of a search for the twentieth-century Holy Grail.

'We are still doing the works of the psalms of David,' Scratch continues. '*Dig me*, man: we are on the same track. Do you know the words to the tune of David?'

I shake my head in the negative.

'If we have a little hutch,' Scratch explains, walking over to the studio door, 'we just hutch out and come like bees. Sting them to death to raas claat.'

He leaves the room.

'It am 'ard,' Wakelin offers, perhaps sensing my disquiet, 'sometimes to relate to Scratch, to deal with 'im. He is so way out. *Freaky.*' He pauses solemnly and then continues, 'Freaky unless you consider, as I read in *Newsweek* magazine, that President Carter right now has a plan to put a solar-energy platform several miles into the sky to supply 75 per cent of the US's need for power without any use for oil. And then power will belong exclusively to just one or two countries.

'But in these times –' he shakes his head as though troubled with some cancer-creating hurt that is almost driving him to tears – 'a solution cannot come like that. It *have* to be spiritual. To get some things properly *heavy*, man.'

Scratch returns. 'So 'ow come you don't ask these usual damn fool questions the other people ask?'

'Because I don't believe it to be ... necessary ...'

'Well,' he smiles, 'you're on the New Wave then. You've got to be a member of the New Wave if you want to find the truth. You've got to be,' he laughs, 'a member of the New Wave if you don't want to be a slave in your grave.'

Then, more portentously: 'If you're not a member of the New Wave, then you're dead. If you want to live you 'ave to be a member of it.'

So Scratch must have been pleased by what he saw of the

English New Wave when he became briefly involved with the Clash?

'Well, right now the whole world got to have a New Wave if it's going to survive,' he pronounces. 'Because Jah coming in a new name and you don't know him. So if you want to know how to go on, just accept the New Wave and then you'll be on a New Wave movement. And the New Wave is Jah Rastafari . . .

'If you're not on the New Wave then you're dead. Jah deal with equal rights, peace and justice and love for ever. That is to say that if you love yourself, then you won't hurt your brethren. When you think about God, you think about Life. So we want more people with Positive Thought.

'I am just showing you how simple it will be: good over evil. It is a *must*. That is a Rastaman − *pos-ee-tive* vibrations. Leave the man who think about negative. Leave that man who talk about belief. Because when there is a *belief* there is a *doubt*. And we have no time for that.'

He pauses. 'You want to know something?' He chuckles, putting a spliff to his lips. 'Then give me a light . . . Ask me any fool question you like.'

'Why do you make records?'

'Because I have to. Because I *have* to make records. That is my job. I was appointed to make records.'

'Why were you given your particular style?'

'That the amount of talent Jah bless me with.'

'Why do you think Jah blessed you with that amount of talent?'

'Mi no know. You 'ave to ask Jah. Cos it 'im that make the decision. 'Im pick me as a honest man and not as a braggart. Because for me to be a braggart in my position would be terrible. And 'Im really must make a man feel it. So 'E must know.'

'True,' nods John Wakelin.

Scratch: 'Them very hard question you ask me.'

'True,' nods John Wakelin.

Scratch stretches his arms in the air above his head and speaks in the tone of someone allowing another into his confidence: 'I am just the man, y'know. Just the man playing the part. But the man in there' – his right forefinger prods his own chest – 'the inner man you can't see, because I can tell you anything but you don't know what I say behind your back. So you must check the inner man. *That* is the man. Y'unnerstand?'

I remark on the volatile state of Jamaica, with strikes breaking out and communications appearing to be breaking down. Scratch, though, is not convinced.

'Well, mi see same things happening all over the world. Most people itemize on Jamaica because it is one of the greatest countries in the world – where all the great people rest. So –' he leans over towards me – 'there must be a reason why so many people look on Jamaica and check Jamaica.

'Check it out if you want to know the Truth, man. Mi say you are very lucky to be here. Look at other parts of the world where people take heroin, people take this, people take that, people make bombs, people make guns. Jamaica never do that: Jamaica not make guns, not make heroin. All we plant is colly weed and smoke it. And gain knowledge. And ask Jah to guide us.

'But check all them nasty thing that man make: them stink out their country.' He laughs. 'Learn that: when Rastafari speak, dig it. Not true?

'Ask me any question you like. The simplest.'

'Where did you get your hat?'

'A friend gave it to me. Right here.'

'It's very good. I like these hats.'

Scratch nods. 'It's one of the best hats I ever have. When I see it I think, Oh! *What* a lovely hat!, then I realize that the man bring it for me. You dig me? Because 'e didn't have to bring it for me. But 'e *did* have to bring the hat for me. His spirit told him to bring the hat for me. This hat belongs to *me* – *that's* why it fits me so much. *Ha-ha-ha-ha-ha.* This hat designed specially for me.

'That's reality, man, dig it.' He laughs loudly again. 'It's true.

Yeah, I feel in a way it's true: Jah did make that man go and pick up that hat and say, "I'm taking it to Lee Perry." He gave it to me as a present. That a favour God does to people who obey him.'

So God gives things to people?

'*No*. Jah not give *things* to people. Him give the whole world to people and then 'Im disappear.'

I step through the doorway, the left-handed gunman behind me. As I cross the three or four steps of my landing which leads to Peter's landing, a woman's voice floats through the dimly lit building, sobbing as though in total hysteria: 'Don' keel me; please don' keel me.'

It would be chilling if I had the mental space to be chilled. As it is everything has gone into a kind of Peckinpah-like slow motion: time is slowed down utterly with everything moving at half pace – trauma and shock, no doubt. I seem to be watching everything from the ceiling, as though I am astral-projecting, an impression that is commonplace, I learn from others who have been in similar peril. What on earth is happening to the kids? There are two of them – very young, less than five years old – living in the house: the children of Donna, the daughter of Ducky, the housekeeper. As I am crossing the landing, the man almost whispers into my ear, 'We're not going to hurt you: we just want to take your things.' For a moment I feel reassured, and a fraction of my tension drops away.

But this slight ease vanishes in less than seconds as I suspect that what is really going on is a game of good gunman, bad gunman. Crossing to Peter's landing, I see him and Ducky face down flat on the floorboards. The shove in the small of my back suggests I join them. My nose is so close to the wooden floor that I can smell the insecticide.

Another man literally stands over us, clearly a far more desperate individual, perspiring with jagged edginess. Behind him is another man, with a very dark complexion and clothing.

'Where the safe? Where the keys to the safe?' demands the man nearest to us.

'I haven't got the keys,' says Peter. He seems in as much a state of shock as I, even more so perhaps since they grabbed him by the balls

39

and yanked him out of his bedroom when he opened the door.

'Where are the keys?' the man asks Ducky.

'I haven't got the keys,' she says.

This guy seems to be operating on a hair trigger: just touch him and he'll go off. Is he coked up? 'Kill one of them now,' he says suddenly. 'Show the others we mean it.'

August 1997

So much has changed in Jamaica in the twenty-odd years since I first went there. In 1978 the island had apparently been reduced almost to some Cambodian-style Year Zero. The little traffic on the roads was from another era of motoring altogether, and a car's performance often seemed to depend on how precisely it was tied together with pieces of string. Taxis were either battered Morris Oxfords from fifteen or so years before or vast, finned American boats-of-the-road of a similar vintage, also falling to pieces. Hardly anyone seemed to travel regularly back and forth from the island to the United States apart from higglers, officially termed informal commercial importers (ICIs), the legions of women who run market stalls and street trading, and hold together much of the Jamaican economy. An import tax of 300 per cent effectively blocked the arrival of any new 'luxury' goods.

In his home off Washington Boulevard 'Scratch' Perry had been waiting for seven years for the installation of a telephone line. Now new subscribers can be hooked up within days, a legacy of the monetarist reign from 1980 to 1989 of Edward Seaga. An anti-Castro free-trader (he visited Ronald Reagan as the US president's first foreign head-of-state), who handed over control to Cable & Wireless, the American company, of the infamously inefficient national Jamaican telephone service. (A friend, calling from London in 1979, found herself enduring an interminable wait as an operator in Kingston seemed to decide whether she could be bothered to make her connection within Jamaica. 'Please could you hurry: I am calling from

England,' she urged her. 'Well, yuh don' haveta,' replied the Kingston operator, cutting her off.)

Nowadays those controlling big business are endlessly accused of hand-in-glove cronyism with the banking system and government: in the 1990s, during P. J. Patterson's second term of office as premier, the 60 per cent interest rates demanded by banks resulted in temporarily cash-strapped companies borrowing a few thousand dollars and ending up owing hundreds of thousands. When, almost inevitably, such businesses go bankrupt, the bank that has lent the money then takes over their business.

Still, nowadays the supermarket shelves are stacked high with goods produced both locally and in the United States – all way out of the price range of any ghetto 'sufferahs'. Yet in 1978 I vividly recall walking into such a store in the Kingston suburbs to find that it had not a single item for sale, except for mounds of pan scourers. Even for those who were reasonably well-heeled, life in that *iwah* – the then current Rastafarian term for era – was not necessarily easier. In the street outside Jojo Hookim's Channel One studio on scruffy Maxfield Avenue, the renowned bass player Robbie Shakespeare begged me for a blank cassette. Fishing in my bag, I inadvertently gave him one that contained an interview with Billy Idol and Tony James of Generation X – I wonder what he made of it?

Now there are acres and acres of shopping malls, notably the endless Edward Seaga-inspired developments in Kingston's midtown Halfway Tree. Vast satellite dishes, sometimes the property of local 'badmen' dons who through them control the omnipresent, unregulated cheap cable TV, give even the humblest ghetto dweller regular access to US news, movie, sport and porn channels. And the snarling traffic jams are composed largely of the most macho modern Japanese four-wheel-drive vehicles with darkened windows, and container-ship quantities of nearly new Japanese saloon cars, dubbed 'deportees' – like Jamaica, Japan drives on the left, and is always anxious to offload year-old vehicles. Kingston today can often appear superficially like a tropical version of the United States.

Although in the United States the men and women behind the wheels of such blustering vehicles are likely to have passed a driving test, whereas in Jamaica at the time of writing the going rate is $JA2000 (around $US60) for an automobile licence and – even more worryingly – $JA12,000 for a bus or heavy goods vehicle permit. (Just as troubling is the allegation that gun licences are sometimes sold for around $JA10,000.) Of course, such corruption creates countless surreal stories. Someone I met kept being failed by a driving-test examiner because, having driven in the UK, he considered himself a capable driver and wished to pass the test legally, without needing to make any payment. And then there was the man who had lost a leg in a traffic accident and required a disabled licence for his automatic car: when the examiner emerged from his office and saw this man, he was horrified. 'I'm not getting in a vehicle with you!' he bellowed. 'Go test yuhself!'

This system of licence allocation may provide some explanation for the interestingly creative standard of driving and the frighteningly high number of road deaths. I always remember hurtling with Burning Spear through Fern Gully, the main road down to Ocho Rios from Kingston, as the great singer delivered his philosophy of driving while accelerating into a gap between two trucks that was growing smaller by the moment. 'Mus' steel yuh nerves, mus' steel yuh nerves,' he recited, as though it was a mantra.

Most driving experience seems to have been obtained by watching car chases on TV shows. Vehicles being driven at night without their lights in order that their owners can save battery power can sometimes be a problem; and when you're proceeding gently along a country lane you may find yourself all of a sudden being overtaken by a trio of left-hand-drive smoke-belching articulated heavy rigs hurtling on the wrong side of the road towards a blind bend. The myth goes that such vehicles are often sent down to Jamaica to the relatives of US-based drug barons as a way of laundering money, no doubt because they look so inconspicuous.

43

On a stiflingly hot Friday night in Kingston in August 1997, I seek a barometer of how things have changed in the almost twenty years since I have first visited the island by spending a couple of hours checking out the two local TV channels. One thing that already has become readily apparent to me is the way in which the once underground culture of Rastafari, considered in the 1970s with scant respect by the establishment media, has become by the middle of the 1990s fully part of the mainstream: now, for example, the dynamic 'conscious' performer Anthony B, the 'poet of Portmore', whose biggest hit has been his 'Fire 'Pon Rome' single, is the fulcrum around which spins a television advertisement for the New Commonwealth Bank. Old and new stars Freddie McGregor and Wayne Wonder are featured in ads plugging the desirability of peaceful elections. And US-style pop psychology attempts to take the stress and volatility out of everyday life with a series of public-service advertisements under the banner of *Mediate Jamaica*, complete with toll-free number, a California-style advance on anything that you might find on British television. *ER*, meanwhile, is the high point of Friday-night viewing.

The news bulletins have their own especial local tang: on the early-evening programme, the lead item announces that new figures show that a staggering 42 per cent of the population is below the age of twenty. The next story is equally culturally devastating, in a country where the stoning to death of 'batty-men' is considered quite socially acceptable: scores of prisoners in the nation's jail population of around 2000 males, comes the official admission, are HIV-positive, with five suffering from full-blown AIDS. (This report leads to prison warders being supplied with condoms to dole out where necessary. As this solution somehow is interpreted by the officials as suggesting that they themselves are gay, the prison officers accordingly go on strike, leaving the prisoners for several days virtually to run the prisons themselves, in the course of which several homosexual inmates are murdered in exceptionally unpleasant ways.) A third item announces that another taxi operator has gone missing after a woman has chartered his white Toyota Corolla in Spanish Town: a rash of murders of taxi-cab operators is continuing unstoppably – during the course of 1997, almost a hundred of them are killed.

The light 'jolly' to wind up the bulletin is a story that seems singularly irrelevant for Jamaica, the news that the Rolling Stones have announced the latest of their interminable tours – except that in the press shots professional 'bad boy' guitarist Keith Richards, something of an occasional local lad thanks to his residence of many years on the north coast near Ocho Rios, is wearing a T-shirt bearing a portrait of *Catch a Fire* era Bob Marley, sucking on the inevitable spliff, beneath the legend RASTAFARIAN in something like 64-point bold.

Just in case the veneer of Americanization should get to you completely, however, there is always the nightly public-service broadcast on IRIE-FM, the local twenty-four-hour reggae station, just before the eight-o'clock news, one that is guaranteed to raise a chill on the back of the spine of first-time listeners: the tremulous words of a young boy deliver the following message: 'Daddy, them say you is a gunman and that one day the police are going to come and shoot you. Then what will happen to little Susie and me? Daddy, if you is a gunman, please don't go to work tonight.'

OK, Daddy-o?

1994–1997

The floor of the club clears for Carlene, the self-proclaimed Jamaican 'dancehall queen'. Dressed in skintight satin next-to-nothing, she languorously rubs her hands between her legs, grabbing her crotch and squeezing it, her hips humping to the pistonlike digital dancehall beat. Around her there is as much

45

lubricious sensuality in the untrammelled movements of other dancers, some miming a cartoon version of the sex act with their partners. Very quickly these participants become reduced to a flurry of flashing, primary colours in flesh-hugging lycra, see-through plastic and sensuous velvet.

It's three in the morning at the Cactus nightclub in the Kingston dormitory town of Portmore and you feel you are probably in the best such venue in the world; the regular Wednesday dancehall night is just kicking in and won't be peaking for another couple of hours, during which time you will be carried along on the waves of energy set off by people having an unalloyed great time. 'What do I say to people who condemn dancehall for being "sexist"?' laughs Carlene. 'I say, "*Get a life!*" '

Before you check out the Jamaican music scene there may be crucial matters to consider. Should you wear a bullet-proof vest to prevent being shot by gunmen? What do you do when people try to sell you drugs?

The answer is to simply keep your wits about you, especially in the first few hours of your visit, when jet lag and culture shock can play havoc with your intuition; smile and be friendly; and don't have so many rum punches that you become a target. Despite the island's reputation for gun battles, flying bullets tend to be restricted to grim ghettos in Kingston. And when approached by the ubiquitous drug hustler ('Sensi! 'Ash! Cork!'), a useful response is an indignant 'But it's illegal!' Word will quickly go around that you are a madman, with all its concomitant status in Jamaica, and you will be left soundly alone to enjoy amazing evenings on the town.

It is worth noting that not only is the smoking of 'herb' in Jamaica decidedly not legal, but the penalties are more extreme than they are in the First World. Along the north coast there are frequent roadblocks, whose function seems to be a slightly more subtle equivalent of those run by the Nigerian police – to boost the weekly wage with as much 'dash' as may be extracted. And woe to any tourist who doesn't have a handle on the rules – the period in a cramped-to-bursting police lock-up that follows the discovery of even the tiniest amount of ganja is not pleasant and is often dangerous to the health. But how, I have always wondered, do you broach the controversial question of whether a pay-off would be acceptable to your arresting officer?

After all, police advice itself is certainly capable of being fallible. Jah Spongey and Patoo, a couple of Rastas I know, are pulled in by such a roadblock. As one of their vehicle's tyres is rapidly deflating from a not particularly slow puncture, the driver expresses concern that the halt might make them unable to proceed much further on their journey. 'Just drive faster, man,' comes the official police suggestion. 'That way you get home before it go down.'

On another occasion, as they are sitting parked in the same car, this pair come close to a larger problem. Having just purchased a pound of weed, they have the ganja spread out on a piece of newspaper on the seat between them as Spongey, in the passenger seat, cleans it. But suddenly a police motorcycle pulls up. As the cop dismounts, Spongey manages in one practised move to bundle the herb into the newspaper and throw it from the car window far into the bush.

When he orders them out of the car, the cop is most perplexed, shaking his head in puzzlement. 'Mi sure mi see a pile of ganja here one minute ago and now it gone.'

'Ah,' says Spongey, opting for a red-herring tactic of partial admission of guilt, 'I am a Rastaman and I did have a spliff. But I dashed it in the bush out of respect for the law.'

The cop walks back to his motorcycle, shaking his head in confusion.

As a seasoned veteran of herb smuggling, Spongey is used to dealing with the law. On several occasions, he claims, he has smuggled ganja into the United States by setting himself up as a decoy. As he steps through the arrivals hall looking as though he has recently descended from the Mount with his tablets of stone, the Rastaman is inevitably hauled up by US customs and thoroughly searched. Meanwhile, his companion, a grey-haired, besuited Jamaican in his early seventies, glides past him with the herb.

Still, the ways of the Jamaican police can surprise even Spongey. 'He is sitting in his car in a backstreet in Montego Bay,' Patoo tells me, 'when he hears gunshots. So, naturally, he ducks down in his seat. The next thing he hears is the sound of running footsteps, and a further shot. Carefully he looks up out of the windscreen and sees a guy in his early twenties lying on the ground. He is bleeding. There is a cop standing over him and he is crying, "Don't shoot me, sarge, please don't shoot me."

'The cop laughs. "Mi not waste a bullet on you," he says. Slowly he begins to unlace one of his boots. Then he takes it off and puts it on upside down over the man's face, holding it there until he suffocates to death. Then he pulls his boot back on his foot.

'Haven't you noticed that in all newspaper reports of gunmen being wounded, they always die on the way to hospital?'

On Tuesday nights in Kingston there's another wild dancehall evening, at Mirage in Sovereign Plaza, just past Bob Marley's former headquarters at 56 Hope Road. And on Thursdays you will find a similar, marginally hipper scene on the main drag of Knutsford Boulevard in New Kingston at the Asylum nightclub, where the Moët flows freely, drunk by large men with shades and girlfriends who look like Caribbean Christmas trees. Outside Asylum vendors selling everything from cones of peanuts to coconut water (and sometimes their bodies) compete for the custom of arriving and departing club patrons. Although the club, which has an admission fee of around four pounds, is only a five-minute stroll from the Hilton, the Pegasus or the funkier Altamont, the dark streets might wisely incline you to take a taxi. (But give precise directions: a friend asked a cab to take him to 'Asylum', and found himself at the infamous Bellevue mental home, in which the legendary ska trombonist

Don Drummond was incarcerated and died after killing his girlfriend Margarita, a renowned rumba dancer.)

Sometimes it is instructive to come across British-born blacks of Jamaican descent who are visiting the island. Invariably, they are far less forgiving of its eccentric foibles of Jamaica than ... well, than I am, for example. 'What do you think to this lot?' complains a girl from Brixton I meet at Asylum. 'Everything takes a bloody age.'

For an island with a population of less than three million people, the effect of Jamaican music on world popular culture has been extraordinary.

A feeling of independence grew in Jamaica after World War II, although politically it was not achieved until 1962. Postwar optimism: you could see it in the music of the late 1940s, the swing sounds of American-style big bands, like those of Val Bennett and Eric Dean, where apprenticeships were served by such nascent stars as the trombonist Don Drummond and the guitarist Ernest Ranglin, two men who would later become part of the backbone of contemporary Jamaican music. On the 'lawns' of Kingston, at venues like Chocomo on Wellington Street and Jubilee on King Street, jitterbugging audiences danced until dawn to tunes adopted from such American artists as Count Basie, Duke Ellington and Glenn Miller. These Jamaican acts contrasted with the island's traditional mento groups. Mento, derived from Jamaican folk music, was similar to Trinidadian calypso, but enjoyed a variety of tempos and song structures. Performances were mainly limited to the north-coast tourist trade. Also still playing in rural areas in the late 1940s were quadrille bands: originating during slavery, these had altered the form of the European ballroom dance by Africanizing it for performances on holidays.

But even the big bands would soon be superseded by the feisty, optimistic new sounds of bop and the shuffle-boogie rhythm-and-blues records that by the end of that decade would float down across the Caribbean from southern US radio stations. Few Jamaicans owned radios, however. Most first heard this new music when it was brought into the island to be played on the original sound systems, run by pioneers like Tom the Great Sebastian. Sound systems were like portable discos for giants: they would consist of up to thirty or forty speakers, each as large as about six tea-chests stuck together, miles of cabling that looped around the venue, and bass lines so thick you could lie on them. Through these the music would thud at spine-breaking volume, interspersed with eccentric comments from the disc jockeys spinning the records. (The characteristic Jamaican phonetic spelling of the 'deejay' job title suggests the jazzy, gaudily silk-shirted individuals who were the precursors of US rap artists, several of whom had Jamaican parents – the former street crack-dealer Biggie 'Notorious B.I.G.' Smalls and KRS-1, for example.)

The system Tom the Great Sebastian started in 1950 established him as the first significant sound-system operator. Many, in fact, believe him to be the all-time giant of sound systems. 'He is the man,' said Prince Buster, who later ran his own system and became one of Jamaica's most innovative musicians. Goodies, Count Smith the Blues Blaster, Count Joe and Sir Nick the Champ were among the other leading contenders, but they never triumphed over Tom the Great Sebastian. This would be apparent at the dances, billed as sound-system battles, in which two or more systems would compete, each playing a record in turn. Tom, with his unique tunes straight off the plane from the United States, the originality of his deejaying and the sheer power of his equipment, would inevitably mash up the opposition. These 'sets', as sound systems became known, would perform in the same locations as the big bands; the records they played initially were 78s – like the 45s that superseded them, these hottest, most underground records would have their labels scratched off to prevent rival sound-system operators from finding out the titles.

Although there was clearly an ironical purpose in the adoption of the various sound-system operators' aristocratic titles, it was also the only way non-white Jamaicans could possibly aspire to such heights. Duke Reid the Trojan's nickname came from the Bedford Trojan truck he used to transport his equipment. His wife had won the national lottery, which enabled them to open the Treasure Isle liquor store and provide the financing for his battery of equipment. Reid set up his sound system a couple of years after Tom the Great Sebastian, and by the end of the 1950s, his was one of the two dominant sound systems on the island.

Reid was an especially contentious figure. Sporting a trio of revolvers in his belt, from which he would indiscriminately fire shots, he was more inclined to destroy the opposition through violence than talent. Ironically, his former occupation of policeman had placed him in close contact with many of the tough characters he would use to threaten the competition. Much of the gangland-style behaviour that later became a feature of the Jamaican music business can be attributed to him. Instead of mashing up the sound-system opposition by playing the heaviest, loudest tunes, he would simply charge into rival dances with his gang, beating up or stabbing people and destroying their equipment. And if that didn't work, he could always resort to a spot of obeah. Reid would even have gangs of tough, sexy women at dances, all dressed in the same uniform, controlled by a female lieutenant called Duddah. But he also had tons of boxes, tons of 'house of joy', as sound-system speakers were referred to.

This was a world in which Tom the Great Sebastian desired to play no part. He packed up his sound system and moved his headquarters from Pink Lane off Beat Street – one of the worst corners in Jamaica – to a less violent venue called the Silver Slipper in Crossroads, where he found he made far more money.

Soon there came another contender for Duke Reid's crown: the Sir Coxsone Downbeat sound system, which took its name from the Yorkshire cricketer Coxsone and was run by Clement Seymour Dodd, whose family was also in the liquor-store business. Coxsone, as he became known, employed Prince

Buster as one of his main deejays; Buster's former occupation as a boxer also ensured he was a sizable deterrent to the gangs run by Reid. (By 1958 Prince Buster was running his own sound system. Reid and fifteen of his thugs went to a dance at the Chocomo lawn on Wellington Street looking for him. But Buster wasn't there: he was playing dice down on Charles Street. Hearing that Reid and his gang were up at Chocomo, Prince Buster hurried up there, and a man immediately pulled a knife on him. In the mêlée that followed, another of Reid's hoods split Buster's skull open with a rock. Later he and Reid became good friends: 'He became a nice man: he was just possessed by what was going on.')

Both Coxsone and Duke Reid soon began recording songs by local artists to use on their respective sound systems. The law of supply and demand proved to be inescapable, and out of this was born the Jamaican recording industry (as well as Coxsone's realization that American record companies like Imperial and Modern did not seem to notice when he blatantly pirated their material). Soon afterwards a pair of white Jamaicans followed this lead. One was Edward Seaga, a Harvard-educated anthropologist who, as leader of the Jamaica Labour Party, would later become prime minister for almost a decade. In 1958 he founded the WIRL (West Indies Records Ltd) label. The other was Chris Blackwell, who started Island Records in the same year, producing his records himself. His initial release was an LP by Lance Hayward, a blind Bermudan jazz pianist; but his first substantial hit did not come until the following year, when Laurel Aitken's 'Boogie In My Bones' became a local smash hit.

Rude boys outta jail! Slower, more languid than ska, the altogether more sultry rock steady sounded like trouble. Unsurprisingly it became the soundtrack for Jamaica's first youth tribe, the ratchet-knife-wielding rude boys – the cooler than cool, hotter than hot Johnny Too Bads of downtown Kingston.

The myth runs that the unusually hot summer of 1966

rendered impossible the faster dance movements of ska. In fact there had been a series of tunes since the spring that vied for the title of the first rock-steady tune – Roy Shirley's 'Hold Them', Derrick Morgan's 'Tougher Than Tough' and Alton Ellis's 'Girl I've Got A Date', in all of which the bassline came in shorter, more pronounced patterns of notes than in ska. The last tune was produced by Duke Reid, the genre's dominant producer. He seized the rock-steady moment with a sure grip that eluded his rival Coxsone Dodd, although Coxsone was to release the classic 'Rocking Steady' by the Wailers.

By 1968, however, a wind was blowing in from Africa: reggae, whose original rhythms can be heard played in lean-tos on the edge of the west African desert. With reggae, Jamaican music began consistently to go outernational: Jamaican music was the voice of the dispossessed and this contributed to reggae's international success.

The first record that year with the word in its title was 'Do The Reggay' by the Maytals. But by that time there had already been several other records with a similar distinctive backward guitar riff. That was part of the point; reggae opened everything: new genres, new producers, new markets. Several different styles vied with each other: fat, jerky instrumental records such as the Harry J. Allstars' 'Liquidator' and 'Return Of Django' by the Upsetters, the group led by the Young Turk upstart Lee Perry (both these records were top-ten hits in the UK in October 1969); the slack pop reggae of Max Romeo's 'Wet Dream'; and the classic three-piece vocal harmonizing of acts like the Heptones, the Cables, and Carlton and the Shoes; the era of the deejay was also ushered in in 1969 with the first sides from the great U Roy. And there was the precursor of the torrent of tunes to come in the next decade with minor chord horn parts and Rasta imagery – the roots revolution, predicted at the time by Burning Spear's extraordinary 'Door Peep'.

In the United Kingdom the market for the fast-paced instrumental reggae of Dave and Ansell Collins or Scratch Perry was the largely racist tribe of skinheads. But a more intelligent audience was also investigating this strange-sounding music, a market that found itself with both the images and soundtrack of a film starring Jimmy Cliff; Perry Henzell's legendary *The Harder They Come*. Along with Toots and the Maytals' 'Funky Kingston' and the Wailers' 'Catch A Fire', this formed the reggae primer triumvirate for the left-leaning middle-classes, looking for what would come to be seen as the seeds of world music.

The modern-day dancehall extravaganzas in relatively sophisticated clubs are a development of the culture of sound systems. The sound may have changed utterly and the outfits may be more outrageous than they have ever been, but 'dancehall' continues a uniquely Jamaican tradition and is utterly accessible to visitors to the island.

As anyone will attest who has tried to get a good Friday night's sleep in Kingston, traditional outdoor sound systems still flourish, seemingly in league with the packs of dogs that yowl along in approximate harmony. There is one particular sound effect with which the night air is perpetually riven, that of a machine-gun-like burst, a no doubt ironic aural development to keep visitors on their toes. Pinned to telegraph poles you will find posters advertising the locations of these forthcoming street dances, each given its own title – *God Bless Promotions with Lexus, Shorty, Snow and Fatta Ranks Present a night called Man Nuh Drink Bag Juice Pon Base*, for example, that sort of thing. (When my friend Buru put on a sound-system dance on the land behind his fish-and-festival shack in Port Antonio, he named it *A Night Called Nuff Gal fe Fuck . . .*)

Such occasions do not necessarily conform to conventional standards of crowd control and safety. At a sound-system dance in a roller-skating rink at Papine on the northern outskirts of Kingston, roots tunes and dancehall were interspersed with Puff Daddy cuts and Queen promising 'We Will Rock You'. Meanwhile, groups of young men, the waists of their baggy pants worn somewhere near their knees, lit the trails of gas from lighter-fluid canisters, firing them off into the air, a cultural development that caused me some concern. (See also: the popularity of putting such poisonous detergents as bleach in plastic bottles labelled 'Lemonade'. A friend of mine has the solution to this possibility of imminent death by 'pisoning' – something that always terrified slave-owners: my friend gives his kids little sips of all available house-cleaning fluids. 'It immunize them, act as a antidote,' he explains, with irrefutable logic.)

A more relaxed evening can be enjoyed at the open-air sound systems you'll find in the country. As the satin breeze cools the air, you will feel there are few better things in life than swaying gently to the latest tunes, Red Stripe in hand, beneath the moon-illuminated mango and breadfruit trees. And at such events there is always one inevitability: even in the most impenetrable bush-hamlet dances, you will find a lone Japanese tourist, intricately aping the styles of the coolest dancers.

In the days when Don Drummond was the featured star with the Skatalites, this first of the modern Jamaican groups would perform almost entirely in the tourist hotels of the north coast. It was taken as a given that there was no real live circuit in Jamaica. Back in 1978 I had to travel across the island to the Trelawny Beach Hotel (driven in the red, gold and green Ford Escort of Horsemouth Wallace, a legendary drummer, who in one backwoods bar declared his general crossness at some imagined slight by waving a machete about) to see a magical bill that included Peter Tosh, Burning Spear, Culture and Big Youth.

If you're looking for live shows nowadays, however, you're in luck: things have changed completely in the last twenty years: In September 1997 in August Town in Kingston, an area that had slid into warring conflict, I watched the cream of the island's musicians put on a free all-night show on the flatbed of an articulated lorry. With a bill topped by Luciano, the king of 'consciousness', the new wave of spiritual roots reggae, and Sizzler, the movement's righteous punk, and cameos from Capleton and Buju Banton, a crowd of 5000 swayed until dawn as the music soared up into the Blue Mountains.

As well as playing to August Town's ghetto people, that same bill toured the island, playing in the tourist towns of Port Antonio, Ocho Rios and Negril. These days current big-name bills – a package of Lady Saw, Bounti Killa and the Innocent Crew, say – constantly tour the island.

Out past the Cactus Club, for example, is Fort Clarence, a beach at the front of the Hellshire hills which regularly hosts day- (and night-) long 'bashments' with fabulous bills; one I saw featured Bounti, Beenie Man and General Degree as well as many other acts: all the hits that fit. The only downside was the vast anthill on which I stood. I had wondered why no one else had chosen to perch on this patch of high ground, and my question was answered after I felt a growing tickling on my lower legs and looked down to find my sneakers and socks filled with crawling creatures. After a time in Jamaica you become accustomed to checking the ground you're about to sit on. Ants – especially 'bitin' ants' – are a genuine hazard: you get used to the sight of people splashing kerosene on the ground and lighting it, as they incinerate entire colonies of what will probably be the earth's next rulers.

(Unfortunately the same tactics can't be used on the chewing gum that also litters the ground at such events: after watching the reggae-soul crooner Ritchie Stevens one Sunday at Boston Beach – famed as the home of 'jerk' chicken – I headed for where I was staying to find the rear of my Paul Smith shorts matted together with a discarded lump of Wrigley's. 'We can fix that,' said the man in the laundry of my hotel. When I got them back later the next day, the chewing gum was gone. But down one leg the shorts appeared to have changed colour. 'I'm say to tell yuh de bleach jes' catch,' said the woman who handed them to me. 'Yuh can wear dem 'bout de house.')

The remote Negril, the loosest of Jamaican resorts, is host to regular shows, often featuring 'revival' artists with guaranteed audience pull, such as Gregory Isaacs, U Roy or Culture. Situated on the most westerly, hottest point of Jamaica, Negril has a seven-mile strip of white beach which slopes into the sea so gradually that you can walk a hundred yards out through its flat water and still find the ocean rising no higher than your thighs. Although much of this spectacular beach has had low-rise hotels built along it, so dense and deeply ingrained is the mood of Negril that these buildings have not managed to damage the spirit of a resort that in the 1970s was the quint-essence of alternative Jamaica. This was when the late Jacob Miller celebrated the prevailing mode of residence in what was still an overgrown village in his Jamaican hit 'Cottage In Negril'. In that era, long before anyone had even heard of 'all-inclusive hotel holidays', the groovers who made it to this hard-to-reach part of the island (it's a five-hour drive from Kingston) stayed in the ramshackle hut complexes knocked up by various local and foreign entrepreneurs. Negril was hippy heaven: dirt-cheap and overhung by a permanent cloud of ganja smoke.

Nowadays music can only enhance the sultry, psilocybinlike effect of Negril at night-time, and the town often has two or three live bills a week. No matter the act, the evenings are special. Kaiser's, on the road to the dramatic cliffs, and De Buss, down on the seven-mile strip of white beach, vie for the best names.

One evening I went and downed a few Red Stripes at Alfred's, the coolest bar on the beach. Then I strolled through the warm night air along the sand to the town square, where I took a drink of overpriced Irish Moss and watched a local being fleeced at the three-card trick of Crown and Anchor. Afterwards I made my way up to Kaiser's.

As amateur hookers and 'rental-dreads' worked the edges of the crowd, I watched Yellowman, the hugely popular 'slack' deejay of fifteen or so years ago. But his set was predictable, going through the motions. Then came a breathtaking per-formance from the prolific Frankie Paul; his soulful voice soared above the sea with a powerful dignity that hushed the hustlers. And as a crescent moon broke through the light cloud cover, I knew I could be nowhere else but in Jamaica.

At the annual SumFest, finding yourself obliged to purchase a 'reggae bed' (strip of cardboard box) for five US dollars to rest your body on the rough rock ground, you may wish you were anywhere but Jamaica.

For the musical archivist who wants to catch up on all the hottest and latest Jamaican acts, however, a visit to SumFest is the one sure-fire method. Take your own seating arrangements; avoid any conversations with people threateningly trying to sell you overpriced drugs; and be content that by the end of the three-day festival, which takes place each August in Montego Bay, you'll have attended a masterclass in Jamaican music.

I was last there in 1997. Every name in Jamaica I hadn't caught was on the bill, and I was thrilled by Anthony B, Tanya Stevens and General Degree, and enjoyed the cultural aberrations of the Scare Dem Crew. A full-blown music festival, SumFest is well run with the acts appearing onstage at the scheduled times – contrary to the prevailing popular image of all Jamaican events as being unpunctual and inefficient, an impression that is increasingly out of date.

Inevitably, it was dancehall night that was the most striking. My final memory of SumFest is of Lady Saw onstage, grabbing her crotch, bumping and grinding into the mike as the sun slowly rose. Rather like when Carlene the dancehall queen hit the floor at the Cactus nightclub.

The second gunman, the one who had suggested the immediate execution of one of us, is obviously panicked, and I can feel his panic seeping into everything and everybody. This is very worrying. I can feel the whole thing could go off and everyone will be slaughtered within seconds. As a matter of fact, I am coming to the conclusion that I was right to think that the reassuring words offered by the gunman who got me out of my room were only to cool me out, and that we are all going to be killed.

I have a solution to this problem of the safe, however. (I am not being entirely altruistic: as I am the only one with no direct connection to the house, and therefore to the safe, I am probably the most expendable.) 'Excuse me, there is a slight mistake being made here,' I say somewhat tremulously, 'the safe doesn't have a key – it has a combination.' I'm trying to take very deep breaths into my stomach to calm any internal trembling that my speech might reveal. 'And Ducky,' I continue, before anyone can reply, 'you know what the combination is, don't you?'

'Yes,' she whimpers, her face in the floor.

'Please go and open the safe for them right now.'

She is led away, and I breathe a slight sigh of relief. Although it still doesn't look to me as if we're getting out of this. After all, I know there is virtually nothing in the safe, which I imagine will increase the mood of general crossness. So although we've got through one problem, we're about to hit the next.

I relax slightly, however. Accordingly, I am not as prostrate on the ground as my captors would like – in fact I am kneeling, my hands on the ground in front of me.

'Get down on the ground, like you white people used to make us slaves do,' says a voice.

Now I am again trying not to look at their faces, at the same time letting them register that I am doing this. As I don't have my contact lenses in, I can't see them too well anyway, which does add something to the soft-focus effect. Everything is still suspended in slow motion, and the solution I was able to create over the safe has restored some calm in me.

Peter is then led over to the other side of the house, where the safe is. After a minute or so, the guy who barged into my room takes me over there too. Now Peter is lying on that wooden floor. Ducky's younger, fourteen-year-old daughter is face down on a cot bed, her body shaking and trembling.

The man who was threatening to kill us if we didn't get the safe open is standing over them, brandishing his pistol. He looks extremely mean. He stands facing me. Behind him are two other figures I haven't previously seen. One is fresh-faced and almost smiling – is this the smile of psychosis? The other, worryingly, is wearing a bandanna around his nose and mouth. I say 'worryingly', because this implies that I may very well know him. Already I am sensing that there is more to all this than meets the eye: somehow we've been set up, either by someone in the house or someone who has seen us eating at one of the nearby food shacks.

Anyway, I try not to let any of these characters think I am registering their features. After all, they don't know I can hardly see them anyway.

The safe – just a metal box, really – has been opened and ransacked: its contents, including an Apple Mac Powerbook, are strewn all over the floor and an adjacent table. Then the gunman points his weapon at me.

'Where de greenbacks?' he demands. 'Where de dollars? Where de jewels? Where de gold?'

August 1997, February 1978, February 1983

Oh, no, Mr Sloe, please don't try and overtake on this corner. In a Nissan bus we – Don Letts, his directing partner Rick Elgood and I – are barrelling along the north coast road from Montego Bay towards Ocho Rios, heading back from the 1997 SumFest. The sensual aquamarine sea is on our left, whitecaps bouncing across it – a beautifully seductive sight – as we turn a corner and are suddenly confronted by the vast Port Rhodes bauxite shipping terminal, red dust everywhere, an eyesore stuck bang in a corner of Discovery Bay. The stretch of coastline gets its name from being the point where Columbus allegedly first came ashore in 1494. 'The fairest island that eyes have beheld,' the great explorer pronounced. Nowadays this strip of road looks more like a toxic waste dump in New Jersey: trucks unload belly-loads of rocks on to roadsides; JCBs shift about bits of coast – there seems to be an eternal preoccupation in Jamaica of moving one bit of the island to another.

Past the port, however, the broad sweep of the bay still takes my breath away (as do so many views and corners that you round in Jamaica) as we swing around it, the warm breeze billowing through the vehicle's windows and caressing our skin and hair. Yet my teeth jam together and my mouth is twisted into the rictus of a death-mask: sheer unadulterated terror is descending upon me as Mr Sloe, hypnotized by herb to further focus his driving skills, hurtles past a cramped church minibus, out of the windows of which arms instructively flap or gesticulate to underline points in their owners' learned disquisitions on arcane interpretations of theology.

It is Sunday lunchtime beachtown traffic. Which means: *Anarchy!* At very high speeds. The greatest danger of all in Jamaica is surely not political gunmen or machete-wielding madmen or ratchet-bladed crackhead rude boys or even badmen dripping with weapons who break into your house: it is ordinary Jamaican drivers, whose collective psychotic aggression and sense of the die-young-leave-a-good-looking-corpse aesthetic would have won them admiration from Sid Vicious. Such a spontaneously creative style of driving, inspired by a frightening blend of random fury and playground fun, is not easily anticipated.

It is noticeable that across the island the potholes in the roads have been fixed, a sure indication of an imminent election, facilitating even more the pleasures of high-speed road racing. Road signs sprayed in acid orange – *DETOUR!* – suddenly flash worryingly past us. The number and newness of the cars on the roads of Jamaica can seem misleadingly like an indication of recent affluence: a pair of white cabriolet three series BMWs squeal upon and past us on a bend, crabbing sideways, jerkily heel-and-toeing.

From what seems to be about 100 mph we suddenly slither to a halt on the loose stones outside a wooden roadside bar where Rick knows a dread who has worked on one of the videos he and Don have made in Jamaica. A shocking pink minibus with 'J and H Special' emblazoned across its windscreen is being washed down in the adjacent river, next to a dark-grey Toyota pick-up truck. As he serves up something called turtle punch, the dread bears important tidings: he tells us that Princes Bekare and Ermias, the great-grandsons of His Imperial Majesty Haile Selassie I, Emperor of Ethiopia, King of Kings, Conquering Lion of Judah, will be arriving in Jamaica next weekend.

But now we are back in the van. Coiled and corrugated cast-off tyre casings punctuate the rough rubble at the roadside. A furl of fresh toilet paper flies in through the window. I wonder if it is bad form to ask Mr Sloe to put on the brakes. He's not so young: what if he has a heart attack – perhaps just as he's ploughing head on towards this trio of big rigs hurtling towards us down the centre of the road, belching smoke as they overtake the inevitable pack of white Toyota Corollas. But then, I'm not a good passenger.

Now Mr Sloe is sitting on the tail of a freshly painted, scarlet Lada, its bumpers removed, a tail-light out, its windows a mottled, time-tarnished purple. I'm hoping that the turtle punch will remain sitting in my stomach: I had thought the term 'turtle' was a metaphor, like that other Jamaican great symbolic drink, Front-End Lifter, for example – I didn't realize until too late that there was real turtle in it. Now I trust it won't be too tricky in a belly that's served over twenty years on a non-meat diet. (There is a tendency in Jamaica to sell drinks and food on their reputed aphrodisiac qualities, a selling point also of turtle punch, I discover. Soursop juice is reputed to 'put back the henergy yuh los' last night'; 'strongback', a bush tea, is alleged to give you more than a strong back.)

Trying to whisper above the racket of the wind and the engine noise, we confess our mutual horror at the pace of our motorized progression. We decide to gravely risk losing face by asking Mr Sloe to slow down. 'No need to brek yuh neck. Take it easy, Mr Sloe,' says Don. Mr Sloe shows his acceptance of our advice by promptly overtaking on a corner. More slowly.

Early in the evening of the next Saturday (16 August 1997), the Bob Marley Museum at 56 Hope Road is a sea of khaki-garbed dreads of both sexes, most of whom are in late middle age or elderly. In a sinewy sort of way they all look tremendously fit, and a palpable aura of sincerity, righteousness and reverence hovers about them like a rich metaphysical soup, enriching and nourishing the parts of our souls few other experiences can reach. For public consumption outside Jamaica, and in as much as Rastafari is personified by Bob Marley, 56 Hope Road seems to be considered the home of the religion. The tall, detached wooden house here was the headquarters of Island Records until 1974, when Chris Blackwell, as part of renegotiating the artist's contract, gave the property to Bob – as he is known everywhere on the island, rather like the way that Castro in neighbouring Cuba has universally become 'Fidel'. Although it's a similar visual icon, Bob's image is even more familiar than that of Castro – ironically as familiar as that of Fidel's revolutionary spar, Che Guevara. (During the Manley era it was fashionable in Jamaica to watch Cuban TV – even if you didn't speak Spanish, you showed on which side you stood and the full extent of your political correctness. When, in 1978, I took Bunny Wailer at his word and went up to his home in Maining, St Thomas, looking for him, his wife and children were sitting watching Cuban television, beaming in from across the ocean ninety miles away, a haze of ganja smoke from Mrs Wailer's pipe hanging in the small living room.)

Although Bob never lived at the property, 56 Hope Road became his headquarters, and a rehearsal studio was built. It was while he was practising here on Friday 3 December 1976 that an attempt on his life took place in which Don Taylor, his manager, was seriously wounded and Bob himself took a bullet in the left arm; his wife Rita was also wounded from a bullet creasing her head as she sat in her Volkswagen Beetle in the car park. Bob vanished to hide out at Strawberry Hill, a small restaurant high up in the Blue Mountains.

Bob fled the island for eighteen months. When he returned to Jamaica, it seemed almost with defiance that he installed himself once again at the property as a regular fixture. Life at 56 Hope Road was like an uptown version of Bob's existence in Trench Town, as it is for many a ghetto don who has moved away from his birthplace.

By ten in the morning the yard would be in a state of permanent bustle. The Tuff Gong record store would have opened and ghetto rankins and junior rankins would be coming up to check Bob or to hustle him for money, or just to cool out: 56 Hope Road was about the only uptown place that a ghetto youth could hang in without experiencing the wrath of the police. During the time of 1978's Peace Concert, which Bob returned from exile to famously hold together the hands of the PNP leader and Edward Seaga, even Michael Manley passed by to idle away an hour or so. Bob, who favoured holding court in the shade of the awning over the front steps, was also extremely welcoming to the 'mad' people who would peer through the white fence, pouring forth their stream-of-consciousness rants. Such individuals are an omnipresent feature of Jamaican life; there is a gnarled dread, stark naked apart from the thick grime that besmears his bony body, who is a regular evening rush-hour feature at traffic lights in New Kingston. Such mental sickness is variously attributed to a surfeit of ganja, overproof rum or simply 'the pressure'. These figures are not without their position in society, considered endowed with shamanlike primal (or highly sophisticated) capabilities. 'It a mad man,' Bob would say, always eager to hear an unorthodox point of view, 'send him in for a reasoning.'

Bob Marley's astrological chart has several points of contact with the chart of Jamaica, which is drawn for 00:00 hours on 6 August 1962, the first moment of independence. This gives the island a Leo Sun, Libra Moon and Taurus ascendant. Saturn sits atop the chart, bringing the island the heavy manners and authoritarian rule it has experienced since independence. Like two smoking barrels, the warlike Mars ascends in the communicative, media-aware sign of Gemini. The Sun, Mercury, Uranus and Pluto are all in Leo, the island's dominant Sun sign: the Jamaican Lion is communicative, controversial and powerful. Venus, the ruler of its chart, is in Virgo in the fifth house, bringing great creativity. Jupiter in the tenth house in Pisces, meanwhile, points to many overseas contacts. Bob Marley's Sun, moreover, is exactly conjunct with Jamaica's Saturn at the top of the chart: he is the king of the nation. His Pluto falls precisely on the lunar north node, linking him to Jamaica's collective unconscious and granting him power and money thereby.

A Leo island: it should hardly be surprising that the Lion of Judah is such an omnipresent image. Or that Jamaicans tend to be warm, open, sensual people who can also be egotistical, self-adoring and blinkered. Part of this latter problem is that of an island mentality – Jamaica can seem like a village, especially in the flashfire area of gossip and rumour.

After the Peace Concert many of the gunmen felt such a debt of gratitude to Bob that they became even more in evidence at 56 Hope Road, to the point where their presence became a problem, even sometimes a threat. 'He grew up with a lot of these guys,' said Junior Marvin, the Wailers' guitarist, 'and he wanted to straighten out a lot of them. He was trying to help them. He was trying to say, "Look, you don't really need violence; if you've got that kind of power, you don't have to use it: you can divert it into another kind of positive energy."'

Bob certainly seemed to feel that part of his role was to be a mediator with and for such figures. In February 1979 I flew to Kingston, my second visit to Jamaica. Arriving late in the evening, I took a taxi to Knutsford Boulevard in New Kingston and checked into the Sheraton Hotel (later sold by the group and renamed the Wyndham, which doesn't have quite the ring of the name that inspired the line 'Natty dread at the Sheraton Hotel' in the Clash's 'Safe European Home'). I was on a press trip, with three other journalists, to write a piece about Inner Circle, a Kingston group that featured Jacob Miller on vocals.

The next morning jet lag meant that I woke early. Seizing the time, I found myself in a taxi at around quarter to eight, chugging through the early rush-hour traffic, rounding the corner at Devon House and into and up Hope Road. 'Bob gets up early,' I had been advised.

Arriving at 56 Hope Road, I found little sign of activity. On the wooden verandah to the right of the building was a group of what looked like tough ghetto youth to whom I nodded greetings, searching in vain for any faces I recognized. In front of the Tuff Gong record shop to the right of the house was a woman who wore her dreadlocks tucked into a tam, sweeping the shop's steps with a besom that scurried around the floor-length hem of her skirt. A sno-cone spliff dangled from her mouth. Wandering over to her, I introduced myself, mentioning that I had been in Jamaica the previous year writing about reggae, showing her a copy of the main article I had written. She turned out to be Diane Jobson, the in-house lawyer for the Tuff Gong operation. (Over the years I was to get to know her well, and her brother Dickie, who directed the film *Countryman*, became a close pal.)

Then a five-series BMW purred into the yard, driven by a beautiful woman. Like many Jamaican cars, it had black-tinted windows, and an Ethiopian flag fluttered in the breeze from an aerial on its left front wing. Out of it stepped Bob Marley. He greeted the ghetto youth and began speaking with them. On his way over he had registered my presence, I noticed. After a couple of minutes, I excused myself from Diane and walked towards Bob. I introduced myself to him, and he shook hands with me with a smile, his attention caught by the Animal Rights badge that by chance I was wearing on my red Fred Perry shirt. Again, I explained I had been to Jamaica for the first time the previous year, and showed him the article. He seemed genuinely interested and began to read it. As he did so, just like Bob Marley should have done, he handed me a spliff he had just finished rolling. Nervously I took it and toked away at it.

After a minute or two Diane came over. Gathering together the youth, she led them in the direction of a minibus parked in the shade. Bob made his excuses – 'We have to go somewhere' – and walked over to the vehicle. Then, as he stepped into it, he turned. 'Come on, come with us!' He waved with a grin, climbing down out of the vehicle and holding the door open for me.

I hurried over. Ushering me into the minibus, Bob squeezed up next to me on one of its two-seater bench seats. I tried to disguise my feelings – a sense of great honour as well as slight apprehension that the herb I had smoked was beginning to kick in, suddenly seeming a million times stronger than anything I had ever smoked in London. I was starting to feel rather distanced from everything, which was possibly just as well. Bumping through the potholed back streets of what I knew to be the affluent uptown suburb of Beverley (*sic*: note the traditional Jamaican misspelling) Hills, I ventured to ask Bob, who was himself puffing away on a spliff, where we were going. 'Gun Court,' he uttered, matter-of-factly.

I blinked, and quickly tried to recover myself. The Gun Court had a reputation that was fearsome. To all intents and purposes, the place was a concentration camp, and certainly it had been built to look like one: gun towers, barbed-wire perimeters, visibly armed guards, a harsh, militaristic feel immediately apparent to all who drove past its location on South Camp Road. The Gun Court was a product of Michael Manley's Emergency Powers Act of 1975. Into it was dumped, for indefinite detention or execution after a summary trial, anyone in Jamaica found with any part of a gun. (Nowadays, it is said, the security forces adopt a more cost-effective and immediate solution: anyone in Jamaica found with any part of a gun, runs the myth, is executed on the spot.) The previous year, when I had been in Kingston with Lydon, Letts and co., the dreadlocked Rastafarian filmmaker had been held at gunpoint by a Jamaica Defence Force soldier while filming the exterior of the Gun Court. At first the squaddie refused to believe Letts was British; only after being shown his UK passport did he let him walk away. What would have happened had he been Jamaican?

'Why are we going there?' I asked Bob, as calmly as I could.

'To see about a youth them lock up – Michael Bernard,' he quietly replied.

Michael Bernard, I learned later, was a cause célèbre – a political activist accused of a shooting.

Having descended from the heights of Beverley Hills, a detour that had been taken to avoid morning traffic, we were soon pulling up outside the Gun Court's sinister compound.

At nine in the morning, beneath an already scorching tropical sun, the vision of the Gun Court was like a surreal dubbed-up inversion of one of the ugly, incongruous industrial trading-estate-type buildings that litter much of Kingston's often quite cute sprawl.

At the sight of Bob emerging from the minibus, a door within the main gates opened for his party. We stepped through into the prison. After we had been standing for some time in the already baking heat of the forecourt, an officer appeared. In hushed tones he spoke to Bob; I was unable to hear what passed between them, which was probably just as well. It was almost a year since I had last heard patois daily, and I could comprehend only about half of what was being said around me.

Then we were led to the left, into the piss-stinking prison building itself. And through a number of locked, barred doors, and into the governor's broad office, like the study of a boarding-school headmaster, which was also the demeanour of the governor himself, a greying, middle-aged man who sat behind the sturdy desk in front of the window. In this office we were seated, on hard wooden chairs, in a semicircle in front of him. I found myself directly to the right of Bob, who in turn was seated nearest to the governor.

Through a door in the opposite wall was ushered a slight man who appeared to be in his early twenties. He was shown to a chair by that door and sat down on it. This was Michael Bernard.

Discussions now began, the essence of which concerned questions by Bob about the possibilities of a retrial or of Bernard's release from prison. Bernard said virtually nothing, and almost all speech was confined to Bob and the governor. I asked a couple of questions, but when I interrupted a third time, Bob wisely hushed me – I was starting to get into a slightly right-on stride here. Most of the dialogue, I noted, was conducted in timorous, highly reverent tones by all parties present, almost with a measure of deference, or perhaps simply hesitant nervousness. (Over the years I was to decide that it was the latter, noting that often Jamaicans called upon to speak publicly – whether rankin' politicians at barnstorming rallies, Rasta elders at Nyabinghi reasonings, Commissioner of Police Joe Williams in an interview I conducted with him, or crucial defence witnesses in the rarefied, bewigged atmosphere of English courts –would present themselves with all the stumbling hesitancy and lack of rigorous logic of a very reluctant school speechday orator. Yet in more lateral philosophical musings and reasonings, there are few individuals as fascinatingly, confidently loquacious as Jamaicans when it comes to conversational elliptical twists, stream–of–consciousness free associations and Barthes-like [or Bart Simpson-like?] word de- and re-constructions.)

After twenty minutes or so, all talk seemed to grind to a halt. Afterwards I was left a little unclear as to what conclusions had been arrived at, if any. At first I worried that this was because at first I had been struggling with the effects of the herb, which seemed like a succession of psychic tidal waves. Then later I realized that the purpose of this mission to the Gun Court was simply to show that Michael Bernard had not been forgotten.

Bidding farewell to the prisoner, wishing him luck, and thanking the governor for his time, we left his office, clanking out through the jail doors and into the biting sunlight. Soon we were back at 56 Hope Road, which by then had become a hive of all manner of activity. 'Stick around,' said Bob. I did. And on a bench in the shade of a mango tree round the back of the house I promptly fell asleep for at least two hours from what was probably a combination of jet lag and some kind of delayed shock.

This visit to the Gun Court with Bob Marley was one of the great experiences of my life. I was in Jamaica for about another three weeks, and saw Bob several more times, often courtesy of Denise Mills, a great human being (now passed on) who worked dedicatedly for Island Records in Jamaica. I watched rehearsals at 56 Hope Road; saw Bob playing with his kids – they had just released their first record as the Melody Makers; found him with one of the most gorgeous women that had ever crossed my eyes at a Twelve Tribes Grounation one Saturday night on the edge of the hills; and interviewed him for an article. Doing the interview, I felt a measure of guilt for taking up so much of his precious time, even though at the time I didn't realize quite how precious and finite it was. Bob looked terribly tired and strained, and it was only just over eighteen months later that he collapsed while jogging in New York's Central Park with his friend the footballer Skill Cole, and was diagnosed as suffering from cancer.

I didn't go back to Jamaica for another four years, until February 1983. By then it was coming up for two years since Bob had passed on, on 11 May 1981; Island Records were about to release the posthumous *Confrontation* album, and I'd gone out to JA to write a piece about this for *The Face*.

Again, jet lag caused me to wake early on the first morning I was there. This time I was staying just down the road from the former Sheraton, at the neighbouring Pegasus. Getting out of bed, I switched on the radio in my room. The JBC seven-o'clock news came on with its first story: 'Released from the Gun Court today is Michael Bernard ...' *Wow! Phew! JAH RASTAFARI!* That Jamaica will get you every time. This island really is a land of magic realism, a physical, geographical place that is like a manifestation of the collective unconscious. Or is it just that Bob Marley, as someone once suggested to me, is very active on psychic spheres and has a great sense of humour? Was this just something he'd laid on for me in the Cosmic Theme Park of the Island of Springs? I found myself wondering, with a certain vanity.

There was more to come. Someone whom I met on that trip was a woman called Valerie Cowan, a feisty, sexy 'Chinee gal'. Despite her affluent background, she had become a kind of downtown fixer. Valerie was a street person, someone most at her ease when dealing with ghetto people. When she asked me if I wanted to go to a cockfight scheduled to take place in Trench Town late that afternoon, I was there like a shot.

Trench Town did not seem especially different. There were the usual constants: the blue sky; the plentiful palm trees; the wandering herds of friendly goats chewing on the grease of discarded boxes of Kentucky Fried Chicken and other scraps of litter. And the mood about the place was as flat as ever.

On Second Street, where Bob once used to live, the cockfight was scheduled to take place in one of the communal tenement yards: a few square yards of dried mud, fringed by chunks of cracked masonry and breeze-blocks, but kept spotlessly clean. Valerie introduced me to Massive Dread, a 'singjay' she was promoting: almost inevitably, considering his name, 'Massive' was of an exceptionally diminutive stature.

The cockfight was very Jamaican Zen: a couple of proud roosters, sharpened spurs attached to their heels, were kissed and caressed by their owners before being let go and sort of pushed at each other. But these guys had transcended their trade, they were hip to the trip; they knew wha' gwan. Desultorily checking each other out, the pair of cocks wandered about each other in circles for a minute or two, then backed off leisurely to opposite ends of the yard, to peck at whatever nutrition they could discover in the earth.

A week or so later I drove up in the customary Japanese rental car with Valerie to 56 Hope Road to check the general runnings. It was around eight in the evening. Valerie lived opposite. After ensuring I made it through the gauntlet of security that was now a fixture of the yard, she introduced me to a couple of dreads who had done some serious hanging with Bob. Then she left me to my own devices.

I squatted down with these two guys on the car-park perimeter to smoke a spliff. Then one of them asked me to give them a lift to the Kentucky Fried Chicken on Knutsford Boulevard, just around the corner from the Sheraton, in New

Kingston. Jamaicans have a particular fondness for 'Kentucky': the ease with which many dreads would slip between a Rastafarianism vegetarian 'ital' diet and this ubiquitous fast food always surprised me. Maybe it was this decidedly un-ital choice of food that triggered (perhaps not the best choice of word) the negative karma. Anyway, we were driving along the four-lane Oxford Road, a few hundred yards before the right-hand turn into Knutsford Boulevard. I had just noticed that somehow a freshly rolled cone-shaped spliff had appeared, as though by magic, on the vinyl dashboard. As I vaguely wondered about its origin, I glanced to my right. Driving parallel to us was an army truck filled with uniformed, helmeted soldiers. None of them looked older than about sixteen – and they were pointing their rifle barrels directly at us. Leaning out of the passenger window was an older man dressed in an officer's uniform, waving at me to pull over.

I felt it best not to question his suggestion.

As soon as I had stopped the car, soldiers were all over us, the muzzles of their rifles pointed at our heads. I edged my eyeballs to the left: the spliff was still sitting there on the dashboard. 'Get out,' the officer ordered, and we didn't waste a second.

He wasn't interested in me at all. The dreads from 56 Hope Road were pushed up against a link fence and told to spread their legs and raise their arms. Then they and the car were thoroughly searched. Concerned for them, for a moment I tried an 'Excuse me, I am a journalist with the *Sunday Times* in London' routine – until a glower from the officer made me button my lip. I knew, anyway, that I would end up spending the night in some horrendous lock-up: the spliff was enough to ensure that. I vaguely wondered whether the British embassy would be able to help me.

But all of a sudden the officer was climbing back into the cab of the truck. And the teenage soldiers were swinging themselves and their rifles over the tailgate. And they were off.

The spliff was no longer on the dashboard. What happened

to it? Neither of the dreads claimed to have taken it. Did one of the soldiers palm it? Or else how on earth could it have been spirited away?

The next day I discovered why we'd been stopped and given such a thorough going-over: about thirty minutes previously, three cops had been shot dead a little down the road.

Dollars? Greenbacks? Jewels? Gold?

Standing there facing Mr Psycho, my eyes ostentatiously aimed at the floorboards, I am very concerned because I know we don't have any money in the house. As well as the laptop computer, the safe had also contained Peter's US$500 in traveller's cheques – but even though they are American Express, I know they are not really acceptable in this situation. Personally, I'm broke: earlier that evening I'd borrowed JA$500 – about ten pounds sterling – from Peter until I got back to Kingston the next day. Again, Mr Psycho is coming out with this stuff about killing us if he doesn't get money. I'm worried they are going to start killing people – maybe the women and children, maybe Peter, maybe me – very soon. I glance at the glittering, fat machete blades being brandished by two of the gang and tell myself that I might have to face these. I don't like to consider this prospect – but I do, and some measure of acceptance of the possibility seems to help.

I decide to introduce another element: I tell them that I have money elsewhere, where I am staying. I have around £500 there, I say.

'Pounds? Mi not want pounds, mi want dollars.'

I find this slightly irritating, though I try not to show it. 'Well, I don't have dollars because I'm not American. But the £500 is worth about US$750. I can take you there to get it.'

Really, my idea is just to get them away. I have crazy schemes, like crashing my rented Toyota Corolla into a police car – the police would probably shoot me, I realize later – or driving them off the mountain and jumping out. (Yeah. Sure.)

'Listen,' I say, 'we can go and get this money I have right now.'

'How long it take to get there?'

'About an hour and a half.'

'Mi not like this idea.'

75

'OK. Take the car.'

'Is rental car?' demands the psycho.

'Yes.'

'Mi not want rental car . . . Where is it?'

'Up the end of the beach. By Raver's food shack.'

'Where dat? Mi not know this person.'

'Up the end of the beach.'

'Wha'?' He is very edgy and irritable, maybe from coke, as though he may go off at any moment. 'Mi not know where that is. 'Ow far?'

'About three hundred yards,' I say. In fact, I am beginning to feel extremely nervous, and it is hard to get those last words out. I feel very exposed, standing there in just my boxer shorts.

1494–1692

Little has changed in Jamaica in the four hundred years since Christopher Columbus first discovered it.

The Genoese adventurer first sighted Jamaica on 5 May 1494, landing at St Ann's Bay after an eleven-day voyage across the Caribbean from Hispaniola, the island on which today are located both the Dominican Republic and Haiti. Immediately Columbus was taken with Jamaica's perfect climate and breathtaking scenery; he declared it to be 'the fairest island that eyes have beheld . . . all full of valleys and fields and plains'.

Xaymaca, or Yamaye, was the name given the island by the Taino Indians, the original inhabitants of the large islands of the northern Caribbean – Jamaica, Cuba, the Bahamas, Puerto Rico and Hispaniola. They feared the god Huracan, who brought fierce storms to the island, and were continually under threat from the cannibalistic Caribs, who had moved into the Caribbean from South America. (The word 'cannibal' itself derives from a Spanish transliteration of Carib into *Calib* and then into *Canib*.) The Caribs were a race of red-painted, tropical Vikings, with an age-old belief in the symbolic power of anthropophagy: they enslaved women and would eat or sacrifice their husbands. (Do we begin to see a karmic logic in the vegetarianism that is part of the faith of strict Rastafarians?)

The Caribs took the southern islands of the Caribbean. With the Tainos, they shared the same language, Arawakan – hence the Native American settlers of Jamaica are often referred to as Arawaks.

There were more than 400 Taino settlements in Jamaica, a

population of 50,000–60,000, when the Spanish arrived. An artistic, creative people, they used the many caves of Xaymaca for the purposes of burial; from these has been learned much of what we know about them. (Considering the impression of the Jamaican as a person with a finely developed talent for relaxation, it seems apt that the Tainos of Jamaica invented the hammock.)

On his visits to Cuba, Hispaniola and the Bahamas (his first landing in the New World had been there, at Watling Island), Columbus had found the Tainos 'gentle, peaceful, and very simple'. But those he met when he landed in Jamaica were hostile, retreating only when deadly crossbow volleys were loosed at them. The next day, accepting that Christopher Columbus's arrival fulfilled an ancient prophecy of men bringing instruments of thunder and lightning, the Tainos offered gifts of cassava, fruit and fish to the Spaniards. (When Columbus found Jamaica, its native fruits were pineapple, guava, sweetsop and star apple. Ackee, the scrambled-egg-like vegetable eaten in the national dish of ackee and salt fish, came from west Africa in the eighteenth century; breadfruit was brought from the Pacific – Captain Bligh's ill-fated *Bounty* had been ordered to fetch the first breadfruit plants to Jamaica.)

After thus making contact with the island's natives, Columbus returned to Hispaniola, from which he set forth for Spain with a cargo of 500 local Tainos, intending to sell them as slaves. Almost half died before they reached Cadiz. In Hispaniola the Tainos were subjected to atrocities, frequently under the command of Juan de Esquivel, the governor. When Columbus first arrived in Hispaniola, 300,000 Tainos lived there: in less than a hundred years they were wiped out, an omen for those in Jamaica.

In 1504 Columbus made a forced landing in Jamaica; his pair of caravels had become too rotten with woodworm for the Atlantic crossing. Foundering in St Ann's Bay, Columbus was stranded for a year with his brother Bartholomew and son Ferdinand. Responding to signs of hostility from the Tainos,

Columbus played a textbook trick: the cunning Italian possessed a copy of the first ephemeris, a table of planetary positions, published by Regiomontanus in 1474, which predicted a total lunar eclipse on the evening of 29 February 1504.

Desperate for provisions, Columbus invited the Taino leaders on board his ship. During the entertainment he explained that he believed in a powerful god who was angry at their failure to help him. As a measure of his anger, the moon would turn blood red before disappearing from view. When the eclipse began, the natives were understandably alarmed, pleading with Columbus to intercede on their behalf.

As mentally agile as he had needed to be to obtain funds for his journey of exploration, Columbus was too smart to agree immediately. Retiring to his cabin, he timed his withdrawal with a sandglass, re-emerging before the end of the total phase of the eclipse, which he knew would come after one and three-quarter hours. He told the Taino chiefs that he had consulted God and persuaded him to stop this shielding of the moon, so long as they promised to behave themselves and supply Columbus for as long as he needed to stay.

Unsurprisingly, the natives agreed: a few moments later, as though by magic, the moon reappeared.

With a Taino crew at the paddles, Captain Diego Mendez, one of Columbus's officers, finally reached Hispaniola after a three-day canoe journey. Bad feeling between Ovambo, the island's governor, and Columbus meant that the former blocked rescue attempts. After some months Mendez managed to rent a ship, and returned to Jamaica in June 1504. Already, however, the Jamaican Tainos had had a glimpse of the future. A group of Columbus's men had mutinied. When heavy seas stymied efforts to sail to Hispaniola, they instead wrought a haphazard path of rape and pillage about Jamaica, before eventually being defeated by men loyal to Columbus.

Columbus never again made the Atlantic crossing.

In 1509 Juan de Esquivel became the first governor of Jamaica:

he was moved by the Spanish king to Jamaica from Hispaniola, bringing with him a small group of Africans. In St Ann's Bay he established the first Spanish capital, Sevilla la Nueva (New Seville), built by Taino slaves. Soon the capital was moved across the island to Villa de la Vega (known by the English as Spanish Town), which within a hundred years had some five hundred houses.

From 1514 Jamaica was governed by Francisco de Garay. Under him it became law that the island's Spanish inhabitants should convert the natives to Christianity, obliging them to acknowledge the pope and the king of Spain. The principal obstacle to such a decree lay in the fact that the Tainos did not understand Spanish, for which they were deservedly punished.

The Spaniards enslaved the Jamaican natives, killing them with overwork, maltreatment and infection from European diseases. Some Tainos did manage to escape and set up encampments in the wilds of Portland, but their number was tiny. Having so quickly killed off much of the local forced labour, from 1517 the Spanish began to import slaves from Africa. By 1534 African slaves expert at sugar manufacture were being imported, the start of an industry that two hundred years later would bring immense wealth to the island.

In the sixteenth century, however, Jamaica was considered almost worthless by Spain: an ill-ruled supply base for the larger Cuba and the conquest of the American mainland. Once it was discovered there was no gold there, exploitation of its natural resources fell away. By a Spanish royal decree that clearly attempted to make as much as it could of little, all Spanish subjects in the New World were obliged to purchase a hammock.

To the ranches they built on the savannah, the Spanish introduced cattle, pigs and horses. These fertile lowlands provided plentiful grazing for farm animals and for growing food for the invading army in Mexico, as well as for the colonists in the other Spanish territories, including Cartagena in what is now Colombia, the walled city that was the capital of the Spanish Main.

Jamaica suffered frequent bloody attacks by pirates, raids carried out on behalf of nations who disputed Spain's and Portugal's assumed right to divide up the New World. After an initial attack by the French in 1506, the Dutch, Italians, Portuguese and English – notably Sir Anthony Shirley in 1596 – all tested Jamaica's defences. There were also English attacks in 1603, 1640 and 1643. It was hard to protect a colony whose Spanish population often numbered no more than a thousand.

By 1655 the English were after more than booty. That year Oliver Cromwell, Lord Protector of England after the deposition of King Charles I, launched his Great Western Design, intended to break Spain's monopoly on the western side of the Atlantic. An expeditionary force of thirty-eight ships and around 12,000 men sailed from Portsmouth in December 1654. The men were drawn from the flotsam and jetsam of London, and further men of similar unimpressive calibre, often indentured labourers, joined from the English settlements in the southeastern Caribbean. A contemporary account was dismissive in the extreme of these recruits: 'Certainly these Islanders must be the very scum of scums, mere dregs of corruption, and such upon whose endeavours it was impossible to expect a blessing.' A handful of experienced soldiers were under the command of Admiral Penn and General Venables, but these leaders were hardly of the standard of the great English pirate Sir Francis Drake, who sixty years before had harassed Spain's Caribbean empire.

Cromwell's fleet launched a disastrous attack on the capital of Santo Domingo in Hispaniola; soundly defeated, it lost a third of its men, Venables hiding from the Spanish behind a tree, from which he later emerged to hector his troops for their spinelessness.

Fearful of the wrath of Cromwell at their failure, the fleet with its remaining force of 8000 men sailed to Jamaica, whose governor, Don Juan Ramirez de Arellano, was known to be ailing and elderly.

The English ships were first sighted off Port Morant, the

island's most easterly point, by turtle fishermen, who sent word of it by horseback to Villa de la Vega. On 10 May 1655 the fleet attacked Caguaya (Passage Fort), the Spanish Town harbour, capturing it with ease after the commander could muster only about 120 men for its defence. While the inhabitants of Spanish Town pretended to be considering surrender, they made a break for the north coast and escaped to Cuba. Furious that they had been tricked, and that the Spaniards had got away with their treasure, the English plundered and destroyed Spanish Town, burning all significant buildings, including churches.

Before they boarded vessels for Cuba, the fleeing Spaniards had freed the 1500 or so African slaves, giving them guns, with instructions to wage a guerrilla campaign against the English, ready for the return of a Spanish force. The fact that the slaves were ready to fight for the Spanish suggests that their treatment had not been too cruel. Under English rule they were considered inanimate pieces of property by the white trash who first seized power there, and by their descendants.

These armed former slaves became the Maroons (from the Spanish *cimarron* – wild, untamed), their ranks soon swelled by fugitives from their English owners. They were beginning a guerrilla war against the English that was to last for the next hundred and fifty years. In March 1656 Major General Robert Sedgwick wrote, 'The Spaniard is not considerable, but of the blacks there are many, who are like to prove as thorns and pricks in our side.' The Spanish commander had escaped to the mountains, along with three hundred of the freed slaves; he harassed the English for two years after the invasion, before finally escaping to Cuba by canoe after being defeated by Juan de Bolas, a Maroon who had gone over to the English. For this perceived treachery, de Bolas was later hacked to death by his own men.

Serious efforts were made by the Spanish to recapture Jamaica; but these finally ended in a significant victory for the English at the battle of Rio Nuevo on the north coast in June 1658. Colonel Edward D'Oyley, the English commander who had whipped into shape the rabble who had arrived in Jamaica in the invading fleet and for a short time became civil governor, sailed around Jamaica to attack the Spanish from behind. In 1670 Jamaica was formally ceded to the English under the Treaty of Madrid.

By then Jamaica had had civil government for seven years, and efforts were being made to attract settlers. In England the monarchy had returned to power in 1660, with King Charles II installed on the throne; a pragmatist, fearful of war with the Dutch and French, the king tried for a trading détente with the Spanish, appointing Thomas Modyford, a successful sugar planter from Barbados, the Jamaican civil governor in June 1664.

To strengthen the English military force, Modyford enlisted the Caribbean's buccaneers, many of whom were escaped English convicts, refugees from religious or political per-secution, or runaway indentured labourers. At first these men had made a living from hunting wild pigs in the Hispaniolan forests: 'buccaneer' comes from the French word *boucan*, the wooden frame on which they cured meat. Hunted by the Spanish, these men had escaped to Tortuga, a small island off the north of Hispaniola, which they had turned into their seafaring headquarters; there they allied together as the *Confederacy of the Brethren of the Coast*. Ruthlessly capturing Spanish ships from their canoes, they built up a substantial fleet, turning Tortuga into a stronghold; although a strictly disciplined organ-ization, the Confederacy enjoyed a vaguely idealistic communal element under which spoils were precisely allocated.

It was to these desperadoes that England entrusted the defence of its Caribbean possessions. As should have been expected from such rough characters, they pursued an aggres-sive policy that amounted to a reign of terror throughout the Caribbean. In time this was to give rise to the swashbuckling pirate mythology popularized by the Hollywood films of Douglas Fairbanks Jr and Errol Flynn.

Strapped for cash, Sir Thomas Modyford gave them legal status as 'privateers'; as far as their wages were concerned, the sky was the limit: all the booty they could seize. The Dutch and French possessed little in the way of prize money, whereas Spanish ships and territories dripped with treasure. Although technically at peace with the Spanish, these pirates, at first ironically led by a Dutch brigand called Edward Mansvelt, mercilessly harassed Spain's territories and vessels – in the West Indies the war with Spain never really ended.

After an attack on Grenada and the death of Mansvelt in 1667, Henry Morgan became the leader of the buccaneers. This stocky Welshman was born in 1635, and had arrived in the Caribbean as an indentured servant in Barbados. Ruthless and tactically brilliant, Morgan was an extreme hedonist tainted with more than a touch of sadism.

Responding to rumours of an imminent Spanish attack on Jamaica from Cuba in 1667, he led a bloody raid on Puerto Principe (later Camaguey), a Cuban inland city that was reached after a lightning forced march, a tactic Morgan would employ again and again.

The next year Morgan attacked and sacked Puerto Bello in Panama, one of the richest cities in the New World. Locking captured Spanish troops in one room in the castle, he set fire to its powder-keep, blowing up the entire structure and killing all the prisoners. After raping the town's women, Morgan and his men feasted and partied well into the night.

The buccaneers returned to Jamaica with huge amounts of booty. In Port Royal, at the entrance to the natural harbour of what became Kingston, the English had established a small city on ground convenient for ship repairing. Port Royal now became the world capital of buccaneering, and within fifteen years was known as 'the wickedest city on earth'; it was also the richest, and certainly the most debauched.

Rather like a precursor of a Jamaican 'don', the godfather-like gangster rulers of the ghettos, Henry Morgan, the close ally and friend of Sir Thomas Modyford, became the uncrowned king of Port Royal. Soon after the raid on Puerto Bello, he led a further expedition of plunder, to Maracaibo in Venezuela. Using fire-ships to destroy a Spanish fleet, he and his men escaped after several weeks of rape, drink and torture. Morgan and his men returned to Port Royal with even more fabulous wealth, which they spent in prodigious quantities on general debauchery. Morgan lived the life of a warrior king, a favourite hobby being to place a keg of wine in the street and sit drinking from it, threatening to shoot any passers-by who refused to imbibe with him. After Charles II expressed his displeasure over the attack on Puerto Bello, Modyford was obliged to reprimand the buccaneer leader, who temporarily moved with his wife Mary Elizabeth to the country.

Morgan had acquired land across Jamaica. As well as property in Clarendon and near Port Henderson, he built a house called Look Out on the north coast, between Oracabessa and Port Maria, at a spectacular vantage point overlooking the sea and much of the north coast. From there he could signal to his fleet, hidden behind a small island, when Spanish fleets were sighted travelling loaded with rich pickings from Cartagena to Havana. Almost three hundred years later, the same site was found to be equally attractive – though for entirely peaceful purposes – by Noël Coward, the English writer, who built his home Firefly on the land.

After a Spanish landing and attacks on plantations in 1670, Morgan was forgiven and recalled to Spanish Town, where he was made admiral and commander-in-chief of all ships in Jamaica. In December that year he sailed with thirty-six vessels for Panama City. After a nine-day forced march through jungle, and a pitched battle on the plains in front of Panama, Morgan and his men took the spectacularly beautiful and wealthy city, looting and burning it and putting all prisoners to death. The expedition retreated to their ships with 175 pack animals of loot, and Henry Morgan was given a hero's welcome when he returned to Port Royal. But there was a slight problem: England had by now signed a peace treaty with Spain, the Treaty of

Madrid, news of which had reached Jamaica only after Morgan had set sail.

His act of war wrecked the treaty, obliging Charles II to publicly rain intense disfavour upon Modyford, who was recalled to London and imprisoned in the Tower; Morgan was also summoned to England. But this official displeasure was only a political sop to Spain: after a decent period of time had elapsed, the king showed his true feelings by granting Morgan the lieutenant-governorship of Jamaica as well as a knighthood; and Sir Thomas Modyford, who had lived a life of leisure in the Tower of London, was returned to the island as chief justice. The close friends and allies were thus reunited.

The era of buccaneering was already almost over; it had lasted hardly ten years. Sir Thomas Lynch, who succeeded Modyford as governor and ran the island until 1675, made a priority of stamping out the vicious trade. Sir Henry Morgan, now an enriched man of property who had become a successful member of the establishment, regularly ordered the hanging of members of his old profession.

Morgan himself had little time left. On 25 August 1688, at the age of fifty-three, he breathed his last, tuberculosis finally having felled him where cannonball, grapeshot and cutlass strokes had failed. He was attended in his last days by Sir Hans Sloane, an internationally renowned physician, who proclaimed that the pirate's life had been shortened by 'drinking and sitting up late' – a salutary warning to mankind. Hedging his bets, Morgan also employed a black medicine man, but he fared no better than the more conventional aristocratic English doctor.

Less than four years later, the final blow was struck to the buccaneering trade, in one of those verdicts from on high that are quintessentially Jamaican. On 7 June 1692 half the town of Port Royal, including Sir Henry Morgan's grave, was thrown into the ocean when a powerful earthquake hit the isthmus upon which it was perched: a quarter of Port Royal's population of 8000 people was killed. Like a metaphor for the biblical scale of this tragedy, one Lewis Galdy was sucked into the ground in an earthquake shock, only to be miraculously spat out into the sea by the next one, like Jonah from the mouth of the whale. Galdy was to live for many more years. It was as though the elements were making a pronouncement upon the wickedness and cruelty that had created the unimaginable wealth of Port Royal: *Judgement 'pon Babylon!*

March 1989–August 1995

There seems to be a causal relationship between the actions of some (or all?) of the people of Jamaica and its elements. Clearly, the Port Royal earthquake is an example of this. In more recent times two seismic shocks were measured on the island the night in February 1978 when the self-exiled Bob Marley flew back into Kingston for the Peace Concert; and lightning flew in through the window of Judy Mowatt of the I-Threes, striking a picture of Bob, at what seems to have been the very instant that he died.

Moreover, should we be surprised that even today the behaviour of some Jamaicans can resemble that of modern-day pirates? After all, piracy was the principal source of the island's wealth in its first years as an English colony. And the padlocked wrap-around grilles and bars that today protect many Jamaican homes from robbery reflect the times when the island's soldiers and settlers were relentlessly harassed by the Maroons.

So effective had been the instructions of the fleeing Spaniards to its freed slaves that for the settlers outside Port Royal, life in Jamaica in the late seventeenth century was a kind of living hell. Tropical diseases, slave revolts, the floods of the rainy season, and endless attacks by the Maroons and Spanish put a considerable damper on life.

For three weeks in April 1989, with my eldest son Alex,

87

who was then six, I stayed at the house of a friend on the beach at Heaven, to the west of Port Antonio. Except for the weekends when half a dozen local families may turn up, its long sweep is empty of people. This small beach offers some of the finest and safest swimming in the Caribbean: ten minutes out is the reef, which surrounds virtually all of Jamaica. (Out by Port Maria, a dread had built a house on the reef, impressed locals told me.) This reef is also the source of the island's shark-free reputation, one that is not entirely based on fact. Just in case any get through, Jamaicans have a basic solution to the problem of large fish that might want to eat you. 'Punch it on the mouth,' advised my friend Buju, formerly in charge of this house on Heaven Beach, 'sharks cowards – them run away then.'

It was the usual sort of deep Jamaica experience, for both of us. 'Dad, why doesn't Gregg have any shoes?' Alex asked me, and I had to explain to him. I watched as the penny dropped – *people don't have shoes because they don't have enough money to buy them!* – and his sensibility shifted for ever.

Eating fish caught from a raft with a hook-and-line and cooked on a wood fire, going early to sleep, rising with the sun, listening over and over again to the same Frankie Paul tape, having conversations of sweet simplicity and colossal profundity. Could there possibly be a better existence anywhere?

Constructed entirely of wood around a central courtyard, in a traditionally Jamaican fort-like design, the house had most of the living quarters on the first floor. There were bedrooms in each of the four corners, with the adjoining landings turned into living space. The open, unglazed windows had shutters, which we were advised to close at night; Peter, the co-owner, casually warned me he had once found someone clambering up the outside wall in the middle of the night. His matter-of-fact tone suggested that this was perfectly normal behaviour and to be expected. Although a sumptuous bathroom had been created on the ground floor, the toilet facilities were provided by the beach or bush. The kitchen was a wooden trestle table and an open-air fire behind the house.

I returned to stay at the house for a weekend in April 1994, when I was in Jamaica for a couple of months researching *Songs of Freedom*, the Bob Marley biography I was writing. By then there was a full kitchen, with sink, stove and fridge, on the ground floor; a flushing toilet had been added on to the bathroom. Even cable TV and a phone had been acquired – of course, money had changed hands to bridge the five-year waiting list for this last item.

The scene had changed, however: Buju, who had built the house from scratch with Mike, Peter's partner in the project, had fallen out with him and been banished. He had retaliated by setting up a fish-and-festival shack up where the main road meets the abandoned railway line that runs for a couple of hundred yards behind the house (Jamaica had a relatively efficient rail network until it was wiped out by the 1980 hurricane.) For a time Noah, his one-time spar, had remained in the building, along with Ducky, a housekeeper, and her two teenage daughters, one of whom already had two children of her own. But now Noah had moved to a bobbadread encampment that had 'captured' the land in the small bay around the next headland.

And the house in Heaven had a further addition: a security guard – which in Jamaica often means an unemployed man with a stick, as was the case here. Was this a sign of the times? Or a sign of the place? There was talk, after all, contrary talk that was hard to get to the bottom of, about another security guard having been shot and crippled at the house a couple of years ago. A small island, Jamaica is prone to petty village-like gossip (*labrish*, as it is known in patois) – in which everyone has their own version of the facts, and in which the narrator is frequently put forward as the leading player in the particular story; inevitably, such creativity with the truth can have dangerous consequences.

So as with so much else, I couldn't find out what had really gone on here. But something had certainly felt amiss on that visit: I hadn't been able to sleep well at all, whereas previously I had never slept so well anywhere in my life.

★

From the beach at Heaven you get a fine view of the unpolluted waters of the local bay. Though countless plastic bottles litter the shore, it is a fantastic stretch of sand. Some miles to the east is Port Antonio's west bay, dominated by Navy Island, a property that Errol Flynn had owned; since the movie star's death in 1959, the island has been taken on by a succession of owners attempting with varying degrees of success to make a go of it as a luxury hotel.

Errol Flynn even had a kind of tangential connection with my return in August 1995 to the area. My intention was to travel down on one of the Rio Grande banana rafts, accompanied by my collaborator on *Songs of Freedom*, the photographer Adrian Boot, and his family and a couple of friends. Boot was staying over at Goldeneye, the former home of the James Bond creator Ian Fleming.

The journey down the Rio Grande that I wanted to make had a purpose of practical research. I was fascinated by the Maroons, and had the idea of making a film about them. In the eighteenth century the river had been the main route up into the hills, and it was along the course of the Rio Grande that the redcoats would move when parties were sent out from Fort George in Port Antonio to hunt down the rebels. The source of the river was the area in which the legendary Nanny had lived: a shamanic figure with alleged supernatural powers. Depending on how respectable or polite your source is, you will be told that she was capable of catching redcoat musket bullets in her mouth, her 'batty' or her 'pumpum'; the bullets would then be expelled back at the redcoats from the particular orifice in which they had lodged themselves.

It was Nanny who had led the Maroon army in the east of the island in a guerrilla war that forced the English redcoats to draw up peace terms in 1739. Such a method of fighting was way beyond the military minds of the English officers, who considered a guerrilla struggle to be extremely ungentlemanly, as well as an inferior form of warfare. As part of the terms of the peace settlement, the Maroons were granted a kind of independence in their own areas, an autonomy that they enjoy even today.

Nanny is buried at Moore Town, where there is still a Maroon colonel in charge of local affairs. On a visit to him in 1989, I'd found a quiet, rather diffident man in his early sixties, unlike the fire-breathing dread I'd romantically been expecting. This colonel, however, recommended that I visit a local healer, to watch her at work.

I was unprepared for what I saw on that day, dry with hot winds dancing up the mountain slopes. The healer operated her 'practice' out of a single-storey Methodist church roofed with corrugated zinc. This agreeable, attractive woman in her early forties showed me what she had removed from people's insides, using a sort of psychic version of keyhole surgery. In a discoloured, off-white plastic bucket she kept skeletons of mice, pieces of steel wool, wodges of Jamaican dollar bills; these had all been plucked, she said matter-of-factly, from the insides of the sick.

As I generally try to expect the unexpected, this didn't overly faze me. At the very moment she put down the bucket, obeying the rules of this land of synchronicity, a minibusload of infirm from Kingston rattled to a halt outside the church. Disgorged from the packed confines of the vehicle, patients poured into the building and lay moaning and groaning on the pews.

And so our bush doctor went to work. Her method employed that crucial element of faith healers – *faith*. It began with chanting and scat singing from her and her two helpers until you literally felt high – a standard method of inducing a trance-like state. (Days after returning to England from that visit, and certainly influenced by this experience, I underwent a similar process as I was inducted into a spot of fire-walking. You know what they say about you not feeling a thing? It's not true.) One by one the candidates for cure would wobble their way to the front of the church. A look of benign confidence about her, the healer would pass her hands over them; her fingers would seem momentarily to disappear inside their flesh, and she would produce – skeletons of mice, pieces of steel wool, wodges of Jamaican dollar bills. And the patients would walk back to their pews to sit firmly upright, apparently cured.

What did she do? Sleight of hand, with the mice, steel wool and money acting as placebos, is, of course, the simplest explanation: her patients believed they were cured, so they became well. Yet this doesn't seem to fit what I saw; I scrutinized her every movement and saw no evidence of trickery whatsoever. When by chance I spoke to the American musician Toni Childs about this, she had a different explanation. She had come across this kind of thing in Brazil, she said. This was her theory: in the first place, the Maroon woman *is* a gifted psychic healer; her knowledge of her gift allows her to remove the suffering of the sick person. Yet she is healing immensely simple, minimally educated people. Accordingly, it is the patients who manifest these objects within themselves as evidence that they have been healed. Although it requires a far greater leap (of faith) and is probably thoroughly bonkers, I prefer that interpretation to all this talk of placebos. After all, wasn't the evidence in the plastic bucket? Or was it all just something in the air?

As is the case with most mythological figures, little is known of the precise details of the part played by Nanny in the Maroon war. Yet her inspirational presence overhangs the island of Jamaica. And there is, in fact, great significance in Nanny being the only woman among Jamaica's seven national heroes. For there seems to be a great truth about all nations that one associates with machismo: Italy, Latin America, Jamaica ... They are all secretly run by women. While the cocks strut proudly around preening themselves and causing trouble, it is the women who keep the whole deal together.

Firmly attesting to this theory, even if often it is an enforced necessity, is the Jamaican concept of the 'baby mother' – the universal Jamaican description for the mother of a man's child, whether married or not. One of the hardest problems that Jamaica has had to overcome is the belief of teenage girls, encouraged by their peer group, that they are not mature adults if they have not given birth to at least one baby by the time they reach the age of twenty.

The traditional explanation for the fragmented Jamaican family lies in the fact that slave owners would separate husbands and wives when they arrived on the island. (This is also given as a psychological explanation of the volatile, anger-fuelled temperaments of some Jamaicans.) In more recent years, driven by economic necessity, emigration to the United States, Canada and Britain has further fractured and extended the Jamaican family. It is commonplace to hear of Jamaicans being brought up for five or ten years of their childhood by an aunt as the parents remain in 'foreign', from where they diligently send back a portion of their pay.

After World War II Jamaicans were welcomed to Britain, Canada and the United States to do the jobs by then disdained by the working classes of those countries: hospitals, transport systems, sanitation departments became dependent on these immigrant workforces. Racism raised its head – sometimes on both sides – but eventually the cultural mix to which Jamaicans added was recognized as an asset: an event like London's colossally successful annual Notting Hill carnival is a highly visible example of this. (Even though the carnival is Trinidadian in origin, Jamaicans have co-opted much of it.) For an island with a population of only 3 million, Jamaica has had a disproportionate effect on the rest of the world. Its cultural influence is discernible in the most unexpected places – in Japan, for example, it has had a huge impact. Moreover, the Jamaican economy was and still is substantially kept afloat by the weekly arrival of cash from workers in 'foreign'; however, second-generation Jamaican immigrants, whose ties to the island are not as strong as those of their parents, are less willing to send those regular crucial £10 or $20 bills to the island.

The tentacles of Jamaica Outernational have had a virtually

global reach. In every significant city in the United States and Canada can be found restaurants with names like *Wi Jammin'* or *Cool Runnings*, and even in Japan, where anything Jamaican is considered quintessentially hip. In Australia, on Sydney's Bondi Beach a sound system, run by a Jamaican who has spent time in London's Ladbroke Grove, operates on bank holidays. In pre-*glasnost* Moscow I met a journalist, the music writer for the trade-union publication *Construction News* (with a weekly circulation of some 18 million), who had the most precise knowledge of Studio One music of anyone I have ever met – a consequence of his studies at Moscow University's African department, which apparently had a complete collection of Coxsone Dodd's cultural heritage. In communist Poland and Czechoslovakia, similarly, reggae's celebration of the dispossessed struck a chord that led to the formation of dozens of local groups playing Jamaican-structured music. The Indonesian paradise of Bali also has not been oblivious to the Jamaican diaspora: as well as various reggae radio shows and groups, three factories work full time at turning out red, gold and green 'reggae clothing' for sale throughout the Western world. In Brazil reggae has caught such a hold that Jimmy Cliff, the star of *The Harder They Come*, is a local superstar and lives there for much of the time. In Africa, most of all, where the music first originated, reggae's rhythms – filtered back from Jamaica – are omnipresent: Alpha Blondy in the Côte d'Ivoire, Lucky Dube in South Africa, Sonny Okusuns in Nigeria, are prominent names. And everywhere you look, on vast wall murals, is the image of Bob Marley, without whose songs of freedom the world might not have been turned on to Jamaican music.

Yet there is a downside to Jamaica Outernational that has a dangerous attraction, one that has a complex symbiosis to the higher form of Jamaican culture. For in the early 1980s, first in the United States and then in Britain, Jamaican posses began running the street end of the drug trade, initially selling mainly ganja and then dealing the superdrug of the 1980s, crack, as well as heroin. Impressed by the immensely creative means that Jamaicans had developed for smuggling marijuana, as well as by their reputation for dealing with any opposition with ferocious violence, in the late 1970s the Colombian cartels actively sought out the cooperation of Jamaican ganja barons. A deal was struck: Jamaica would become a staging post for the importation of cocaine into the United States. The agreement runs to this day. This is the explanation for the regular reports in the Monday editions of the *Daily Gleaner* of women being found on flights to the United States and England over the weekend – it always seems to be women on weekend flights – with substantial quantities of cocaine concealed on or in their bodies. American citizens are also lured down to the 'Isle of Springs' with the promise of a few days' vacation in exchange for becoming mules: unaware of the stringent anti-smuggling measures for those exiting Jamaica, many end up in the hell of Jamaican jails with their gross overcrowding, open sewers and frightening levels of abuse from both guards and fellow inmates.

A large amount of the coke comes in from freighters passing along the Jamaican south coast from South to North America. Always fond of the latest technology, Jamaicans in the trade would ride out the five or so miles to the ships on jet-skis and tow back bales of cocaine, wrapped in waterproof plastic – until jet-skis were outlawed. Down on the south coast a while ago a dealer was bringing in an especially large consignment and was anxious as to what might happen to him when he hit the beach: so he arranged for his friends in the local police force to act as his bodyguards when he arrived at the shore. Out by the keys off Kingston, fishermen from time to time come across bales of cocaine floating in the water.

The first English settlers in Jamaica fared much the same as frontiersmen in America: they were forever liable to be attacked. The Maroons, their number continually swelled with escaped slaves, would steal down from the hills at night to rustle livestock, burn sugar cane and attack properties, which is why they were built like forts. The rebels maintained an underground network with slaves on nearby plantations, who gave them food and warnings when soldiers were moving against them. As early in the English occupation of the island as 1663, there was an attempt at a peace treaty with the Maroons: they were offered land and full freedom in exchange for surrendering, but unanimously rejected the proposal.

African slaves continued to be imported into the island to work the sugar plantations. Their grim labours may have caused their owners to become rich men, but their growing numbers were bringing the slave masters closer to the likelihood of a bloody death. In 1703 there were 45,000 African slaves and 8000 whites; the census of 1731 showed the whites had decreased in population to 7648, while the slave population had grown to almost ten times that, at 74,525; and the number of rebels living on the island was assessed at 2000. In terms of natural justice, it is nice to think that the presence of the slaves gave their owners life experiences that ranged from extreme discomfort to terror.

Strong and naturally stroppy – a trait not uncommon among Jamaicans today – the Gold Coast Coramantees stood out among the slaves, almost every revolt being inspired or led by members of this tribe, who came from the area around what is now Ghana. 'Bringing with them into slavery lofty ideas of independence, they are dangerous inmates of a West Indian plantation,' wrote one Codrington, a West Indian planter.

Almost as soon as slaves started to be imported by the English into Jamaica, they began to escape. In 1673, two hundred slaves killed their owner and other whites in St Ann's and headed for the mountains, forming the basis of what became the Leeward

Maroons – those who lived in the largely inaccessible western interior of the island. In 1685 another 150 slaves broke out of an estate near Spanish Town and also made for the mountains.

But it was not until 1690, in what became known as the Sutton revolt in Clarendon, that there occurred the first major slave rebellion and mass break-out in Jamaica. It was led by Cudjoe, a teenager who was to grow into an inspired military tactician. This group linked up with the Leeward Maroons and began a full-scale campaign against the English; this was to grow into the First Maroon War, which lasted until 1740. All this time, the Maroons in the west of the island were led by Cudjoe. Although short in stature, this Maroon chief was physically impressive: massive shoulders and thick limbs, underpinned by the charisma and indomitable spirit of a shaman. Camouflaged and fighting from ambush, the Maroons wrought havoc on the English regulars. If these professional soldiers were having success, the Maroons would simply retire and fight back from elsewhere, constantly shifting their positions.

As almost all Maroons at this stage had been born in Africa, they continued with their African religious beliefs, principally those of animism or spirit worship: animism, with its fondness for 'fetishes', later became interwoven with the Christian religion, especially the pomp and ceremony of Catholicism, leading to what in Haiti is known as voodoo and in Jamaica as obeah. Both forms can be benign or not, according to the needs of the practitioner. Even in those parts of Jamaica that were reasonably peaceful, the island's slaves were imbuing its very soul with a culture rather separate from anything within the experience of the English white settlers. This culture continues to this day, its presence felt in the form of the most hi-tech digital dancehall rhythms. 'On one hand,' Linton Kwesi Johnson, the poet, performer and academic, said of dancehall,

this music is totally technological; on the other, the rhythms are far more Jamaican: they're drawn from Etu, Pocomania, Kumina – African-based religious cults who provide the rhythms used by Shabba

Ranks or Buju Banton. So despite the extent of the technology being used, the music is becoming even rootsier, with a resonance even for quite old listeners, because it echoes back to what they first heard in rural Jamaica.

In their eyries deep in the mountains, the Maroons developed entire towns, guarded by strategically placed lookouts who at the sight of an enemy would blow on an *abeng*, a cow horn with a hole at the tip and a blowhole on one side, whose sound could carry for miles.

By its very nature the life of the Maroons was hard, constantly endangered. In the numerous expeditions sent out against them, their towns and provision grounds were often overrun by troops: when their towns were stormed, moreover, the Maroons would simply set up new ones; sometimes they would even win back their old towns. In those days of single-shot weapons, the fights that took place between the regular army soldiers and the Maroons were invariably bloody: terrible cutlass fights would take place when Maroons and soldiers had the misfortune to meet, hacking each other to pieces after the first volley. Despite the terrible pressures to which they were subjected, however, the rebels hardly ever surrendered, and won battles at least as often as the English soldiers, frequently fighting off the troops and literally forcing them back to base. Or they watched as the soldiers were defeated by the flooded rivers and torrential rains so characteristic of Jamaica's tropical climate. For raw recruits sent out from England, life in Jamaica sprung constant surprises: malaria and yellow fever took a terrible toll on the troops, although not so much as the effects of rum. The Maroons ambushed the English so often that the troops rode two to a horse, the front man facing the rear.

The island's white residents were the soldiers' only allies: most slaves naturally supported the Maroons, and yearned to join them. After 1713, moreover, Jamaica stewed with the heady atmosphere created by the knowledge that a huge number of imported slaves were kept in transit in Port Royal and its environs: under the terms of the Treaty of Utrecht, which ended the War of the Spanish Succession that year, Jamaica became the slave marketplace for the entire West Indies as well as Central America.

Relations between the various factions on the island were more complex than might be imagined. 'No simple division between master and servant or white and black was ever made,' writes Frederic G. Cassidy in *Jamaica Talk*.

From the beginning of English settlement there were indentured white servants whose condition was very close to slavery; on the other hand, many blacks earned or were granted their freedom. The position of the individual in the scheme of things, then, was more important than his colour; and those negroes who were born in the island, spoke English, and had better kinds of employment considered themselves almost a different order of beings from the newcome Africans.

Further war officially broke out with Spain in 1718, lasting for three years – although most inhabitants of the Caribbean would have been oblivious to any peace at all existing between the two nations.

The death of Henry Morgan had once and for all brought an end to the *Confederacy of the Brethren of the Coast*. A life of out-and-out piracy, however, still offered considerable attractions to those with financial ambitions. So great was its lure that a proclamation in 1717 promised a King's Pardon to any pirate willing to surrender and give up the trade.

Yet there were always those whom such offers failed to impress. 'Calico' Jack Rackham, for example, whose nickname derived from his partiality for calico undergarments, terrorized Caribbean shipping for two years until November 1720. That month he made the tactical error of remaining too long at Ocho Rios on the north coast. When Sir Nicholas Lawes, the governor, learned of this, he despatched a fast Royal Navy ship, under the command of a Captain Barnet. Following Calico Jack around the coast, Barnet came upon the pirate's ship anchored off Negril, on the west of the island. Although the pirates were sleeping off the effects of a rum party, a vicious fight ensued before they were killed or captured.

At that point it became clear that Rackham operated an equal-opportunities vessel: two of the most bloodthirsty pirates turned out to be women disguised as men. Anne Bonney and Mary Read were both sentenced to death. Read died of fever in prison at Port Royal, and Bonney escaped the gallows when it was discovered that she was pregnant. When Calico Jack was executed, however, his body was left dangling in an iron cage on a sandbank by Port Royal, a warning to other pirates.

As always, the elements continued to ravish the island. After a hurricane hit Jamaica on 28 August 1722, forty-four out of the fifty ships in Kingston harbour were sunk. The skirmishes with Maroons were by now without surcease. In 1720, to help track down the rebels, the government brought in fifty Mosquito Indians from Nicaragua, although they proved largely ineffective other than in low-lying swampland.

Throughout this time the Maroons in the west of Jamaica continued to be led by Cudjoe, a man who was growing old at the head of his people, assisted in his military art by his brothers Accompong and Johnny. But of all the Maroons even Cudjoe was not as revered as Nanny, the obeah woman leader of the Windward Maroons. Hidden away in the Blue Mountains above Port Antonio, her stronghold was Nanny Town, which she ruled over with Cuffee, her able second-in-command.

In 1729 Robert Hunter, a Scotsman born in 1667, arrived in Jamaica to become governor of the island. From 1710 to 1719 Hunter had been governor of New York and New Jersey, where he had made an impressive reputation, being described as the 'best-loved and most able of the Royal Governors of Colonial New York'.

At the time of his appointment, the Spaniards again threatened the island; and the conflict with rebel slaves was about to reach crisis proportions. Even among the whites there was hardly any unity. In September 1729 Hunter, who poured his own fortune into the organization of militia and defences, wrote to Thomas Pelham-Holles, the Duke of Newcastle and English secretary of state. 'The Irish here,' he informed him, 'of which our servants and lower ranks of people chiefly consist, are a lazy useless people, who come cheap and serve for deficiencies. Their hearts are not with us.' He cited an instance: Captain Loughton, an officer in his command, had been standing at the door of a Port Antonio punch house filled with Irish militiamen, and heard them say that they had no quarrel with Spain and would not fight the Spanish.

Many of the whites in Jamaica were indentured servants, labour that was in great demand in Jamaica in the eighteenth century, considered a practical means of increasing the European workforce and keeping a balance between Europeans and Africans. And the law of the island positively encouraged it: the Deficiency Laws of 1703, for example, required anyone owning 300 African slaves and 120 head of stock to keep a quota of 17 indentured servants.

That same year a further law was passed exempting ship's masters from paying port charges for voyages on which they brought in thirty 'white men servants'. Accordingly, hardly a ship arrived from England without its quota of indentured workers. Although a great many of these were Irish, there were also English, Welsh and Scots. Such individuals had either sold themselves into service – £20 for a three-year contract was the going rate – or were kidnapped by 'man traders'. Given bills of lading, they were shipped across the Atlantic like merchandise, great numbers perishing on the voyage. In the same manner as incoming Africans, they were lined up on the docks to be sold; for the smallest of misdemeanours, indentured workers could be punished with years of extra service, and were sometimes treated with even greater brutality than slaves, their finite contracts inclining owners to extract the maximum amount of labour.

Following their term of contract, however, indentured servants were free to pursue their own fortunes. And as early as 1680, ran an official report, 'many a convict from Bridewell or a young plough man from the Midlands, who had been sent out under seven or four years indentures, was in possession of a valuable plantation making his thousand pounds a year, and owning a coach and horses'.

In November 1730, Governor Robert Hunter sent a further 'Address and Representation' to the king in London:

We are more convinced of the weak and defenceless condition of the island by the defeat of several parties which have been lately fitted out at a great expense of men and money in order to reduce those rebels, but by the want of experience in the officers, and of discipline in the men, they have always miscarried or met with little or no success, which hath encouraged our slaves to that degree that we are under the greatest apprehension of a general insurrection, which may be the entire ruin of this colony there being so great a disproportion in the number of whites and blacks.

The governor had no choice but to step up the war against the rebels. In February 1731 a party of troops and militia left Port Antonio to attack the nearest rebel town, which it took successfully, with the loss of only two killed and some wounded. Although the Maroons fled to the mountains under cover of smoke from buildings that they had set alight, the troops did not follow them, but remained in the town for three days, before burning its 106 houses to the ground. Not a single prisoner was taken.

Hunter was furious at what he saw as the wilful dereliction of duty of this failure to pursue the Maroons. Reporting again to the Duke of Newcastle, he said he believed the rebels were so numerous and well armed that he suspected they must be receiving help from elsewhere; Jamaica, he added, was in such a weak and defenceless state that it was quite conceivable that the colonists might become prey to their slaves. As if to prove his point, rebel groups on the run marched to the parish of St Elizabeth in the dry, hot southwest of the island, and attacked two plantations, killing the owners and carrying off slaves.

A full-blown, bitter war now raged across the island. Nowhere in Jamaica could whites enjoy safe travel: the Maroons killed just about anybody they could lay their hands on. And in revenge the whites meted out vicious reprisals to any adult Maroon who was captured, torturing them before finally putting them to death; any children who were caught were sold into slavery on other islands.

By March 1732 Governor Hunter was close to cracking up from the stress of his Jamaica posting: pleading poor health and fatigue, he applied for six months' leave to go to England. Not only were the Maroons running rampant, but also the local planters and attorneys were wilfully obstructing the safety measures he was trying to put in place. Reeling from the blows delivered by the rebels, Jamaica suffered a corresponding decrease of public credit and trade.

Speaking to the island's council, Hunter announced:

Your slaves in rebellion, animated by their success, and others ready to join them on the first favourable opportunity; your Militia very insignificant, the daily decrease in the numbers of your people and the increase of rebel slaves: these circumstances must convince you of the necessity of entering upon more solid measures ... for your security, all former attempts against the rebels having been either unsuccessful or to very little purpose.

It has been suggested at home to His Majesty's Ministers and the Lords Commissioners of Trade, that a treaty with the Rebels, by which they are to agree to be transported to some of the Bahama Islands, or the employing again of Mosquito Indians against them may be of use.

Clearly, Hunter was at a point of desperation; the very thought of the possibility of peace terms indicates precisely how serious the situation in Jamaica had become. In 1733 the Jamaican legislature noted that the Maroons had greatly increased in number, and Hunter glumly wrote home:

The danger we are in proceeds from our slaves in rebellion. We have for several years been put to an extraordinary and almost insupportable expense in endeavouring to suppress them ... But our attempts ... having been in vain, only convinced me of our weakness. Instead of being able to reduce them, we are not in a condition to defend ourselves.

In early 1734 the Maroons in the east of Jamaica were so strong that they were able to temporarily capture three plantations within eight miles of Port Antonio; troops sent up the Rio Grande were ruthlessly attacked.

On 31 March 1734 Governor Robert Hunter died, without having achieved a major defeat against the Maroons. He was succeeded by John Aysegough.

The victory Governor Hunter so desperately had sought was in fact only weeks away. Nanny Town had always seemed invincible to the efforts of the English regular troops to take it. But in May 1734 a Captain Stoddart led his men, dragging small cannon, up the mountains above Nanny Town, from where they bombarded the Maroon settlement, destroying the buildings and driving its inhabitants into hiding in the bush. Finally, Nanny Town was stormed, taken and occupied. Reports of the death of Nanny herself, however, were greatly exaggerated.

Perhaps the stress of the job of governor should not be underestimated: John Aysegough was to serve in this position for less than eighteen months before he joined Robert Hunter in the great plantation in the sky. Dying on 21 September 1735, Aysegough was succeeded by John Gregory.

To this day the site of Nanny Town is said to be haunted by the ghosts of those who died in that fight in May 1734. Its destruction struck a great psychological blow to the Maroons throughout Jamaica. Fleeing Portland after being driven from their town, about 300 men, women and children of the Windward rebels marched to the west, crossing the island at its highest, most impenetrable points, until they reached Cudjoe's people.

In 1737 the Jamaican assembly resolved to bring in 200 more Mosquitoes. Arriving with their own hunting dogs, these men, paid two pounds a month, were like supertroops, guaranteed to track down any Maroon whose trail they discovered. The government built heavily fortified advance posts from which to seek out and destroy the rebels. Broad footpaths were hacked through the woods.

The target was Cudjoe. The troops began a war of attrition, finding the rebels' provision grounds and destroying them one by one, exposing Cudjoe's people to the danger of slow starvation. Early in 1737 a wife of Cudjoe's, an escaped slave, went over to the government troops, acting as a guide against the rebels: she was given her freedom, her former owners, the Barbados Valley estate, being paid £40 in compensation.

Cudjoe and his Maroons shifted camp, retreating to the landlocked cockpit country in the west of the island. Since the island was first formed, Jamaica's soluble white limestone has been dissolved by the intensity of the tropical rainwater that falls on the island, creating sinkholes and underground caverns and a characteristic honeycomb appearance; in certain areas deep depressions or glens have been formed that are called cockpits. The area's ease of ambush meant that troops might suffer casualties – often from rocks hurled at them – while not seeing a single Maroon. Although the war against the Maroons effectively had been won in the east of the island, in the west the situation seemed to become even worse.

Cudjoe placed a strong group of rebels under the command of his brother Accompong, who set up a camp in northern St Elizabeth, which was to become the Maroon town of Accompong. Nearby were many English cattle farms, which were frequently raided. Never realizing how hard-pressed the Maroons were, the English felt the weight of the absolute failure of their forces to defeat the rebels, the colony's morale having been completely undermined by Cudjoe's years of warfare. The new offensive from the town of Accompong encouraged an atmosphere of great fear and fatalism in Jamaica: slave owners were deeply nervous that their slaves would lose all respect for them and rise up and kill them.

Accordingly, Edward Trelawny, the acting governor, decided to try to make a peace treaty with the Maroons. 'I know but two ways of dealing with an enemy: either by force or treaty. The first we have often unsuccessfully tried,' he wrote. For his part, Cudjoe was ready for peace. He was now more than sixty, having been in the bush for forty-eight years, eighteen of which had been a time of ceaseless fighting. In February 1739, a Colonel Guthrie set out to look for him, to discuss a truce.

Over several meetings near Accompong, Guthrie and Cudjoe fenced and parried over peace talks. When they finally decided to formally go ahead with them, Cudjoe spun off in an impromptu dance, whirling about and hugging the amazed colonel. Rising to the occasion in a very English way, Guthrie drew his sword and laid it on Cudjoe's head in a mock knighthood ceremony. The historic treaty with Cudjoe was finalized by Colonel Guthrie on 1 March 1739, under a large cotton tree in the centre of a cluster of Maroon huts by Petty River Bottom Cockpit.

The treaty called for a final end to hostilities. Freedom and liberty were guaranteed to Cudjoe and his people and they were given 1500 acres of land; 100 acres was assigned to the Accompong Maroons around the site of their town. The Maroons were given the freedom to sell their product and livestock anywhere on the island; for their part, they were to cut, clear and maintain roads from Cudjoe's town to Westmoreland, St James and St Elizabeth. Cudjoe was made chief of his community for life: he was also given the power to inflict punishment for crimes committed by his men, all except the death penalty.

Tucked away in this agreement, however, was one extremely contentious article: the Maroons were obliged, it said,

To use their best endeavours to take, kill, suppress or destroy, either by themselves or jointly with any other number of men ... all rebels wheresoever they may be throughout the island ... If any negroes shall hereafter run from their masters or owners and fall into Captain Cudjoe's hands, they shall immediately be sent back to the Chief Magistrate of the next parish where they are taken.

This piece of expedient cunning on the part of the English administrators of the island was to change for ever the relationship between the Maroons and the rest of the African population. Apart from peace, the treaty gave the Maroons little that they did not already have; instead they were placed under the jurisdiction of their former enemies who, while giving the former rebels the appearance of autonomy, really had final authority. The treaty also provided the colonialists with a ready-made and well-trained mercenary force to help maintain iron control. What did it say about the war's wearing-down of the Maroon's psyche that they had been prepared to go along with this clause?

The next month the House of Assembly voted £1500 to Colonel Guthrie for his part in bringing about this peace settlement. He did not have long to enjoy this substantial fortune: on 13 June 1739, at the age of fifty-two, Guthrie was killed while on an expedition against the surviving Windward Maroons. The following year a treaty was struck with these Blue Mountains guerrillas. To all intents and purposes, the First Maroon War was over. It was the first time that the English army had been defeated by such an irregular force.

February 1978

Surrounded on three sides by a raw, harshly primeval terrain that combines austere, Brontë-evoking moorland with the dense verdancy of northern California, the Jamaican Tourist Board showcase of the Trelawny Beach Club is built right down on the edge of the Caribbean.

The Peace notwithstanding, business is not good. Epitomizing the way emergent nations must play the whore to their once colonial masters and their buddies, the hotel – a couple of miles out of Falmouth in the parish of Cornwall on the north coast – solicits North American newspaper readers that they may 'Experience Ecstaticism Here', with all the New Colony implications thereby suggested.

Even though they may be heartened to find that rumours that 'the Rastamen come down from the mountains to attack white people' are not exactly correct, US and Canadian holidaymakers courageous enough to invest in a week-long Beach Club package holiday must be distressed to find that it's far closer to a Torremolinos tower block than the quasi-Club Mediterranée paradise the name suggests.

It offers three six-storey buildings, each linked by concrete open walkways, translucent soft pink plastic sofas by each lift, Falstaffian feasts of Americanized Jamaican food, and a heavily fenced-off beach.

No doubt aware of the possibilities of being pillaged or plundered, few of the pink- and blue-rinsed holidaymakers venture far from the hotel's precincts. Besides, the heat and humidity in this part of the island are none too conducive to rapid leg-muscle action. If you come direct from an air-conditioned WASP world, you may soon wish you could strip the flesh off of your body and shove it into a spin-dryer.

If you are a black Jamaican, however, you have come to terms with it a long way back. You have understood that the brain-twisting humidity and black clouds and afternoon downpours that accompany it are simply part of the life-giving forces to which you are allied. The humidity is the provider of the water that nourishes the land, the goats, the sugar cane, the bananas, the ganja.

Which is a way of saying that there is some heavy culture shock going down when these polyestered innocents abroad amble their cheeseburger behinds through the hotel lobby. Suddenly they may come face to face with a dreader-than-dread congregation – tammed, locked and spliffed to the hilt – squatting down in a corner and making crazy jungle rhythm on some bongos.

Culture seem as confused as I am as to why they, along with Burning Spear, Peter Tosh, the Heptones and Big Youth, should be playing at the Beach Club this weekend. The reality, according to Winston Rodney, the Spear himself, whom I catch backstage before his gig in the hotel ballroom, is that the three-day event is being put on by the owner of the Long Island club My Father's Place. All the acts playing the Trelawny Beach Festival have played or will be playing that oddly named prestige gig in New York State. And written into their contracts has been an agreement to work the festival.

As a matter of fact, bizarre setting aside, this gathering of Jamaican musical heavies for weeks now has been the talk of Idlers' Row, the side street off North Parade in downtown Kingston close by Randy's Record Store where, most days, any number of name musicians can be found reasoning or blowing 'erb or just plain hanging out. Over the course of the three-day event such luminaries as Augustus Pablo and half the Bob Marley band, including the I-Three singer Judy Mowatt and the keyboardsman Tyrone Downey, will be sighted.

Culture's main man Joseph Hill agrees that this set-up seems none too rootsy. But then, along with Kenneth Days and Ralph Walker, the first bass and tenor harmonizers to his own anguished, impassioned, scrunched-up vocal expressions of undiluted freedom, Hill had played Madison Square Garden just a few months ago and that wasn't too rootsy either.

Still, he had fully understood that – as he'd told the police the time they stopped him in a roadblock, took him to the side of the road and cut off his locks – his purpose in life was to be an entertainer, and the fulfilment of this purpose involved playing such venues.

Besides, these upmarket concrete jungles don't screw up the head of JA's hottest vocal group's lead singer too much. How can they? He knows he has them licked. 'I am fa-a-ar wilder than Babylon!' He laughs happily. 'I just can't be tamed. I will not get weary.'

And Joseph and his brethren have, he tells me, 'made a written intention not t' change from being a Rastaman for ever: a covenant which shall never be broken. I wouldn't know how to break it for I love this way. I don't think of trying another way because … Look, I am at my final point of religious liberty. The spot I have reached has a clean pathway. It is just the best way for I and I to live.'

It is that impassioned clarity of purpose that forms the core of the *Two Sevens Clash* album, the beautiful and remarkable LP, a Joe Gibbs production, that is largely responsible for Culture's late 1970s status as the island's top vocal group. The title refers to the year 1977, the seventy-seventh year of each century being regarded by those versed in numerology as loaded with import – and we know of Rastafari's inbuilt mystical leanings. As Alfred Douglas writes of the number seven in *The Tarot* (published by Penguin), it is 'a prime number which signified unity within complexity … a number of far-reaching symbolical significance: the seven Classical planets, the seven virtues and vices, the seven ages of man, the seven days of the week, the Seven Seals of the Book of Revelation'.

And when the two sevens clash, a time of major change is signified, a time of heavy restructuring of what has been going down. Looking back on 1977 in the UK, the year when the punk movement erupted into glorious chaos, who could deny that? Equally, glance over at Jamaica and see what happened as the sevens ceased clashing: the Peace was declared. Yeah, mon. Culture is HEA-VEEEE. Them is hard!

And just to make the point doubly clear, the vocal trio's second LP carries the title of *Harder Than the Rest* – not to be confused with *Africa Stands Alone*, the bootleg of rough-mixed tapes said to have been spirited away from the same sessions.

Anyway, heavy and hard and extremely prestigious as these rankers may be, they live a very different lifestyle to that of successful white rock bands. In such comparisons, it is worth considering that the population of Jamaica is approximately 1 per cent of that of the United States, which clearly affects the earnings potential of local acts. All the same, it certainly would not fit the game-plan of most major UK or US acts to be shacking up three to a room, as Culture are at the Trelawny Beach Club – four to a room, in fact, as a cot has been set up in a corner for the drummer Horsemouth Wallace.

Maybe the American promoters imagine that Culture will find it cosy and reminiscent of home – which, considering the crowded Jamaican housing conditions, is probably correct. And there is a nice view of the sea if you peer hard to the left out of the corner of the window.

Culture are scheduled to tread the stage boards in about thirty minutes' time. In an astounding display of almost non-Jamaican timekeeping, the trio are already decked out in most natty black three-piece suits and shirts. (The reality, however, is that although the group is ready, the venue is not: they will not be performing for over three hours.)

Kenneth, who does not have much of a reputation for making his presence felt in interviews, is stretched out on the furthest bed eating a star apple (something like a cross between a Cox's orange pippin and a peach): the far more vibrant, vocally active Ralph, who spreads his benevolent aura over all those whom he encounters, is putting together a spliff. Joseph, meanwhile, stares down at the bedspread. As he fills in background details on the group, his voice crescendoes, dips, falls and rises with a strength that recalls Hollywood interpretations of biblical prophets. Or, more appositely perhaps, tub-thumping Baptist preachers.

It is only when he glances up to take the joint from Ralph that I notice he is totally cross-eyed: a less sensitive fellow than I might describe it as a supreme stage gimmick, for Joseph's eyes are as integral an aspect of the band's stage set as Mick Jagger's lips are to the Rolling Stones.

Culture is the first group to which any of the three have actually belonged. In 1973 Joseph Constantine Hill cut the 'Behold' 45 for Coxsone Dodd's Studio One label. Engineered by Maurice Goodall, it featured the Heptones' lead vocalist Leroy Sibbles on bass, a role in which he was habitually employed by Dodd, and Anthony Morgan on drums. Speaking of it, Joseph half-smiles and shrugs philosophically: 'I am sorry to say I was financially disadvantaged.' Both the Wailers and Burning Spear are among the artists who did not grow rich working with Coxsone Dodd: yet rarely is ill will expressed towards him. Spear, for example, prefers to define this period with Studio One as his 'university of musical knowledge'.

In 1976 Joseph Hill, who plays both guitar and drums, came together in Culture with the two guys with whom he'd grown up in Stony Hill, just outside of Kingston on one of the two main roads to the north coast. After the release of 'Behold', Hill, who was 29 years old in 1978, worked as a sign painter for the Kingston Public Works during the day while singing at night with an unrecorded group known as the Stepping Stones. Ralph, the youngest at twenty-five, was an electrician and twenty-seven-year-old Kenneth worked in the building trade.

Up to the first time they went into the studio together, the three singers had been using the working name of African Disciples. However, as Joseph points out, 'I'll tell you a plain thing true. It is that the cultural experience . . .'

In perfect intuitive vocal-harmony counterpoint Ralph takes over the next four words of the sentence: '. . . that we have inside . . .'

Joseph: '. . . causes us to make a certain kind of music for which we thought that the name African Disciples was best. But on that particular day when we went to make our first recording the other artists heard the sound that was leaving our mouths and the type of lyrics that we were putting together and they asked, "What is the name of this group?" '

Joseph told them. 'But they said,' he continues, a wistful grin opening up the lines around his face, ' "Brother, I'm going to tell you something better. Have faith and it will turn out to be the best. Better call this group Culture." And everyone there say "Irie." '

'Yeah.' He leans closer to me and the grin broadens into a blissful smile. 'A top-ranking name, mon. A *re-mark-able* name. Not true?'

'Quite remarkable.' I nod.

'And physically I and I must live up to that name. Because my religion and my only concept is that I will say hereby, Every knee shall bow unto the tongue of confession that is Jah Rastafari. So that must be the name.

'To be,' he continues, 'a Rastaman is to be a reincarnation of the entire world. Seen? The years and the days and hours and the moments and the calculation of the appearance of the idea from the day I was.'

'Irie,' agrees Ralph softly. 'Any man 'oo 'ave a good name 'as been given a good name. And any man 'oo 'as been given a bad name 'as been given it for 'is works! We 'ave only one way to deal with them: just know 'oo is yourself. Just pray to the Father and keep on doing the work. That will survive it.'

The work that Culture will keep on doing – the music, which Joseph writes and Ralph arranges – includes mixing and finishing *Harder Than the Rest*, which is being produced by the group's new manager, Mrs Pottinger.

'Put some lickle more dub on it.' Ralph smiles. 'And some more percussion. Gonna be plenty nicer than the first one. Already working on the next after. Want to release lots of records and are doing so.'

In fact, since singing with their manager's High Note label, the rate at which Culture have put out 45s has been prodigious. 'We work super-quick,' Joseph smiles. 'Is no need for a brother to sit down and t'ink, "Ow is it Culture get through songs so fast?" It is because we 'ave our t'ing –' he clicks his fingers – 'so-o-o-o STRONG. Everybody's spirit is well equipped.'

Although he lists Aretha Franklin, James Brown, Wilson Pickett, Joe Simon and Barry White ('Barry White has a whole lot of arranging experiences, and I dig his baritone voice') as prime influences, it is relevant in terms of the band's highly visual stage act that Culture are the only reggae artists I have spoken to who really rate rock. 'I lo-o-o-oove the rock bands when they are saying something,' says Joseph, 'and the Rolling Stones are my favourites for some reason.'

Culture's stage act, says Joseph, 'is just part of an in-born concert. Whenever I start to work with a brother' – a blissed-out cosmic grin – 'I just can't keep still.' He shudders into an onstage spasm.

'This is true,' agrees the soft-spoken Ralph.

'I love to work on the stage,' Joseph continues. 'I love to play for the people who make me what I am . . . I help to build myself but other people are the main builders.'

That love comes across onstage as it shifts about the gears of the Culture vibe until you're feeling as warm and cosy and totally at ease with your existence as the first time you fell in love with just one human being, let alone the whole of the species.

Much as they are loved, however, the audience still get only a short set, no longer than those performed for package-tour ticket-holders in America and Europe in the 1960s. Onstage for not much more than thirty minutes, Culture deal out the 'Two Sevens Clash' track itself; both the Joe Gibbs 12-inchers, 'Zion Gate' and 'Baldhead Bridge', three of the Pottinger-produced cuts: 'Stop The Fighting', 'Peace Truce' and 'Natty Never Get Weary'; plus maybe five or six more songs from the *Two Sevens Clash* album and the new LP. There is hardly a single second's pause between numbers, as the trio hit the audience between the eyes with their varied songs like an ace deejay adept in the usage of twin turntables. Each member of

Culture dances in a thousand directions at once: the superficially anarchic movements of each group member come together and visually harmonize with a natural spontaneity. And just wait until you see Joseph's eyes caught in the glare of the spotlights: wilder than Babylon? Not true?

On the evidence of his shows in London in October 1977, you might reasonably expect Burning Spear (a.k.a. Winston Rodney), who tops the bill over Culture on the first night, to be somewhere between superb and magnificent.

He is. With his soul brother musicians Phil Fullwood on congas and Bobby Ellis on trumpet, as on the British tour, and most of Soul Syndicate providing the backing, the sounds from Burning Spear are as blissfully exhilarating and beautifully elevating as ever.

Performing a similar set to that on his *Burning Spear Live* album, Winston Rodney proves yet again that his is some of the most magnificent music being created anywhere in the world. We talk a little before the show, but as most of the conversation consists of stoned telepathy, there isn't much to transcribe. Just dig Winston, though. Go out and buy all his records if you've never heard them: you owe it to yourself to give head space to a man who is one of the least known greats in contemporary music. And wait and see what you will get out of it, too.

After Spear's show outside the hotel, in the distance I see that a pair of uniformed police are rousting down a spindly, slight individual whom they have slammed face-forward against a wall of one of the hotel buildings. After searching him, they release him.

This diminutive figure is Augustus Pablo, creator of the 'far east sound', one of the greatest musicians and recording artists ever to come out of Jamaica. Although his pre-eminent period was during the 1970s, he later adapted ably to computerized technology. This master of the melodica first appeared on record in 1969 on a single, 'Iggy Iggy', recorded at Randy's.

There, working with the producer Clive Chinn, Pablo made his classic instrumental LP, *This is Augustus Pablo*. Shortly after, for his own Rockers label, Pablo made *King Tubby Meets Rockers Uptown*, a magnificent dub album and one of the finest records made in any field whatsoever. *East of the River Nile* (1978) was an instrumental set that rivalled his first album. Always sickly, however, Augustus Pablo died in 1999.

The biggest group in Jamaica in the 1960s, the Maytals, comprised Frederick 'Toots' Hibbert, Nathaniel 'Jerry' Matthias, and Henry 'Raleigh' Gordon. They first recorded as ska artists in 1962 for Coxsone Dodd's Studio One. Performing with all the gusto of a revivalist minister, Toots asserted his throaty lead vocals, which often earned comparison with those of Otis Redding, over the galloping instruments of Coxsone's house band, which in 1964 would become immortalized as the Skatalites. After briefly working with Prince Buster, they moved on to Byron Lee, for whom they made Jamaican musical history in 1965 when both sides of 'Daddy'/'It's You' topped the charts.

After Toots was jailed the next year for ganja possession, the Maytals moved to Leslie Kong's Beverley's label; their first release was a huge hit, '54–46 That's My Number', the story of Toots's prison experiences. That same year, 1968, they recorded the crucial 'Do the Reggay', 'Sweet And Dandy' and 'Monkey Man', which made the UK charts. Their *Funky Kingston* album for Byron Lee was one of the handful of Jamaican records that converted white rock audiences to reggae, and the follow-up *Reggae Got Soul* made the UK album charts. By now the group was known as Toots and the Maytals. Despite many superb records, Toots, who parted from Jerry and Raleigh in 1982, remains a man with a reputation greater than riches.

As it turned out, the Heptones were not destined to tread those Trelawny boards that night.

However, the man Naga Heptone had spoken of as 'a

respected man of the country and dreadlock', Peter Tosh, most certainly was. With Bunny Wailer, Peter Mackintosh quit the Wailers after working with Bob Marley for ten years, in order to follow his own individual and militant musical course. Backed by, among others, the rhythm team of Sly Dunbar and Robbie Shakespeare, with Touter on keyboards and Al Anderson on guitar, Peter Tosh provided a musical experience that at the time seemed to surpass the last performance I had seen from his previous musical bredren with Bob. (Unfortunately, in later years Tosh would not maintain such a standard.)

Playing material from his two Virgin albums, *Legalize It* and its masterly successor *Equal Rights*, Tosh deserved every one of those ultimate Jamaican accolades: cool, heavy, hard.

The perfect control Peter Tosh exercised over the near-magical music he and his group created suggested that all the forces he had for so long been attempting to muster within him had finally come together.

Before the superlative show, after watching an almost equally inspirational soundcheck, I talked with Peter Tosh in his hotel room. He proved to be a solid blend of controlled warm passion and a dignity that in a lesser man might slide into unseemly arrogance. I was interested to learn that he is a karate expert. Perhaps the inner strength he evinces emerges as much from that as from his Rastafarian beliefs.

Tosh is certainly the coolest person I saw on the island, resplendent in a pink press-stud shirt, the sleeves torn off at the elbows, khaki pants and beret. As you would expect from the man who recorded *Legalize It*, and who declares himself to be Jamaica's 'Minister of Herb', Tosh smokes giant spliffs of colly weed, rolled for him by one of his brethren who sits on the floor.

We start in a relaxed manner, speaking about the tour of the Caribbean islands which Tosh, playing with virtually the same band, had made the previous month. On it, he sighs incredulously, he 'went back to the seventeenth century'. Is this a man who in some herb-induced halo has overcome the petty limitations of time itself? Disappointingly this is not the case.

'It's so incredible to explain,' murmurs the soft-spoken voice that is capable of rising to thundering crescendoes of passion.

Yeah, mon. You know, I used to watch *Time Tunnel* on the TV and would think it was just fantasy. But it became so real to me because when I trod out into the rest of the West Indies it was like treading back in the sixteenth and seventeenth centuries. That's how backward the System [the soft tones transmute into a sneer] – the Schism is in those places. Seen?

When I went into those places, man, the amount of humiliation and hassles that you have to go through [he sighs, toking deeply], especially when you are militant and black and stand fundamental for your constitutional rights ... Well, they don't like that: no one must come and tell black people they must get up and wake up their slumbering mentality.

Leaning back on his right elbow on his bed, Peter Tosh tells how his tour took in Guadeloupe and Martinique before he hit Trinidad where 'I went to jail. For herb. Some po-lees –' his lips curl derisively again – 'arrange up some t'ing because they say according to my philosophy I am the Minister of Herb in Jamaica.' (Grunts of 'Nah true' come from his brethren on the floor.) 'And they don't like that. So they say they goin' to interrogate me.'

Tosh relates how, while on that island, he met the vice-president of the Trinidad radio station:

A blind, old Indian of sixty-five or seventy. He told me that the Indians in Trinidad have legal rights that permit them to raise herb – which they call marijuana – for their religical purposes. Yet [the volume control on his voice-box rises a couple of notches], that bumbacla'at government t'ing is so out of existence it does not give the same rights to black men. It is *pure bullshit*.

What they teach: 'Black man must die and go to heaven.' They are just there to talk to him, to give a command, to work up in the hotels where it is oh-so-green-and-nice. But I say is all bloodcla-at. Them guys say we must go to a heaven. To all that cow jump over the moon and dish run away with the spoon fuckin' shit.

'But I and I [he gestures to his brethren] come to break down those barriers of inferiority and fantasy to build up something constructive out of reality. And [Tosh's voice takes on a tone of aggressive frustration] if there is anything wrong with that, then tell me. For anyone who opposes that in this time shall surely feed the worms.

I tell Peter Tosh that since I have been in Jamaica, on this my first visit to the island in February 1978, some people have talked to me of the need for armed revolution, and others speak of a revolution in the spirit that is under way at this very moment. He himself, however, appears almost conveniently ambivalent about where he stands. Could he perhaps clarify his position?

The Minister of Herb is an excellent political orator:

Yes. There have to be a revolution. Because a revolution means a change. Seen? a change from up to down or from down to up. So there must be a revolution irrespective of how they want to look at it. The revolution can be a small revolution, if the downpressors will use their discretion.

And if they've got any heart left then they must use it. For it has reached a stage where people just give up. People just don't care no more.

900BC

As the Kingston headquarters of Bob Marley, the house at 56 Hope Road has become a spiritual power point: without Bob

Marley, after all, most of the world would never have heard of Jah Rastafari or entered into any debate whatsoever about the possible divinity of Haile Selassie, a central tenet of the apparently curious religion of Rastafarianism.

In Jamaica the image of His Imperial Majesty Haile Selassie I, King of Kings, Lord of Lords, Conquering Lion of the tribe of Judah, is inescapable. And across the island you hear its ubiquitous soundtrack, the addictive hymns of praise to his divinity that make up most of the material of the 'roots' reggae of the 1970s and the 'conscious' reggae of the 1990s. This music owes everything to Bob Marley, a man who never wrote an indifferent song, and who united masses around the globe in a love of what is essentially the earliest form of Christianity – which, give or take some contemporary cultural add-ons, like the consumption of marijuana as a sacrament, is essentially what Rastafarianism is.

Legend has it that this early Christianity was established in Ethiopia by the 'black Jew' descendants of Solomon and Sheba, who adopted the teachings of the disciples of Jesus Christ, who had fled into the upper Nile to evade persecution. So was born the Ethiopian Orthodox Church. In the autumn of 1980, when he had less than a year to live, Bob Marley himself was baptized into the Ethiopian Orthodox Church, so acknowledging it as the ultimate source of the faith for which he had rigorously proselytized in the form of what were superficially Jamaican pop songs.

But how did this insistent mythology of Ethiopia, a subtle subtext to more of world thought than we might imagine, come about? Firstly, the country is part of a region where humanoid fossil remains have been discovered of a type older than anywhere else in the world – this has led many to consider it to be the birthplace of mankind. Events in this perhaps oldest populated area of the earth seem always, moreover, to have moved apace: 'No other region of Africa fostered the development of an indigenous literate civilization, and its history spans more than 2000 years,' writes John Reader in his seminal work *Africa, a Biography of the Continent*.

Such distinctiveness begs a number of questions: Why Ethiopia? Why not other regions? Are Ethiopians inherently different from the inhabitants of other parts of Africa; genetically predisposed, perhaps, towards the pattern of behaviour from which civilizations evolve? Or is the region they occupy the determining factor? Does the landscape of Ethiopia offer opportunities that would enable any group of people – regardless of origin – to create an indigenous literate civilization, simply by exercising the universal human capacity to exploit the potential of whatever resources are available?

Reader's conclusion is that it is the last reason that led to the ascendancy of Ethiopia: although it covers only 4 per cent of the surface of Africa, Ethiopia has 50 per cent of the continent's land above 6500 feet and just under 8 per cent of the land above 10,000 feet. Its tropical regions, at altitudes over 6500 feet, tend to be free of the diseases that blight the lowlands in such climates and are conducive to the development of human-friendly ecosystems.

Yet the foundations of the faith of Rastafari come from far before this civilization developed. The basis of this apparently contradictory religion in the chronology of Christianity left it open to the influence of earlier beliefs and creeds into which it had bumped. Implicit within Rastafari are the sort of arcane practices that may be found in *The Egyptian Book of the Dead*, the core of the Egyptian mysteries. There is the acknowledgement of Ra, for example, revered by the Egyptians as the god of the sun, as a life-giving force, and the acceptance that mankind is not separate or different from God, or Jah, an abbreviation for Jehovah. (Jahweh was employed in place of Jehovah in the English Bible from 1539 until 1758, including the King James Bible of 1603, which would have been widely available in Jamaica.)

Moses became the personification and archetype of this philosophy; after being adopted by the high priest's daughter in Egypt, he was taught the principles of Osiris, Isis and other Egyptian gods. Then for his final initiation he travelled to

Ethiopia, synthesizing what he had learned. The source of Judaism was the teaching of Moses. As tradition has it, Moses was author of the first five books of the Bible (arcane legend has it that Moses' sixth and seventh books were not included in the Bible because they were considered too complex for the common man to comprehend: *The Sixth and Seventh Book of Moses* is the title of a famous obeah textbook, celebrated in a 1968 Toots and the Maytals song of the same name.)

The connection between the Horn of Africa and the Bible goes back to the ninth century BC: the Queen of Sheba travelled from her Ethiopian palace to meet Solomon in Jerusalem, as depicted in the Old Testament in 1 Kings 10:

And she came to Jerusalem with a very great train, with camels that bore spices and very much gold, and precious stones: and when she was come to Solomon, she communed with him of all that was in her heart . . .

And she gave the king one hundred and twenty talents of gold, and of spices very great store, and precious stones: there came no such abundance of pieces as these which the queen of Sheba gave to king Solomon.

And king Solomon gave unto the queen of Sheba all her desire, whatsoever she asked, beside that which Solomon gave her of his royal bounty. So she turned and went back to her own country, she and her servants.

The Ark of the Covenant, the most sacred object of Old Testament times, was a wooden box covered and lined with gold: it contained the two tablets of stone on which God had written the Ten Commandments. The Ark had accompanied the Israelites through the wilderness, helping them to victory and the conquest of Palestine. King Solomon later bestowed the Ark of the Covenant on the temple he built in Jerusalem.

Queen Makeba of Sheba was converted to the God of Abraham by King Solomon; until then she had worshipped the sun in the person of Ra. When she returned to her capital of

Axum in Ethiopia, Queen Makeba changed the religion of her empire to Judaism. Pregnant on her return journey, the Queen of Sheba gave Solomon a son, David. He succeeded his mother to the throne as Menelik I, the first emperor of Ethiopia and founder of the Solomonic dynasty of which Haile Selassie was the last incumbent. David spent a year at his father's court. When he left he stole the Ark of the Covenant, taking it to Axum, where it remains.

Or so the legend runs. There is no evidence whatsoever that this heisting of the Ark of the Covenant, or the stashing of the loot, actually took place. And in fact the city of Axum was founded several centuries after this was supposed to have occurred. None the less, monks still act as guards at the sanctuary inside which is said to be the Ark. Although no one is ever allowed to see it, the Ark of the Covenant has generated a huge body of myth, supported by the priests' assurances. Today there are more than 20,000 churches in Ethiopia, and in each there is a replica of the Ark, known as a Tabot. (On a more temporal level, those modern myth-makers Steven Spielberg and George Lucas exploited the Ark's legend to impressive populist effect in the film *Raiders of the Lost Ark*: diabolic Nazis steal the precious treasure for their own evil ends from a land that looks like Ethiopia.)

But how precisely did the Orthodox Church first catch hold in Ethiopia? There are two main accounts. At the very beginning of Christianity, according to the most resolutely mythological version, Philip the Apostle converted an Ethiopian eunuch, a high-placed, respected rabbi of orthodox Judaism, to Christianity. When he returned to Ethiopia, this eunuch rabbi changed the country's religion to Christianity.

The second version ties in with an era in which Axum, powerful in business, military force and intellect, finally grew to become sub-Saharan Africa's first indigenous state. There is specific historical evidence that King Ezana of Axum adopted the Coptic Christian faith in the fourth century. Nestling in the cool, temperate highlands of northern Ethiopia with two rainy seasons a year, the city was the heart of a civilization and an empire that rose to a peak in the fourth and fifth centuries. The Axumites developed Africa's only indigenous written script, Ge'ez, from which the written form of languages spoken in modern Ethiopia is derived. Trading with Egypt, the eastern Mediterranean and Arabia, Axum used gold, silver and copper coinage, the only coinage in sub-Saharan Africa until the tenth century, when Arabian coins began to be used along the east African coast.

Axum, the capital of the northernmost province of Tigre, was an eight-day journey from Adulis, a seaport forty miles away on the Red Sea. Among the exports of the city-state were ivory, rhinoceros horn, gold dust, frankincense, elephants and slaves.

Even after climatic changes led to the Ethiopian power bases moving down from the highlands – by AD 800 Axum had ceased almost to exist as an economic force – the city retained its position as a seat of religious authority. Subsequently, Ethiopian kings acquired divine status as priest-kings; by the thirteenth century the powerful African Christian nation was legendary in European learned circles. Records show that in 1306 Ethiopians travelled to the Holy Sees of Rome and Avignon, conversing with locals in Latin. But it was not until 1407 that the first European, an Italian – which is ironic, all subsequent developments considered – called Pietro Rombulo, arrived in Ethiopia.

The Ethiopian Orthodox faith adopted by Axumites 1600 or so years ago is essentially the same as that practised in Ethiopia today, a pure form of Christianity that maintains its connection with its Judaic and Egyptian pasts, all elements within Rastafarianism. Although still a religious centre, by the end of the nineteenth century Axum was no longer a capital city: Emperor Menelik II, who had united Ethiopia when his armies swept across its various provinces and conquered them, moved his seat of government to Addis Ababa (Amharic for New Flower) which became the capital of the entire country.

The notion of the priest-king was indelibly stamped on the ruling monarch as part of his job title: all such Ethiopian rulers were supposedly descended directly by bloodline from King David, who, in turn, was descended from Moses. And the 225th king in this tradition, the only one to be crowned in the twentieth century, was Ras Tafari, Emperor Haile Selassie I.

Before his visit to Jamaica on 21 April 1966, Haile Selassie (his name means Power of the Trinity) had already established the Ethiopian Orthodox Church there, in answer to a request from the island's Rastafarians. Many of these insisted on the historical inevitability of 'repatriation' to Africa. In 1958 land had been granted in Shamani in Ethiopia by His Imperial Majesty to a visiting deputation of Rastafarians, including the revered Mortimer Planner. In 1966 he emerged from the teeming mass of rapturous matt-haired faithful who surrounded Haile Selassie's plane when it landed in Kingston and led His Majesty off the flight – after a wait of around an hour, so local legend has it, while the tiny Ethiopian remained on the Royal Ethiopian aircraft in a state of shock at the delirious reception.

April 1994

In April 1994, at the suggestion of Rita Marley, Bob's widow and principal flag-bearer of the faith, I went to try to find the venerable Mortimer Planner. The now ageing man was living, Rita told me, in a Nyabinghi Rastafarian settlement at Scotch Pass in Clarendon; I later discovered that this hamlet was built on land that she had donated. As one of the Trench Town Rastafarian elders, Planner had acted as manager and spiritual mentor to Bob Marley in the second half of the 1960s. 'Planner was someone we would listen to,' Rita told me.

He was a community elder, someone who everyone would respect for what he stood for in the Rastafarian faith. And he used to sell herbs – that was his trade. And he would talk about Rastafari.

He was respected in that sense of communicating with the people and being able to tell us what was happening in Africa. And he was a great reader, and a good psychologist; he had a lot of head: to survive in that type of community he had to be something of a psychologist.

He had been into Rastafari for a long time. When we knew him, he was established into organizations like the World Federation and Rasta groups that went to Ethiopia and visited His Majesty. He had a great past in terms of what he used to do.

Planner grew up that way: in the ghetto as a bad boy and come up tough and then found himself. Not bad in terms of doing wrong things. But growing up in that kind of community he had no chance but to be tough.

On my mission to find Mortimer Planner I was accompanied by Jah Stone, a wrinkled Rasta poet, considerably venerated, who was then seventy-six years old, and who had generously offered to be my guide; his nephew also came with us. Jah Stone lived in Kingston's rather upmarket Constant Springs, just around the corner from the Manor Park shopping centre. In some ways the select environment reflected his state of great inner grace; but all Stone actually had in the way of property was a tiny plot of land on the bank of a gully where he had built the exterior breeze-block walls of a small, single-storey house, corrugated zinc sheeting forming the roof. It was the usual tale of one-man land development in Jamaica, one familiar in fact throughout the Third World, where half-built block buildings, their metal guiding rods waving like clusters of directionless antennas, are omnipresent, their owners' commendable ambitions having outrun their supply of funds. Stone was seriously strapped for cash, and wherever you moved in the interior of his home, you stirred up small clouds of the all-pervading dust that building work always creates. But at least his place existed, and it seemed likely that at some point, at

God's blessing, the funds would appear and everything would be put in order.

His soul, certainly, was free of all dust. Jah Stone's very existence glowed with the righteousness of his Rasta belief, and there was a perceptible aura about him, like a halo. For our journey to Scotch Pass, Stone had dressed himself in priestly 'i-ficial' raiments of immaculate white.

Suitably accoutred, with a moderately excited mood not unlike that of setting off to the English seaside on a bank holiday, we squeezed into my tiny Hyundai rental car and headed down Constant Springs Road for Washington Boulevard; then we skirted the sprawl of Spanish Town, before chugging along in thick traffic to Old Harbour. There, past the clock tower permanently set at ten minutes past eleven, we stopped for delicious fried fish and bammy (cassava biscuits), a speciality of the town. As you pull up to the dozen or so women selling the food, fish-bearing hands stab through the car window, and the interior of your vehicle becomes an instant marketplace. The unwritten rule is: if you're purchasing several fish, buy one from each of the different vendors – spread the money around.

Our bellies full, we headed for Scotch Pass, which lies at the base of the Santa Cruz mountains in which the town of Mandeville is located. Heading along a narrow straight stretch of road, overhung with a canopy of leaves, I noticed that we had hit a line of fruit stalls. Behind them was an abandoned stretch of railway line, with which the geometrically straight route on which we were travelling ran parallel. 'Turn left here,' said Jah Stone.

Crossing the railway track, I made a further left, doubling back on ourselves for a few hundred yards before a bend to the right led me up a hill. On the right was a gateway. 'Through here,' directed Stone.

At the end of another short rise was a large covered awning, like a venue for small concerts. In front of it was a flat grass parking space. Pulling up, we climbed out of the car. Around the perimeter of the site, I could make out a number of small one- and two-room wooden houses. Taking my video-8 camera out of the car, I panned about the property.

Through the viewfinder I saw a dread walking towards me, waving a hand of protest. I took the camera from my eye. 'Yuh cyan film here.' He shook his head.

'Is all right, man, 'im mi bredren,' protested Jah Stone, with whom the man was evidently acquainted.

'Yuh cyan film here,' he repeated.

'Is Rita send him here, fe look fe Mortimer Planner,' Stone told him.

'Yes, I'm writing a book about Bob Marley. I want to meet Planner, but also I want to understand the nature of Nyabinghi to assist me in my understanding of Bob.'

This was not the correct thing to say. The dread, a man in his middle forties or thereabouts, was visibly angered by this information. 'Planner not here,' he declared, disappointingly. Then he brought up the name of Timothy White, the author of *Catch A Fire*, the superb Bob Marley biography published in 1984, a book that was very much a labour of love. He soundly and unfairly cursed the writer. ''Im sell millions of books and 'im keep all the royalties for himself,' he declared, furious. (In considering of the veracity of this information, it is worth pointing out here that it was at Scotch Pass on this occasion that I heard for the first time a story, which I later discovered everyone in Jamaica seemed to know, that Cedric of the Congoes, the group whose 1976 Lee Perry-produced album *Heart of the Congoes* is one of the greatest of all reggae records, had won $10 million in a lottery in the United States. The truth was that he had received one of those envelopes which wise men immediately chuck out that declare on their cover that the recipient has won $50,000 – if, if, if . . .)

A wise, sensitive man, Jah Stone excused us. 'Well, that is not our predicament.' He declared that he would go and check on one Granny Ivy, and moved across the encampment away from the car.

By comparison with Granny Ivy, Jah Stone was a mere slip of a lad. A spliff in her hand, this sprightly eighty-six-year-old Rasta elder sat on the step of her one-room wooden house: she and Stone immediately became embroiled in a reasoning about arcane matters of Scripture. Unable to comprehend the daunting combination of thick patois and toothlessness, I strolled round to the rear of Granny Ivy's home. A small boy, his youth clearly having been no deterrent to the growing of copious locks, ran ahead of me. In front of a nearby hut he paused, waiting for me to catch up, and pointed at it. 'That Planner's,' he declared. I peered through cracks in the door and windows, but could see that there was no one inside.

While Jah Stone and Granny Ivy were speaking, a convocation of dreads had gathered beneath the covered awning. They were there to discuss important matters of doctrine. I told Stone I would be very interested to hear what they were discussing. Nodding with his customary sagacity, Stone understood this would be important for me. We must address these dreads, he told me, leading me towards them, to see if I might observe their collective reasoning. So, after Jah Stone had given me a reference, I raised myself to my feet and spoke to the thirty or so assembled elders. Yet my request to listen to them speak was soundly dismissed, on what seemed to be the sort of point-of-order grounds you might find in a university debating society. Afterwards I realized the full extent to which Jah Stone was his own man – he was quite unimpressed with the arguments against my sitting in on the various discussions.

We left and headed back for Kingston, taking Granny Ivy with us. At one in the morning I dropped her off in a downtown area, a tenement yard where people seemed to be sleeping six to a room. Locking the doors of the car from the inside, I headed off through the deserted streets of Kingston back up into the mountains where I was staying.

Six days later by chance ('There is no such thing!' – Carl Jung) I met up with Granny Ivy again in the yard of 56 Hope Road. I was delighted to see her as I had been touched by her purity of purpose when I drove her up to Kingston, realizing she was a lovely person. Granny Ivy's business in Kingston was now complete, and she wanted to return to the Nyabinghi encampment. Hoping that I might again encounter Mortimer Planner, I said I would take her back there, and arranged to meet her at eleven the next morning. Accordingly, under an overcast sky, heavy with imminent rain, I found myself once again on the road to Scotch Pass. By the time we had hit Spanish Town fat drops of rain had begun to fall, and on the road to Old Harbour I was driving at no more than ten miles an hour, for the road had turned into a river.

In typical tropical manner, the storm suddenly passed, and by the time we were nearing May Penn, crossing the railway line that carries the goods trains to the Alcan works, we were under clear blue skies, the sun beaming down on us. Granny Ivy lit and relit a suitably massive spliff, drawing in huge puffs that filled the entire car with Burning Spear-like quantities of smoke. From time to time she loudly honked mucus out of the open window of my vehicle.

By the time we reached our destination the sun was at its zenith and it was extremely hot. Swinging off the main road across the rail tracks, I drove up into the encampment. 'Park over there,' Granny suggested. Grateful to avoid the full glare of parking in the centre of the property with all its concomitant potential for hassle, I tucked the Hyundai away by the side of her small house.

As Granny Ivy made herself at home, I went round and looked at Planner's place. Someone seemed to be inside the one-room shack. I stepped forward and peered through the half-open door. 'Excuse me,' I said to the large, bulky man sitting on the cot. 'My name is Chris. I am writing a book about Bob Marley. Rita said I could find Mortimer Planner here. Do you know where he is?'

'I am Planner,' he announced with biblical portentousness, his voice guttural and croaking.

The body and head of the owner of the voice resembled a

gnarled, ancient oak; his locks were like dangling vines. In truth, Mortimer Planner did not look too well, an impression emphasized by the fly-strafed, phlegm-filled bucket at his feet into which from time to time he would drop further expectorations. (He and Granny Ivy both brimful with gooey mucus: did this, I wondered, have something to do with the long-term effects of herb inhalation?) Though the exact illness was never specified, I was later told that Planner was 'very sick'.

As 'Sister Rita' had sent me to search him out, Planner expressed his willingness to help me. Sitting on the edge of his bed, speaking in laboriously slow, sonorous tones, Mortimer Planner began to tell me his story.

Born in Kingston in 1920, he was one of the founder members of the Jamaican capital's first Rastafarian encampment in the Dungle. In 1939, as an early convert to Rastafari, he had moved to Trench Town. His devout studies of all matters connected with the faith, combined with his exceptional intellect, established Planner, or Planno, as he became known, as one of the elders of Rastafari.

According to Rita Marley, he was part of the 'natural mystic' within the orthodox Nyabinghi school, the branch of Rastafari that through hand-drumming keeps the sovereignty of ancient, sacred African rhythms. Planner had played drums all his life. Carrying these rhythms to recording studios, he would harmonize with whatever the other musicians had to offer.

After the construction of the government yards in Trench Town, he had become a tenant at 5 Fifth Street. Planner was consulted on all matters of serious import by the 'clean, poor people' of Trench Town, as he called them. The true nature of his neighbours was essential in attempting to arrive at any solution. 'They were not particularly law-abiding,' he explained. 'That was how the society have the people. That was one part of the people's predicament.'

Selected as a member of the deputation sent to pay homage to His Majesty in Ethiopia in 1961, Mortimer Planner was honoured and delighted. He loved Ethiopia. In the unpolluted atmosphere of Addis Ababa he breathed in the clean air and gazed in awe at the city's tall eucalyptus trees. Most inspiring of all was his visit to Haile Selassie I.

So it was Mortimer Planner, his Kodak Brownie camera dangling around his neck as though he were a tourist, who had ascended the steps of His Majesty's plane when it landed in Kingston in 1966 to extend a welcome from the brotherhood of Rastafari. Tears had come into the Emperor's eyes when finally he stepped forth from the plane. The mystic breeze that blew from this moment was to dominate the rest of Planner's life. Gradually it showed him, he believed, how to teach the world. Specifically, Planner paid heed to Haile Selassie's parting words of advice: *International cooperation will quicken progress.* Planner prayed – literally, of course – that the people of the world would become receptive to such a simple truth.

He had seen the effect that His Majesty's visit had had on the people assembled in Kingston. And was aware of its effect on Rita Marley, who on the day of the Emperor's arrival in Jamaica had had a revelation. Seated in Governor-General Clifford Campbell's purring official limousine, Haile Selassie had been driven into Kingston from the airport. Rita eased her way to the front of the crowd on the Windward Road and stood in the warm, light rain, waiting for the car to approach nearer. Rita was anxious. She had made a secret pact with herself: if, somehow, she saw the sign she was looking for, she would accept the divine status of Haile Selassie.

As the Daimler limousine drew parallel with her, Rita's thoughts were not positive. 'How is it they saying that this man is so great,' she wondered, 'when he looks so short, with his army hat over his head in such a way I can't even see his eyes. Then I said to myself, "What am I even thinking about? Jesus is a spirit."' At that exact moment Haile Selassie raised his face: he looked directly into Rita's eyes and waved.

And I looked into his hand and there was the nail-print. It was a mark, and I could only identify that mark with the scriptures of history, saying, 'When you see him, you will know him by the nail-print in his hands.' So when I saw this, I said to myself that this could be true, this could be the man of whom it was said: before the year 2000 Christ will be a man walking on this earth.

Like his brethren, Mortimer Planner believed that democracy had run its course: the time of theocracy was now coming. (Jah Stone was also firmly of this belief.) Planner had no doubt of the role that Rastafari would play in the time of change and world crisis leading up to the year 2000. He had read it all in Revelations.

At the time of His Majesty's visit to Jamaica, he said, he had been living in Trench Town. With a warm glow in his heart, he observed the effect that the Emperor's visit had on many of Jamaica's citizens. People were wandering about the streets of the capital, visibly perplexed by these matters of profound spiritual and theological importance. So many people were asking themselves the same question that Rita Marley had puzzled over: Was this really the man the Rastafarians claimed him to be? The more that His Majesty remained metaphorically in their midst, Planner noted, the more people started having different considerations about their lives and about the world.

In August 1966 Rita Marley flew to Delaware to visit Bob. Her stories about the visit to Jamaica of His Imperial Majesty hit a sharp nerve within him. When he returned to Kingston two months later, it was with two specific purposes: as far as his career was concerned, Bob Marley had resolved to set up his own record company and become a self-financing musical artist. His other main intention was to pursue his quest for knowledge about Rastafari. As it turned out, the two became interlinked.

Bob had already encountered Mortimer Planner in his day-to-day runnings in Trench Town. Now he was impelled to seek out this elder of the ghetto. In his nervous request to Planner to provide him with instruction in the great truths of Rastafari, the singer's natural humility prevailed.

'Him learn so much from the experiences of people who suffer,' Planner said, explaining to me why Bob had so readily absorbed his teaching. 'Bob was taught in a Rasta university. And him understood well. Him a bright student.'

As Bob's 'mentor and tutor', as he described himself, Mortimer Planner guided that profound but unformed sense within the musician. 'It had for long been coming to the conscious thought within his soul: *Serve Rastafari!* Understand how you have to hear it and see it and feel it to come free. How you have to let it pilot you and open your eyes and see within your life how you want to live.'

Planner's teaching took many forms. He would explain to Bob the links between Egyptology and the Coptic Church, for example. But he would also describe the symbolism at the heart of various international systems in intricate detail: such mysteries as the reason for the image of the Egyptian pyramid on the US dollar note; or the true significance of the English crown, and its relation to the Church of England and to that of Rome.

This was crucial, the Rastaman sage believed, in helping Bob come to terms with who he was: a hybrid of the United States and Britain. 'His mother is a green-card American, and his father was British. So Bob came out a British–American. And him have to move far from there to be the successful universal figure that him end up to be.'

Something had shifted within Bob's unconscious, at the very deepest level. It was as though he doubted the validity of the paeans to rude-boy culture formerly sung by the Wailers. Rastafari, he began to instruct the ratchet-knife wielders of Trench Town, was the only course. At this time, Planner observed, Bob had a strong influence on shaping the youth out of their rude-boy image.

But these large-scale changes within Bob were not without considerable struggle. Early in 1967 he appeared to undergo something of a minor nervous breakdown, and became unable or unwilling to speak to anyone other than Rita or Planner. If others attempted to talk to him, he would reply only through Rita or Planner. Planner came to the conclusion that this withdrawal was motivated by a need for psychic self-protection that might ultimately lead to extended mental powers.

Whatever the cause, this syndrome vanished as quickly as it had arrived. As well as becoming Bob's spiritual coach, Mortimer Planner began to take on the role of his business manager: in a country where there is virtually no music-business tradition or infrastructure, the task of management very often falls to the artist's closest friend. Planner backed Bob to the best of his abilities, although this help consisted of little more than moral support. He did, however, produce a tune called 'Pyaka': a 'pyaka', a word with African origins, is a hawkish person, and the song was a social comment on the current situation in Jamaica at the time, as well as on the group's deteriorating relationship with Coxsone Dodd.

In 1968 Bob Marley managed to scrape the cash together to buy a second-hand Hillman Minx car. One day when he was out with Mortimer Planner, he let the revered elder drive. Surely the man who was important enough to greet His Imperial Majesty could steer Bob's car through Kingston, even if he didn't have a full driving licence? When they were stopped by the police and this offence was discovered, the pair were imprisoned overnight.

Bob had got the cash for the car as a consequence of a deal that Planner had struck for him with Danny Sims, an American who was resident in Jamaica. Sims, who promoted concerts throughout the Caribbean, ended up managing Johnny Nash, a Texan-born singer with a sweet, powerful voice who had had a number of big-selling records in the United States.

Many of the musicians Nash met in Jamaica were Rastafarians. To find out more about their religion, Nash had gone to west Kingston to a Grounation, a ceremony at which the Nyabinghi rituals of drumming and chanting were taking place. Mortimer Planner and Bob and Rita Marley were also there at the Grounation. Greatly impressed with the number of beau-

tiful songs, his own compositions, that Bob sang, Nash immediately told Danny Sims about them.

When Sims got in touch with Bob, the musicians sent
Planner along to negotiate. After Planner and Sims had had 'a
few lickle rough talks', the American ended up addressing the
dread as 'chief', and an agreement was struck: Sims would
apply himself to helping Bob break through as both a songwriter
and an artist in his own right.

Having given me his story, Planner lay back down on his cot.
He was exhausted. Thanking him, thanking Granny Ivy, I
climbed into my car and drove back to Kingston.

They appear to consider the idea of taking the car. But then it seems to be forgotten: I am told to lie down on the floor, next to Peter. When I am face down, all I do is pray to God for guidance. And it goes beyond that: I am atoning for all my sins, I am asking for forgiveness for all that I have done wrong, and I am saying goodbye to everyone. The circumstances are terrifying.

Still they are tearing the place to bits, looking for money. Then the one to whom I made my offer of getting the money from where I am staying starts to do something to Peter; I realize he is tying his hands behind his back. This seems very ominous: it draws up visions of victims of death squads on the Central American mainland, not very far from here.

Then they tie my hands behind my back. The man doing this is annoyed with me because I don't push my wrists tightly enough together, and he curses me, punching me in the kidneys. Then he pours some kind of liquid over my wrists, presumably to tighten the cord – it's some kind of electrical cord – and I fear it is petrol: I'm aware of some of the sinister tricks that get pulled here.

I also have a cloth pulled over the top of my head, which makes me suspect this is a prelude to being either smothered or shot. It still seems doubtful we're going to get out of here. Especially when I realize that they are fastening something around Peter's mouth: is this also a prelude to execution? Peter seems very frightened, and I don't blame him. I am too, but I am fighting not to let them see it, and I kind of wish he wasn't letting them see it so obviously. Though maybe that's a good thing: the fact that their terrorizing tactics are having an effect may be to our advantage.

'OK, we're going to kill one of these white niggers now. We'll kill this one.' The speaker kicks Peter. Peter looks entirely white, but his

father is black, as a matter of fact, born and raised nearby. Yet this doesn't seem the moment to point this out.

1887–1940

The notion of repatriation to Africa was not exclusive to followers of Rastafari. In Jamaica the idea had most successfully been promoted by the revered and esteemed Marcus Garvey, an icon of Rastafarianism often mistakenly understood as its direct founding father, largely owing to his eminent position in the highest heights of reggae subject matter.

Garvey certainly was inspirational to the beginnings of Jamaican Rastafari, but the force of his personality went far beyond this. Indeed, according to the preface of the 1968 Atheneum reprint of *The Philosophy and Opinions of Marcus Garvey*, originally published in 1923, this Jamaican is

the most important predecessor and spiritual father of today's American black nationalists. Much of his philosophy and program are widely accepted today: pride in being black, epitomized by the chorus in a current hit of the black 'soul' singer, James Brown: 'Say it loud, I am black and am proud' . . .

However, Marcus Garvey was not the first to promote a vision of Back-to-Africa, always one of the central tenets of Rastafari (much debate has arisen over the opposition between literal and metaphorical interpretations). During the second half of the nineteenth century, this was a recurring current of thought in the United States and the Caribbean. Henry McNeil Turner was the most persistent campaigner for a Back-to-Africa movement in the United States, but he never organized any repatriation scheme. In 1878 Dr Martin R. Delany had formed the Liberian Exodus Company; although he succeeded in resettling two hundred American blacks in Liberia, the venture fell apart. Alfred C. Sam, an Ashanti trader, the founder of the Chief Sam Movement, landed around sixty American blacks on the Gold Coast in January 1915.

But none of these leaders had the impact of Marcus Mosiah Garvey. Born on 17 August 1887 (like the island of Jamaica itself, in the fixed sign of Leo) in the north-coast fishing town of St Ann's Bay to parents with Maroon blood, he learned much when the white daughter of the local Methodist minister was forbidden to play with him because of the colour of his skin. His love of words and language provided the young Marcus Garvey with the weaponry he would require to become an orator, writer and editor. And he also learned printing. In Kingston he became a leader of the Printers' Union and organized an unsuccessful wage strike, briefly putting out his own publication, *Garvey's Watchman*.

In 1910 Garvey went to Central America, where he was shocked by the exploitation in the fruit trade of black workers, many of whom were Jamaican. The migration of Jamaican workers to Central America had become commonplace: the building of the Panama Canal, for example, had been heavily dependent on Jamaican labour; and in Bluefields on the Nicaraguan Caribbean coast and in Costa Rica there were Jamaican settlements. Garvey became a spokesman for these migrant workers, establishing workers' unions wherever he could.

Moving to London in 1912, where he became a docker, Garvey met Duse Mohamed Ali, a black Egyptian proselytizer of African independence, who proved a great influence. Garvey attended lectures at the University of London's Birkbeck College, and buried himself in the stacks of the British Museum's Reading Library. There he read Booker T. Washington's autobiography *Up from Slavery* and became inspired. It was Washington who set Garvey on his pan-African path.

In 1914 in Kingston he launched the Universal Negro Improvement Association (UNIA) with the motto 'One God!

One Aim! One Destiny!' Its stated purpose? An ambitious, revolutionary and ennobling philosophy, to unite 'all the Negro peoples of the world into one great body to establish a country and government absolutely their own'. But it was small beginnings: despite his adept oratory, Garvey at first attracted only a small group of followers.

On 23 March 1916 Marcus Garvey arrived in New York City. He travelled across the United States, lecturing to black audiences, whom he found empathetic and inspiring, and meeting the country's black leaders, with whom he was disappointed. Within three years of the end of World War I the United States was in a miasma of economic malaise, and the black population fared worst: twenty-six race riots ravaged US cities in 1919 alone. For a prophetic figure, ready to lead his people to freedom, it was a propitious time. The UNIA flourished in the United States, by 1920 claiming a membership of over a million. Across the nation UNIA branches flew the association's red, black and green flag – red for the race's shed blood; black for skin colour; green for the lush vegetation of Africa's tropical pastures. 'The Universal Negro Improvement Association and African Communities' League,' Garvey declared, 'is a social, friendly, humanitarian, charitable, educational, institutional, constructive and expansive society, and is founded by persons, desiring to the utmost, to work for the general uplift of the Negro peoples of the world.'

Fear of the successful Russian Revolution meant that all radicals were considered potential Bolsheviks. From 1919 onwards Garvey was shadowed by US government agents under the control of J. Edgar Hoover, then a leading figure in the Bureau of Investigation, a forerunner of the FBI. Mired in anticommunist hysteria, Hoover made it a personal quest to have the Jamaican deported.

On 1 August 1920 a month-long UNIA international conference opened in Harlem, New York. Delegates from twenty-five countries paraded in impressive military-style uniforms with marching bands – this must have troubled Hoover even more – and 25,000 people packed Madison Square Garden to hear Garvey's address on racial dignity and African independence. 'We are the descendants of a suffering people; we are the descendants of a people determined to suffer no longer ... We shall organize the Negroes of the world into a vast organization to plant the banner of freedom on the great continent of Africa,' he proclaimed. Crucial to his later legend, he also spoke of 'Ethiopia, land of our fathers', and proclaimed that 'negroes' believed in 'the God of Ethiopia, the everlasting God'. Threatened by dwindling congregations, many traditional black clergymen in the United States attacked the resulting African Orthodox Church, founded in 1921 under the auspices of the Greek Orthodox Church, a cousin of the Ethiopian Orthodox Church.

Garvey was hardly circumspect: 'Honest students of history can recall the day when Egypt, Ethiopia and Timbuctoo towered in their civilizations, towered above Europe, towered above Asia ... Black men, you were once great; you shall be great again.' As well as a spiritual programme, Garvey had an economic plan. In 1919 the UNIA had founded a publishing house, tailoring establishments, laundries, restaurants and a chain of grocery stores. Garvey announced a plan to pour $200 million into Liberia, the Liberian government understandably being delighted.

Garvey declared that the UNIA would develop its own shipping line, the Black Star Line, to link together the black world. This ambitious project would be a principal cause of Garvey's ultimate downfall. But at first it took off: within twelve months, the Black Star Line sold stock worth over $600,000. The three steamers it bought, however, turned out to be rotten hulks. By 1922 the Black Star Line Corporation had debts of almost half a million dollars, and charges of using the US mail for the purpose of fraud, a federal offence, were levelled at Garvey. With characteristic Jamaican distaste for rules, Garvey had taken a legal short-cut, ignoring the US attorney-general's office's edict that it was illegal for a company not formally incorporated to sell shares by post.

At the time of his arrest, Garvey wrote, 'There is an old adage, that says a thief does not like to see another man carrying a long bag, and thus the dishonest ones of our preachers and politicians believing that I am of their stamp, try to embarrass me by framing me up with the law.'

The next year Marcus Garvey was convicted and sentenced to the maximum of five years' imprisonment. Although his appeal failed, it was not heard until 2 February 1925, and in the meantime he remained on bail and was undeterred in his course: he even set up a further shipping line, the Black Cross Navigation and Trading Company, with the SS *Booker T. Washington* as its sole vessel. But pressure was brought on Liberia by the US government to ban Garveyite immigrants.

This utterly blocked Garvey's scheme and the UNIA went into decline. After Garvey began his sentence at Atlanta penitentiary, his plans were further stymied. But fortitude only strengthened the Jamaican's soul: from Atlanta he declared that he had 'planted well the seed of Negro or black nationalism which cannot be destroyed by the foul play that has been meted out to me'. In December 1927 Garvey's sentence was commuted, whereupon he was deported back to Jamaica.

Marcus Garvey brought back with him to his homeland one of the island's most comprehensive collections of books on African and international history, art, science and religion. Immediately he set about reorganizing the UNIA. But squabbling between Garvey and his American officers led to the two national branches going their separate ways. Little more of significance emerged from the UNIA.

In Jamaica Garvey threw himself into local politics, forming the People's Political Party in 1929. It called for Jamaican representation in the British Parliament, a minimum wage, more local industries and a Jamaican university. When Garvey attempted to challenge the courts' practice of doing deals behind closed doors, he was charged with contempt and sentenced to three months in prison. Afterwards he enjoyed success as an elected politician, taking on the United Fruit Company by organizing exploited dock workers.

In 1935 Marcus Garvey moved with his fragment of the UNIA to London. There he called on all blacks to join in the fight against the Italian occupation of Ethiopia. But he also hectored the Ethiopian emperor for his exile in Britain, calling Haile Selassie 'a great coward who ran away from his country'. In terms of the legend of Rastafari, this seems superficially confusing and highly controversial; for was it not claimed that Garvey already had declared, 'Look to Africa for the crowning of a Black King; He shall be the redeemer.' (Later there was some debate about this: was it Garvey who uttered these words? An associate of his, the Reverend James Morris Webb, author of *A Black Man will be the Coming Universal King, Proven by biblical History*, had spoken to the same effect at a meeting in 1924.)

The struggles Marcus Garvey had undergone seemed to have worn him down: on 10 June 1940 he succumbed to the stroke that had laid him low the previous January and died in hospital in Hammersmith in west London.

In one of those synchronous twists that appear in much that is connected with Jamaica, his hospital bed was next to that of a man whose grandson was to end up almost fifty years later working at Island Records. Late one afternoon in the autumn of 1987 I found myself at a moving small ceremony at Island's west London headquarters: the man's grandson presented Jamaica's prime minister Edward Seaga, who was visiting London, with the Rod of Correction, a wooden staff that Marcus Garvey had given his grandfather on his deathbed.

Although Marcus Garvey's star may have been waning when he died, time has more than resurrected him. Two years after Jamaican independence his body was reburied in Kingston. Today in Jamaica his image and impact are omnipresent; interwoven with no great accuracy into the mythology of Rastafari, he is part of Jamaica's holy trinity with Haile Selassie and Bob Marley. Moreover, Garvey became a widely respected figure in Africa, an inspiration for the political leaders Jomo Kenyatta and Kame Nkrumah, among others.

1950–1992

On a clammy evening in the last week of February 1992 Neville Garrick, the director of the Bob Marley Foundation, drove in his Jeep to a club in the affluent, uptown part of Kingston. Sixties ska and seventies rockers pumped out of the sound system. It was a 'revival nostalgia night': loping, slurred reggae from the days when Garrick met Marley and the Wailers and designed their artwork.

By the bar he saw Valerie Cowan, a friend from the same musical period, the same woman who had taken me to Trench Town ten years before to see the cockfight. Cowan's face, for years often flushed with the effects of alcohol and cocaine, now flashed with the fervour of her latest addiction: fundamentalist Christianity. Even over the sound of the music, Garrick could hear that her voice – cajoling, boastful, having three conversations at once – was as loud and hyped up as ever. But of late much of her hectoring concerned born-again doctrines, and the energy level rarely came from drugs.

A small legend in Jamaica, Valerie Cowan had lived at a fierce, glamorous pace. On first-name terms with gunmen and police chiefs, politicians and revolutionaries, and artists of all kinds, she was probably the best-connected person on the island. She was much loved, partly because of the love that she herself gave out. 'Valerie just loved people,' said Robbie Shakespeare, the great Jamaican bass player and one half of the hugely innovative production team of Sly and Robbie, 'especially people she thought she could help.'

Lithe, razor-witted, with high cheekbones, Valerie Cowan could be a Rastafarian mother, a gangster queen or a prim Kingston matron, switching parts with chameleon ease. At the urging of her three children, increasingly worried about their wayward mother, she had joined a 'charismatic' gospel organization, the Church on the Rock. An ironic choice, perhaps? An alert woman with a strong humour, she had, after all, been snorting and smoking 'rock' cocaine for over a decade.

But of the various drugs that drove her, there was none that she was addicted to more than danger. And, despite having got religion, she still could play rough in business, almost as a point of principle. But sometimes you worried that things could go badly wrong, that she was skirting disaster, that the whole deal could collapse. Yet her spirit was so positive, her energy so impressive and uplifting, you hoped this might guide her from further self-inflicted traumas. Valerie Cowan was loud-spoken and pushy, but at the best of times these characteristics, which served her well in her nonspecific role of music-business hustler, were obscured by a purity of energy and spirit as invigorating and revitalizing as a breeze blowing off the nearby Blue Mountains.

Valerie Cowan and Neville Garrick were two of the few survivors of the era of music that was playing that night in the club. Of the Wailers alone, three were dead: Bob Marley of cancer; Peter Tosh, his former vocal partner, killed in a home invasion; Carlton Barrett, the drummer, murdered by his wife and her lover. Gun law had ruled the world of reggae, its leading players risking violent ends.

Of late Valerie's income had come from the illegal exchange of US and Jamaican dollars, a trade not at all uncommon on the island, and one into which she had flung herself with gusto with her new boyfriend, Ricardo Reynolds. Business was good; she looked rich. There were those who expressed concern about the boyfriend, to whom she was engaged to be married.

'I didn't like his spirit,' said Shakespeare, 'and I told her so.' Reynolds, who was thirty-five, had been deported from Miami for cocaine dealing. Seven years younger than his lover, he gave his occupation as 'real estate speculator', but his true sources of income were the illegal selling of currency and cocaine.

This evening it seemed Valerie was the one sailing close to the wind. Since taking up with Reynolds, she had begun to lapse back into her old ways. And on this night her haughty, proud face was flushed with alcohol. She was edgy and aggressive, perhaps betraying an intake of the second of the commodities supplied by the man to whom she was engaged to marry. 'It seemed obvious that the Church on the Rock wasn't the only rock she was involved with,' Garrick quipped. He left the club 'early, at around 3 a.m.'. Later that night, he heard, Valerie's attitude and perpetually dubious business practices had landed her once again in a sticky situation. With that almost magical suddenness with which events can turn in Jamaica she found herself facing a man she had crossed in business. 'She got into an altercation with some guy she had had dealings with in a money transaction. She'd bounced a cheque on him for US$20,000. He slapped her.'

Existing in a wide-screen gap between tragedy and farce, her life's script like that of one of the spaghetti westerns so popular in Jamaica, Valerie Cowan sometimes seemed to draw violence to her. But that incident was surely a temporary convulsion in a recent success story that, despite its 'underground' nature, many saw as directly connected to her dedication to the Church on the Rock.

Two nights later she was in another uptown joint, a bar called Pepper's, sufficiently high-society for its customers to consist almost entirely of light-skinned Jamaicans. She had been drinking alcohol; and her exaggerated gaiety suggested that she might again have been dabbling in cocaine. But then she had reason to celebrate: as she bragged to almost everyone she met that night, she would be changing US$170,000 into Jamaican currency the next day. After many years in a decadent wilderness she seemed to be back in the financial big time.

The Jamaican national motto is 'out of many races, one nation', and Valerie Cowan embodied this maxim. Her maiden name was Chang, revealing her family's mix of Chinese and Afro-Caribbean blood: her father was pure 'Chinee', her mother a 'brown-skin lady'; the Changs were a large Catholic family of five brothers and four sisters, with Valerie the second youngest, born on 13 October 1950. When she was two, her father died.

Based in the county of Manchester, a central region of the island, the Chang family was a small financial dynasty: they owned shopping plazas in the towns of Mandeville and May Penn, haulage firms, pharmacies and the West End chain of sports stores, which had the Nike concession throughout the Caribbean. Despite such a background, the second-youngest daughter had an intuitive sense of right and wrong, invariably taking the side of the underdog. 'She had a great, deep feeling for poor people,' said her former husband, Tommy Cowan. All the same, the family wealth was to bail Valerie out of tight situations on several occasions in the ensuing years.

Raised as a Catholic, Valerie was sent to Kingston to board at the leading convent school, Immaculate Conception High School. After she left school she took a secretarial course, and went to work for a firm of motor dealers. Nearby were the offices of Byron Lee, a legendary reggae entrepreneur. Working for him as head of promotions was Tommy Cowan, a former member of the Jamaicans recording group, who was four years older than Valerie.

They married in 1971, when 'Cherry Oh Baby', a song that Cowan had produced, later to be covered by the Rolling Stones, was a Jamaican hit. Over the next five years Valerie bore Tommy Cowan three children: a son, Che (the name reflects the Cuban influence in Jamaica of those PNP-dominated years), and two daughters, Sara and Shikisha. Valerie had had little interest in music when Tommy met her. With her husband, however, an interest was kindled in what was to become one of Jamaica's principal legal exports. 'But even more than the music,' remembered Tommy Cowan, 'she enjoyed the exciting people she'd met around the scene.'

In 1976 Tommy and Valerie Cowan founded a company called Talent Corporation. From its offices in the post-independence development of New Kingston they promoted concerts – as 'gateman', Valerie would collect the money – and distributed records and posters. 'At the time she was like a businesswoman, on the ball with everything,' recalled Robbie Shakespeare.

Next door to their premises was an 'ital' health-food bar. The location was a favourite with uptown Rastas keen to rub shoulders with the likes of Bob Marley. There was a freshness and vitality about the Cowans' operation, a sense of optimism about the new times that seemed just around the corner for Jamaica's musical artists.

The heart of this mood was the faith in Rastafarianism that had been reignited in Jamaica since the visit to the island of Haile Selassie. Both Tommy and Valerie Cowan had surrendered themselves to the poetic religion. Valerie threw herself into its doctrines. 'She became much more involved in the understanding of Rastafari than myself, even though I was into it first,' said Tommy Cowan.

It was Valerie who joined and then introduced her husband to the Twelve Tribes of Israel, the intellectual, Jesuit-like branch of the faith. In many ways the 1970s version of Rastafari, with its imprecise mysticism and reverence of marijuana, was very much of its time. The position it allotted to women, however, hardly accorded with prevalent notions of feminism. But perhaps this aspect of the religion was simply an acceptance of the traditional place of the woman in the distinctly matriarchal country of Jamaica.

Like the rest of the 'sistren', Valerie Cowan maintained a background role, wearing a headdress and a long skirt, playing out a motherly role to their three children. In a documentary about reggae made by the director Jeremy Marr in 1977 there is a sequence with the group Inner Circle in which she appears as a subdued figure in the background, respectful, humble, knowing her place.

But an intelligent, feisty woman like Valerie would put up with such a role for only so long. When the former convent girl finally rebelled, a torrent of repression burst out. By 1980 her marriage was in trouble. 'She basically freaked out,' said Colin Leslie, a figure in the Jamaican music business. 'She didn't start to behave in any particularly insane way, but she seemed to decide she wanted to lead a far more colourful life. There were a lot of affairs – with men, women, young, old. And also a lot of drugs. This put a lot of pressure on her relationship with Tommy.' Vivien Goldman, the English writer, who came to know her during this period, described her as 'the wildest woman I ever met'.

Valerie's husband's faith was sorely tested. 'She was a very independent person,' he said. 'She told me that she wanted to try a separation. I said that my spirit and culture as a Rastaman could not allow me to agree with that. And I told her that although I knew it would hurt me a lot, we should end our marriage altogether rather than just separate for a time. I didn't think I could deal with seeing her with other people.'

Valerie Cowan left the family home, leaving her husband in charge of their three children. 'I think Tommy thought she wasn't stable enough for the kids, but more because of the drugs than because of her sexual behaviour,' said Yvette Hussey, a Jamaican writer who had known her since those times.

In a kind of inverted migration, this Jamaican high priestess began to spend much of her time in the ghetto areas of Trench Town or Rema or Jonestown. 'I remember our son pointing out to her how she'd moved from Cherry Gardens, the richest part of Kingston, to the poorest, without blinking an eyelid. But her heart always went out to the poor,' said Tommy Cowan.

There is no distorted romanticism here from a grieving former husband. It's a description you hear again and again. Familiar with the 'runnings' of both uptown and the ghetto,

Jamaica: the young lion roars.

Peter Tosh, 1944–1987.

Turtle punch anyone?

A late-seventies sound system: a serious business.

Above Welcome to the uniquely Jamaican art of go-go dancing.

Right Obeah or not to be.

The ubiquitous Jamaican hand cart, a vital part of the ghetto economy.

I'm in a dancing mood – but the woman is hard to catch.

When people in Jamaica speak of record shops, they are not always thinking of Tower Records.

Serious title contenders? Jamaica digital-style at
the première bashment for the film *Dancehall Queen*.

Valerie Cowan won her spurs as an influential power-broker. She numbered several of the island's leading political gunmen as lovers. Was there an element of slumming or voyeurism here? According to Robbie Shakespeare, himself a man of the ghetto, it was more a fact of her environment. 'Valerie loved ghetto people – her heart went out to them. And there'd always be a couple of gunmen around in those kind of neighbourhoods. But,' he added in a telling metaphor, 'Valerie not care what gun you fire.'

During the 1980 election, it was widely rumoured that gunmen working for Edward Seaga's victorious JLP Party received CIA funding; this, so the story ran, was in exchange for letting Jamaica become a conduit for shipments of cocaine from Colombia. Events such as Irangate and the activities of Panama's General Noriega lend credence to the conspiracy theorists' line on why the 1980 Jamaican general election became the most murderous campaign in the country's history: over eight hundred people died in an election run-up that took the country to the brink of civil war. Edward Seaga won a landslide victory over the incumbent Michael Manley. Manley, who had declared that Jamaica would not be a fiefdom of the United States, had announced a policy of allying with other Third World countries like Cuba, and had nationalized the American-owned bauxite industry. CIA files reveal a deliberate policy of destabilization – even Bob Marley was closely watched.

Whatever the provenance of the drug, it was from around this time that Jamaica became riddled with cheap cocaine. 'Michael Manley freed up herbs,' Valerie told me in 1983. 'He was for the poor people. Seaga turns the place into a coke culture – he's for the rich people.' By now Valerie herself had a serious coke habit. Sitting in her uptown apartment on Hope Road, with an armed guard by the gate, snorting line after line and slugging back vodka, she would gaze across the road at the headquarters of the late icon of 'ital' living, Bob Marley, the red, gold and green colours of the Ethiopian flag flying at all four corners of this heart of the reggae empire. But in this paradox she was not particularly unique. Half of the ghetto seemed to have succumbed to the lure of the cheap white powder, snorting it or freebasing.

In fact, Valerie had started snorting coke several years earlier in fashionable uptown circles, with the likes of musicians like Third World and even some of the Wailers. But the sudden availability of cheap cocaine in Jamaica brought out the worst side of her addictive personality.

Violent, unpredictable behaviour on the island became more common. Perhaps linked to the same lack of self-worth (or love of a good time) that led to her ferocious consumption of drugs and alcohol, Valerie Cowan seemed to put herself in situations in which she drew violence down upon herself. Arriving in Kingston in February 1983, I found her with a badly blacked eye, the cause of which was the source of much gossip. After a fling with Gregory Isaacs, the Jamaican king of soulful crooning, Cowan had badmouthed him over his alleged mistreatment of her. Isaacs, already under pressure from an expensive freebasing habit and a police charge of possessing a machine gun, which carried a life sentence, had run into her in a hotel car park and punched her in the face. It was a mark of her standing in the community that, notwithstanding Isaacs's vicious reputation, people from all ranks of Kingston society were openly express-ing how 'vexed' they were with him.

In the early 1980s Valerie Cowan had worked for a time for Island Records, helping the artists managed by the company, particularly Black Uhuru. Her friendship with Michael Rose, the group's singer, brought about the end of this business relationship. Mostly, after that, she was hustling, and having a hard time, you felt. The men she became involved with may have been interesting, but hardly seemed reliable hunter-gath-erers. 'When you're broke and you're pretty,' said Yvette Hussey, 'that's the kinda guys you run into – people who deal with smoke and coke.'

From time to time she would pick up a well-paying gig. When the British television programme *The Tube* ran a special from Jamaica, Mick Sawyer, one of the researchers, encountered various aspects of the personality of Valerie Cowan. Slugging back his duty-free Armagnac with scant regard for its vintage, she discussed the terms of her contract; the prankster in her then arranged a sound-system evening in the unlikely location of Kingston's snobbish Constant Springs Golf Club.

Here she played to the hilt her rebellious part. 'The golf club was full of affluent Jamaicans, trying very hard to be respectable,' said Sawyer.

They really weren't expecting half of the roughnecks of downtown Kingston to turn up. And next door was the convent school that she'd been to. As with all good sound systems, this one went on until dawn, which caused a lot of problems for the nuns. So she was extremely pleased with herself for having scored a double coup. And although *The Tube* set up the sound system at the golf club, she announced that she was going to charge money on the door, which she took herself and spent on cocaine. It was always extremely difficult staying straight around her.

Valerie then insisted on taking the researcher with her to score coke.

When she'd bought the stuff, which she did by sounding her car horn in this suburban road, she suddenly announced that the police were always waiting at the other end. So she reversed out at about 50 mph: I've never driven so fast going backwards – she told me it was a police chief who had taught her to drive like that.

I found her enormously good fun. One was quite happy going along with anything she suggested. There was something quite innocent about her. She was extremely guileless, even though she knew every dodgy person in Kingston.

Cowan had arranged for Sawyer to acquire his own bargain-bin Jamaican currency before he left the UK.

I had to get in touch with this import-export guy based in Hastings. I wrote him a cheque, and there was all this Jamaican money. Actually, the difference between the official rate and the Valerie rate was not that great. It's worth mentioning that everybody in Jamaica seems to be into currency deals. Certainly it had been going on for a while with her.

Things seemed to be beginning to take a downturn, however. Increasingly, Valerie was spending time in Washington, DC, a city with a large Jamaican community. She was involved in 'business deals' in the American capital, she said, although only the sketchiest details would emerge. However, connections she made there set up one of her most dubious enterprises. In exchange for flying into Trinidad with a large quantity of US dollars – unbeknown to her, she claimed, these were counterfeit – she would be paid in cocaine, which she would offload for cash on an acquaintance on the island.

The money was to buy arms for revolutionaries intent on overthrowing the government, though she later claimed that she was unaware of this too. When Valerie arrived at her rendezvous in a middle-class suburb of Port of Spain, the gunrunners were already there with their samples, waiting for a down-payment. Under the terms of her contract, she was given the cocaine. As she was leaving the house, however, the police swooped – they had been watching the house for days.

After being held in solitary confinement for seventy-two hours, Valerie was transferred to a women's prison to sit out the miserably indeterminate length of time cases take to come to trial in Trinidad. After four months, she was – unusually, in a case as serious as hers – granted bail. She was also allowed to keep her passport and return to Jamaica. Valerie Cowan never went back to Trinidad; later she alluded to help given to her from very high levels in Kingston.

★

No doubt about it, Valerie was a tough broad. She turned up at the place I was living in Ladbroke Grove one day in December 1988 as the guest of my flatmate, arriving from the airport several hours later than you might have expected for a flight from Jamaica. Immediately she immersed herself in a series of furtive phone calls. Her energy seemed clouded, and a harshness had crept into her face (the consequence of cocaine?); the oval eyes of her Chinese ancestors seemed to be trying to avoid my gaze. I had the feeling that maybe things were not going well for her, that she was tired of hustling, that the hustling was not even successful: money was clearly tight. But wanting to give her the benefit of the doubt, I came to the conclusion that her strangeness was due to jet lag.

After a night's sleep she was fresher, energized. There were a few more calls, I noticed, but thought little more of it. Then, after she'd been staying with us for about a week, Valerie decided to let me in on a little secret. 'I didn't fly over on my own,' she confided. 'I came with a friend.' The 'friend', she said, had brought 'a few t'ings' in his suitcase; when she told me that these 't'ings' were 'hidden in a place no one thought of looking before' I found myself shaking my head in disbelief – that line was a stock hippy drug-smuggling joke, almost worthy of a Furry Freak Brothers comic. Just to confuse things further, there'd been some effort at switching identical suitcases at the Heathrow baggage carousel.

Needless to say, the guy had been busted. He'd been given bail, and Valerie, I now learned, had been on our telephone trying to get him a passport to get out of the country. Scarcely believing the naivety of her actions, I began to fear the worst, and it didn't help when I heard her solution to a quarrel between two women: 'Do what we do in Kingston,' she recommended to one of them, 'cut her!'

Such an approach to life seemed a matter of course to her. Eventually she was indefinitely banned from the United States for altering the US visa in her Jamaican passport – very inconvenient for an inhabitant of an island whose more well-to-do citizens like to consider themselves as commuters to Miami. But Valerie always approached life with scant regard for legality.

When Valerie turned forty, in 1990, a sea-change took place in her attitude to life. In what some considered an almost inevitable act of rebellion against his mother's lifestyle, her son Che had studied for a degree in theology at an American college in Jamaica, and was about to enter the church. At his urging Valerie joined the Church on the Rock. 'I was surprised,' her former husband admitted, 'but when Valerie throws herself into things she really gets involved.'

She took some kind of saleswoman job. And she approached life with the zeal of a convert, giving particular help to those with drug problems: with the church's pastor she would counsel addicts, and was acclaimed for bringing an overdose casualty back to life through her prayers. Unable to give up her fondness for nightclubbing, she would use such visits to spread the church's message.

Mick Sawyer, the researcher from *The Tube*, found himself in Jamaica again later that year. 'The transition from the Valerie I'd previously met to this model was remarkable. Suddenly she was this highly respected figure in uptown society, a friend of Michael Manley.' In fact, Valerie had the ear of both Prime Minister Manley and senior figures in the opposition JLP, an impressive juggling act in a country where an expression of the wrong political allegiance can result in death. As though pulling together the most positive strands of her upbringing, Valerie Cowan became a regular feature in the society pages of the Jamaican press. No longer locked into a drug user's dietary patterns, she put on weight and wore her hair in a pert perm.

Over Christmas of 1991 an old female friend from London arranged to meet her at the Kingston home of Yvette Hussey. Now the perm appeared somewhat bedraggled, and there was a harshness about her that suggested she might be slipping back to her old ways. Accompanying her was her new boyfriend Ricardo Reynolds, whom she'd been going out with for some three months. It was the first time either of the two women had met him.

'Even though some people had been saying that her drug problems were not yet totally behind her, Valerie seemed very happy,' Yvette Hussey thought.

She was talking very excitedly, a bit too excitedly perhaps, about the church. But the boyfriend . . . My spirit didn't take to him. He seemed very restless, not a very friendly type. All his talk was about money. He rushed her out, away from us, as quickly as he could. I had been told he was selling cocaine. What else could he be doing? He seemed to have plenty of money and wasn't working. Valerie said that if we had money to exchange, she was in business for it.

With the value of the Jamaican dollar at an all-time low, the pair were living high on the hog from the illegal exchange of banknotes. Both Tommy Cowan and Neville Garrick believed that they were working directly for some banking institution, bringing foreign currency into the economy through the back door. In any case they had rented an expensive, lavishly furnished house in Stony Hill, an isolated suburb just outside Kingston on the 'Junction' road to the north coast, and drove the priciest, most fashionable Japanese four-wheel-drive, equipped with every conceivable gadget. Some felt that they flaunted their wealth in an ill-advised manner.

The morning after she had been in Pepper's, in 1993, Valerie made her deal for the US$170,000. Then she took the rest of the day off, spending much of it with her former husband, with whom she'd remained close friends. 'Even though she'd made all this money, she told me that she was tired of this dollar-trading, that she was going to leave it,' he said. After trying to persuade him to take her to the movies, she left, excusing herself from taking their youngest daughter to stay the night with her; there were problems between herself and Reynolds, she said, problems sufficiently bad for her to have asked the police to make sure he didn't come near her.

All the same, some time after a final eleven-o'clock call she made from her home to Tommy Cowan, Reynolds turned up to spend the night with her. Perhaps he thought he was protecting his investment. If so, it was not a wise move.

Three men came to the door of the remote Stony Hill house at eight the next morning. Although their live-in maid had not seen them before, they were known to Valerie and Reynolds, who let them into their home. Then the men pulled out guns and knives, and demanded the money. They were given a large bundle of notes, JA$100,000, worth just over £2000. But this hardly satisfied them. 'Where is the US currency?' they screamed.

When Valerie and her boyfriend claimed not to know what they were talking about, they were tied up, along with the maid. At first they were just beaten. Then the torture became barbarous. They cut off Reynolds's genitals and one of Valerie's breasts. Then they stabbed Reynolds to death; Valerie was split from her crotch to her throat with a machete. The murderers left the house with only the Jamaican money, without harming the maid.

Valerie Cowan did not die immediately. Even now, the survival instinct that had so long protected her let her tear a hand loose from the tightly knotted cord with which she was tied. She crawled across the floor towards the phone but couldn't make it, collapsing and finally dying from loss of blood.

No charges were ever made.

'Valerie would always go to these places where there was danger,' said Tommy Cowan. 'Probably that's what brought about her death, because it seems the people who killed her were from those areas.'

Before she'd left his home on the day before she died, Valerie had confided a secret ambition to Tommy. Her next project, she told him, was to see if she could promote a tour of the Caribbean with some of Jamaica's leading musical acts to raise a million dollars for the children of Trench Town.

'Valerie loved people,' Robbie Shakespeare affirmed once more. 'I never heard her talking bad about anyone who'd done her any harm: she'd just say, "I leave them to God." '

After I learned of her death, I seemed to feel Valerie's presence for some weeks, as though her shocked spirit was roaming angrily. Other people I spoke to had similar feelings. Perhaps unsurprisingly, many of the details of her killing flash through my mind as I lie on the floor.

I am ignored again. Then one of the guys who I'd thought was kind of OK says, 'Don't worry, I won't let anything happen to you. Mi know you work with Bob Marley and study him and try and help. Just put your head down and go to sleep.'

But I'm unconvinced by this display of charity. This guy may mean it, as perhaps did the guy who got me from my room. The psychos around him, however, may have different ideas and plans. Anyway, I lie down, slightly on my side, so that they can't see that I've got my hands completely free. Worried that my bonds were going to tighten so much they would hurt, I tried to hold my wrists a little apart when I was tied up, and the liquid that was meant to tighten the cords instead had the effect of creating a loose, unravelling slide.

I spend some moments considering whether I should jump over the balcony and race out the front door. (It is a very good thing that I decide against this – or, rather, don't work up enough nerve to do it – because in fact the front door is not open at all. It is securely padlocked, as I find out later.)

Then the very dark-skinned man speaks: 'We're going to treat you like you used to treat us slaves.'

'Well, a lot of bad things went on in those days. I hope people don't think like that any more.'

Suddenly a gang member who has not spoken before tries to hold a conversation with me; he has a very put-on English accent, of a type you might learn in the United States. 'Hey, which part of England yuh fram?'

'London.'

'Which part of Landan yuh fram: east, west, south, north?' It is the sort of accent that immediately fills you with dread, like the forced, fake American accents of Viet Cong calling out to GIs to surrender.

I decide it is prudent to keep my sentiments about his elocution to myself. And soon I find myself in a surreal conversation with him about the greenhouse effect and world climatic changes. At the end of each thing I say to him, I quietly take as big a gulp as I can of oxygen, trying to will my voice not to betray any of the internal trembling I feel.

August 1997

As throughout the Caribbean, the 1930s were years of social ferment in Jamaica. Trinidad, Cuba, Puerto Rico, St Kitts, St Vincent, St Lucia, Barbados and British Guyana also all experienced labour unrest.

In Jamaica, where people were starving to death, Alexander 'Bustamente' Clarke, the leader of the new Jamaican labour movement and sometime associate of Marcus Garvey, formed the Workers' and Tradesmen's Union in 1934. ('Bread! The people want bread! B-R-E-D!' Bustamente would exhort at political gatherings.) Labour unrest on the island culminated in the vicious suppression of striking sugar-cane workers at Frome, near Negril in Westmoreland: at the beginning of May 1938 four strikers were shot dead and dozens rounded up and jailed. (At the height of the unrest, a baby boy was born in Kingston to parents so enamoured of Bustamente's populist appeal that despite the child being named Cecil Campbell, he was known by everyone forever more as Prince Buster, becoming one of the handful of founders of modern Jamaican music.) In response, the Kingston dockworkers downed tools three weeks later, with other workers following, a general strike grinding the capital to a halt. The events of 1938 led to the foundation of the contemporary Jamaican political system. The Workers' and Tradesmen's Union developed into the right-of-centre Jamaica Labour Party (JLP), while another, more left-wing party was formed by an Oxford-educated lawyer called Norman Manley, a cousin of Bustamente ('Norman W. Manley, that brilliant young barrister who looks like the younger Pitt in yellow skin' is how the great American writer Zora Neale Hurston described him in 1938), and grew into the People's National party (PNP). After enraging the British authorities with a rabble-rousing speech – 'The niggers in this country shall rise. This will be war. We want revolution in this country and before whites destroy us, we will destroy them' – Bustamente was given a four-year prison stretch. Adopting a more sagacious, statesmanlike stance when released from prison, Bustamente steered the JLP to victory in the country's first elections, severely trouncing the PNP.

But there were some outsiders who already had mentally divorced themselves from the oppressive social system – the Rastafarians. Masters of wordplay, they held no truck with 'politricks'. The cult of Rastafarianism thus became cast as a religion of the dispossessed – but this failed to acknowledge the depth of intellectual rigour of many practitioners. (Though the oratory may be hesitant and awkward, the depth of biblical and historical knowledge displayed at a Rastafarian reasoning is impressive indeed – though you can hear similar 'reasonings' among any random pair of middle-aged women standing laden with shopping at any Jamaican bus stop . . .)

In the hills of eastern Jamaica – in Wareika, which overlooks Kingston, and above Bull Bay, a few miles along the green, hilly coastline from the capital, out past where the Harbour View drive-in cinema now sits on the edge of the sea – Rastafarian encampments sprang up: for the religion's followers a life of asceticism and artistry became their armour against Babylon. Leonard Howell, one of the island's chief propagators of the religion, founded the Pinnacle encampment in an abandoned estate between Kingston and Spanish Town. Eventually taking thirteen wives, Howell finally decided that it was not Haile Selassie who was Jah but himself. In 1954 he was thrown into Kingston's Bellevue mental home, and Pinnacle was closed down. The 'dreads', as Rastafarians became known colloquially, spilled out into the ghettos of west Kingston. Around the time of independence in 1962, there were a number of violent incidents involving firearms between Rastas and the police, making headlines in the *Daily Gleaner*, the main national newspaper.

At a grassroots level, the movement was now spreading with the speed of a bushfire into the popular psyche of Jamaica. But it took the unceasing efforts of Bob Marley to popularize the apparently crazy idea that the emperor of Ethiopia could be the living deity: a man who had grown up in Kingston, hearing the orations of dreads in the shantytowns of Dungle and Back a Wall. Many of Bob's brethren in the faith of Rastafari felt that this was why he had been blessed with this talent – to spread the message of Jah. Others believed that Bob Marley was capable of such a task because of his spiritual closeness to His Majesty himself, on whose right-hand side he deserved to sit.

This then is something of the background to what is happening at today's event. Which, slightly curiously, is a prelude to the Jamaican premiere later this evening, in the cinema at the Bob Marley Museum, of Spike Lee's film *Get On the Bus*, a screening at which the special guests are to be none other than Haile Selassie's great-grandsons, the princes Ermias and Bekare.

Unsurprisingly perhaps, the occasion even has a connection to the Nation of Islam in that the subject of the Lee film is the Million Man March, organized by Louis Farrakhan.

'Today is the fulfilment of the dream and prophecy of our beloved father Marcus Garvey,' declares Rita Marley, opening the proceedings with something of the air of someone throwing a private party at home – which, in a way, she is. 'He asked, where is the black man's king? He finally found his fulfilment in Ethiopia.

'*Yes, Jah: give thanks!*' she calls out finally.

Prince Bekare raises himself at the podium, which is set in the same doorway awning under which Bob Marley was fond of catching the shade and partaking in a spirited reasoning. 'To stand here at the Bob Marley Museum for the Jamaican premiere of *Get On the Bus* is truly an honour,' declares the prince. 'Who can deny the devotion of Bob Marley to my great-grandfather His Imperial Majesty Haile Selassie?' The air is rent with chants of 'Jah Rastafari!' 'Bob Marley also was in the Solomonic tradition. Africans must not only liberate their soul but free their minds.'

Bruce Golding, a former JLP politician who has launched an ultimately ineffective third party, is introduced to speak to the assembled multitude. The moment he tries to speak, however, the public-address system goes dead. 'Fire! Judgement!' call out the dreads.

At eight the next morning the faithful are gathered on either side of a curved driveway. They are in the grounds of a former school off the somewhat rough Hagley Park Road, which has been redesignated as the Kingston Ethiopian Orthodox Church, awaiting the arrival of the two princes at the regular Sunday-morning service. Everyone – men, women and children – is dressed in white, females in modest dresses, males in uniform-like garments; understandably, considering the cultural chronology with which we are here dealing, there are a sizable number of ancient dreads with medals attached to their breasts, crocheted red, gold and green tams covering their locks. Many of the faces here were evident at 56 Hope Road last night.

At first they sing 'Rivers of Babylon', movingly and achingly beautifully, several times. Then they essay a song that is new to me: 'Bring them, bring them to the Orthodox Church (bring-them-bring-them)' seems to be the entire sum of its lyrics. It would have seemed suitably momentous and portentous if, after a couple of choruses, the princes had then driven into the church grounds. But they don't: we are talking Jamaica time here, cross-fertilized with African time and adding up to erratic time-keeping, so you feel the assembled throng may be singing this for a long time. And indeed they are. After about twenty minutes of waiting and hearing the same chorus lines, as the sun grows hotter and beats down on the gathering, our faith is tested. By 8.30 the archbishop is pacing back and forth. Perhaps the princes are locked in at the cinema at 56 Hope Road.

Finally, at ten minutes to nine, a Mercedes sweeps into the driveway. Trilling tongue sounds greet this final arrival at the church of the princes Bekare and Ermias.

The service takes a form that seems close to Greek Orthodox services. It is several hours long, with much swinging of incense and purple colours; the men and women are divided into separate sides of the church; and the various priests keep disappearing behind the altar curtain as if for some mysterious conspiring. The entire business is unquestionably moving and uplifting, reaching those parts of the soul only hinted at by lower churches.

A four-year-old boy is christened, and Prince Bekare steps forward. 'We are very honoured to be here that we can share this month in the spirit of One, thirty years after the visit to Jamaica of our grandfather,' he says in his slight US accent. 'We are Orthodox Christians. It is a cornerstone of our existence. You are witnesses that this culture has expanded. I pray for the Oneness.'

Standing there in the midst of such heightened thinking I feel crucial issues rising from the depths of my unconscious. The big question for me is precisely *why* Haile Selassie I is considered to be God? What has led his adherents to the conclusion that this man, clearly made of flesh and blood, is the personification of the deity? Or am I even getting it wrong here: is he God-in-living-flesh? In fact, if I'm honest I don't really comprehend the deification of His Imperial Majesty in any way at all, apart from at a symbolic level. Nor do all his followers consider him to be the Father. Is he, as some suggest, merely God's representative? (But in that case, isn't everyone?) Is he a top of the Premier Division prophet, or a Son-of-God type like Jesus? The more I think about it, the more confused I become.

Don Letts had been a member of the Twelve Tribes of Israel,

and went to a meeting of a London branch with Ari Upp, the singer with the Slits; because she was having her period, she was forbidden to share the chalice of herb as it was passed around. Unable to accept this ruling, Letts left the organization. (Ironically, the dreadlocked Ari, the stepdaughter of John Lydon, is a familiar face in Kingston, having now lived in Jamaica for almost two decades.)

When I ask Letts to explain *why* Haile Selassie, he gives me his opinion: 'I always thought it was because he was the alternative to the blond, white, blue-eyed version of Jesus.'

But why is he God?

'I was never completely sure. Isn't it because he was descended directly by blood from David?'

Look, I know the blood lineage and wouldn't presume to dispute it for one moment: except that the Bible's King David wasn't God.

'I know. Do you know what they say – if you want to know about the details of Rastafari, ask a white man.'

I decide I had better ask someone who is not a white man. Who better than Haile Selassie's great-grandchildren?

The next day I drive with Kwesi Dickson, a Cambridge-educated Jamaican who works in the film business, over to Ocho Rios on the north coast where the two princes have scheduled a meet-the-press-and-people event. I am going to interview the princes, with Kwesi shooting it, for the pilot of a television programme. I follow the fantastic, wild scenery of the Flat Bridge Pass through the mountains. As I crawl in heavy traffic up a mountain slope somewhere past Bog Walk, a tailgating minibus driver rams into the back of the Toyota Tercel I have rented this morning.

(A friend of mine was once on another minibus to Ocho Rios on this same route. Suddenly it hit a man walking along the edge of the road. He staggered and collapsed on the roadside.

'Mi not know what to do,' said the driver.

'Gwan, man! Gwan!' The passengers urged him to drive on

and speed them to their destination, leaving the man to stagger off into the bush, where he later died.)

At the first police station we find, we report the accident. We are shown into a grey-painted room with pink floral curtains. A large cluster of green bananas sits on the floor against the wall and above it there is a tourist map of the area. Otis Redding's *Otis Blue* album is playing loudly on the ghetto-blaster in the office.

The traffic cop lets us know what a favour he is doing us: we should have gone to the nearest police station, at the small town of Moneague, to report the accident. But generously he agrees to deal with it here instead. 'I am grateful for that,' says Kwesi, with no hint of the irritation he's feeling.

The cop is tediously pedantic, giving the impression of a person who has not risen well to power – a global rather than local phenomenon, of course. Eventually he lets us go.

A mile or so to the east of the centre of Ocho Rios is the Hibiscus Lodge, a small ocean-front tourist hotel. There we find gathered another small clump of khaki-uniformed dreads, men and women both, many of them the same characters who had been at 56 Hope Road and the Orthodox Church. Benign contentment surrounds them like a collective aura. Just as well, as this is a further example of the great Jamaican tradition of hurry-up-and-wait.

Kwesi and I decide to go and eat at the Great Wall Chinese restaurant on the opposite side of the road. From a table by its upstairs window we can see everything that is happening at the front of the hotel. The owner, a middle-aged man, and his attractive daughter, in her early twenties, tell us something of their history, which seems typical of Chinese Jamaicans. Arriving in Jamaica during the last century as indentured labour, the Chinese came to form what is now a considerable 'Chinee' community on the island; they run much of the island's commerce, and as a consequence have borne their share of resentment from the rest of the community. 'People complain about the Chinese having all the money, but they don't accept that it's because they work so hard. We've got to change this attitude,' said a Jamaican friend.

The family running the Great Wall restaurant have returned to the island only within the last five years. The daughter was educated almost entirely in Hong Kong, where her father and mother had relocated during the Manley years: after several of their Chinese friends had been held up, some of them even murdered, they had realized that the Chinese were being targeted by gunmen, and had joined the exodus of intelligentsia from the island. Now that times in Jamaica are more stable, they have returned to the country they consider their home.

Three hours later than its scheduled 2 p.m. kick-off, the media conference and flesh-pressing appearance by the two princes finally gets under way.

Seated behind a row of dining tables, the princes are flanked by a pair of self-consciously anonymous white Americans, who have the air of CIA agents in a Graham Greene book – this naturally leads to a certain whispered speculation among the assembled throng about their true roles. Prince Bekare, I realize, bears a distinct resemblance to Gamal Abdel Nasser, the Egyptian leader. The likeable Prince Ermias, regarding the proceedings with a permanent baffled smirk, has an immense spot glowing in the middle of his left cheek: so at least we know he is human.

After a number of questions of a quite staggeringly banal nature about church procedure and church politics, we get down to nitty-gritty matters directly pertaining to Rastafari. The most contentious of these is voiced by a very dark, very righteous, very round woman in full Ethiopian Orthodox military regalia. 'There is no DNA evidence that has been found to prove the death of His Majesty,' she keeps insisting. The two princes are obliged to concur, although you suspect they believe that their great-grandfather has quite definitely shuffled off his mortal coil. Satisfied, however, that they appear to agree with the possibility of her supposition – that His Majesty is still alive – she once again sits down.

Then it is the turn of a tall, thin dread in his early forties wearing a red, gold and green patchwork shirt to stand up. 'What instrument is not an instrument of society, but is an economical instrument?' he asks and beams. It is like a moment from a medieval court, the joker stepping forward with the key advice, couched in mystery, that can save the times. Yet he is soundly ignored. Everyone in the room looks utterly flummoxed, slightly embarrassed, as though wishing this riddler would go away for ever.

'We don't know the instrument you are talking about,' eventually says Prince Ermias, looking even more confused. Choruses of 'Shut up and sit down, man' ring round the room.

Just in time to save embarrassment all round, one Jah Stumpy, as a one-legged Jamaican dread inevitably would be known, hops forward with his acoustic guitar and performs Bob Marley's 'Iron Lion Zion'. Then – just in case we haven't got the idea – he performs it again.

The press conference comes to an end. Then, according to a prior arrangement, I interview the princes at the rear of the hotel, on a stone terrace above the sea, in the last light of the day. During the faintly surreal question-and-answer session in which they have just taken part, I have been immensely impressed with their benign and courteous demeanour. As I speak with them now, I am taken even more by their palpable sincerity and energy. First I enquire what they heard at the time of their great-grandfather's visit to Jamaica in 1966.

'Personally, I was very young at the time,' Prince Bekare answers. 'I was four years old. But we had a great relationship with our great-grandfather.'

'I was privileged to have heard about the visit first-hand from my cousin Prince Daiz Makonen, who had accompanied His Majesty, who passed away some time back,' says Prince Ermias. 'And he often talked about how moved His Majesty was by this experience. And having also watched the video of His Majesty's visit to Jamaica, we got some flavour of what His Majesty must have gone through.'

'The visit had a great impact, because it led to the development of strong relations between Jamaica and Ethiopia, and His Majesty was able to donate land for people who were interested in repatriation, and also to the establishment of the Ethiopian Orthodox Church in Jamaica.'

Did you understand why the people of Jamaica would revere him in the way they did?

'Well, you see,' Prince Ermias continues, 'His Majesty was a larger-than-life figure. He had enormous receptions throughout the places he visited outside of Ethiopia. He had had the courage to face fascist aggression at the height of fascism, when Ethiopia was weak. But I think Jamaica was special in that the outpouring of emotion was enormous. And of course it all ties in with the tremendous charisma and historical play that His Majesty had throughout his lifetime.'

Did the support of the Rastafarian community come as a surprise?

'I think the Rastafarian community goes way back before the visit,' replies Prince Ermias. 'And they had sent delegations to Ethiopia. His Majesty knew of the Rastafarian movement, and had met with the delegations prior to his arrival. But I think he was still surprised.'

Prince Bekare: 'Very surprised. He knew, but he wanted to pay the respects for the credit he was getting from the Jamaicans and the Caribbean. And I think that was initiated way before the visit. And then when he did, the impact it had ... Well, history speaks for itself.'

What has been the effect of Bob Marley in bringing the ideas of Haile Selassie, Rastafari and Ethiopia to the world?

Prince Ermias: 'The first event we held on this visit was at the Bob Marley Museum on the evening of our arrival. And really it was to honour the tremendous message that Bob Marley has done to spread the message of love, of oneness, and also of Ethiopia's heritage. And his music transcended barriers of race, of distance. I was very privileged to have known Bob Marley personally, and I have very warm memories of the way he was able to move people. And his legacy will remain with all of us.'

Prince Bekare: 'The respect we have for Bob Marley is colossal. He talks about war, he talks about unity, more or less everything my great-grandfather spoke about. And we have a lot of respect and admiration for him and his efforts.'

But how do you feel about the notion of your great-grandfather being referred to as God?

Prince Bekare: 'We cannot judge someone's belief – we cannot judge that. Everyone looks for a God, for whatever cause, for whatever reason it may be. We personally are Orthodox. We believe in Jesus Christ.

'Our great-grandfather was a human being like you and I, OK? But he had a lot of faith. And for what he has done, and his accomplishments and his foresight ... For his time he was very, very advanced in his vision – if someone considers him a God in that sense, no one can deny him that right.

'Like I said, we don't think he's God – he's our great-grandfather. We believe in what he's done and everything he stood for. Which is precisely what we are trying to continue.'

1990–2000

In case you thought that Rastafarian roots culture was date-tied to the life of Bob Marley, the cyclical theory of the religion should go some way to dispelling this. The theory is that Rastafari returns with greater strength each alternative decade: in the thirties, in the fifties, then in the seventies and nineties, Rastafari has flourished, is self-regenerating.

But the cyclical theory, one that I have heard before, may be somewhat simplistic. Certainly it is the case that Jamaican culture has always been two-sided, that there always have been two opposing components, the spiritual and the carnal. In

Jamaican music, much of which is the popular expression of Rastafari, those elements are omnipresent: in the era of spiritual reggae dominated by Bob Marley, a 'slack' element was also forever on display – for example, amidst Marley's hymns to Jah on *Catch A Fire*, his first album on Island Records, there was also the presence of the tune 'Kinky Reggae'; and then there is his earlier song 'Guava Jelly', in which he promises to rub something on his girlfriend's belly, 'like guava jelly'.

Even in more recent ragga dancehall days, spirituality always has been present – for example, in the music of Yellowman, renowned as a slackness deejay, there is always a dimension that is both spiritual and radical. It doesn't really matter whom you mention, you will find that those two elements are always present, working in a kind of balance. It is the nature of the larger moment, what is happening on the island and elsewhere in more general political and economic terms, that determines whether the spiritual or the carnal is uppermost in Jamaican culture and its music.

'It is an interesting question,' says the dreadlocked [Cecil] Gutzmore, one of Kingston's leading cultural academics, a former lecturer at the University of North London,

whether what might be called roots-and-culture and what might be called slackness are parts of a cycle, one of which is dominant at any period. I think to call it cyclical oversimplifies it. For example, the moment in Jamaican music that is most celebrated, the time of Bob Marley, was one of a kind of radicalism which wasn't just made by Bob Marley and the other griots of whom we are enamoured. For they were supported in that moment by the fact that revolutionary things were happening in this society, a reaction to the 1960s, the dominance of the JLP in politics, and the coming into focus of Michael Manley and that experiment which he tried. It wasn't just in Jamaica – things were happening worldwide. And so in that moment there were a great number of factors supporting the radicalism that made that moment. In the 1980s we might say that things changed: we had a conservative movement taking place worldwide, symbolized by

Thatcher and Reagan and in the Caribbean by the return of Seaga and Eugenia Charles. At least part of the analysis of the music of the 1990s, and the dominance of slackness, is that it was appropriate to the moment, and also it was the music that the moment allowed. So what we have is that the domination of slackness in the 1980s is argued by some to have been a representation of the nature of that moment, of the brutality of the state, of the way in which the economy seemed to be reorganized against the poor. But side by side with it there is also going on that much more representative roots-and-culture dynamic which survived and resurfaced in the 1990s. We're not just talking cycles, we're talking the fact that at any moment what you have to do is look at the pressures on the musicians, and the pressures on the culture, and if you look properly at what those pressures are, you begin to understand why one tendency is dominant.

Cycles mean nothing to the most visible manifestation of Rastafari as the millennium turns: the young punk zealots known as Bobbadreads disdain any form of transport by walking every-where. Bobbadreads have taken a 'Nazarene vow' of poverty, and espouse the humblest of lifestyles. All over the island, but especially in Kingston, the Bobbadreads are visible on the streets, wearing their characteristic tightly wrapped head-cloths, selling mats, brooms and Rasta badges on the pave-ments – except for on the Sabbath, when they refuse to work, as they disdain employment by anyone or anything other than their church. All the money made by Bobbadreads goes to their church, except for what they spend on food – and these are guys you tend *not* to see down the KFC.

'My Lord!' is the traditional greeting of the Bobbadreads, the right arm crossed to the heart. In Jamaica there are maybe 2000 members of this rigorous community, many of them living communally in the long-established semi-autonomous Rastafarian encampments in the hills above Bull Bay, an area that has a reputation as being extremely, sometimes lethally, anarchic. For example, when I suggested in 1994 to Ziggy Marley that I might go up there to pay my respects and peruse the scene as research for my book about his father, he advised me not to go. Later I learned that up there not long before, Ziggy had been making a video: the brother of the director, who was a white painter from England's West Country who had moved to Jamaica, had been shot because he refused to hand over his watch when a modern-day highway robber stopped his car on the way to the video location. Now, in a twist that is readily apparent, any non-Bobbadread visitors must present themselves at the police station in Bull Bay itself, and await constabulary accompaniment up the hill.

'It can get very heavy up there,' says Carl Bradshaw. 'Many of those guys living up there are ex-convicts. You can rob all the banks in the world as long as you cleanse yourself through Rastafari. The punishment is the purification through righteousness.'

'How can you be so ungrateful / After all that God has done for you ...' Unlikely lyrics for a Jamaican smash hit in 1995? Earlier in the 1990s, when celebrations of ghetto gun-battles, cocaine culture and 'slack' sexual lubricity ruled the dancehall, it might have seemed from another time altogether. Now, however, as Luciano's Sam Cooke-like soul voice intones the religious words of praise of his latest local hit for a video shoot, he is surrounded by almost the entire community of the holiday town of Treasure Beach. It is as though he's fulfilling a very precise need.

Which he unquestionably is: Luciano, who has had hits with a seemingly endless supply of his own spiritual songs, is Jamaica's king of 'consciousness', a musical shift in thinking that seems too important to be merely a trend. 'Conscious' means exactly what it says: being awake, having your eyes and head open, embracing the numinous rather than the negativity. 'With relation to the various tendencies with consciousness in Jamaica,' Gutzmore points out,

the first thing to accept is that Rastafari is the central element. Rastafari

176

is an incredibly complex, contrary, even contradictory phenomenon within society. It is important to understand that it is a society that essentially consists of a number of different elements. Different perspectives on Selassie, different perspectives on Jesus, on Ethiopia and so on. When you first encounter this, it might look as if you are in the middle of a confused movement. But the point is not that that movement is confused, but that it is so diverse. And it is the diverse elements that make up this very different and dynamic and quite radical reality.

You may encounter the difficulty particular performers have within their music: Luciano is a good example. There is a religious context which celebrates both Haile Selassie as God and Jesus Christ as God as well, and manages to run that rather complex and contradictory theory together. You will encounter other griots who have a less rich and less complex conception of what the theology is about, who think that you cannot combine Haile Selassie and Jesus, the one with the other. But I don't think of it as confusion, but as rich complexity.

So the subject-matter of conscious music dramatically reverses the glorification of the dystopian badman lifestyle that for almost a decade has ostensibly dominated 'dancehall', the commercially guaranteed digital blend of reggae and rap favoured by artists from Shabba Ranks to Ninjaman. 'But how could those ghetto deejays write about anything but the material they were singing?' Luciano says to me. That was their world, all they knew: they were victims themselves.

'It seems,' Luciano offers an explanation, with humility, 'that of late consciousness in mankind has raised up to a higher dimension. For some reason myself and other artists began to feel a need to ameliorate the subconscious human condition down here in Jamaica: we realized the impact that music has on young minds.'

In the controlled anarchy of the Kingston ghetto in the middle of the 1990s, life is tougher and deadlier than ever. And the guntoting braggadocio of much dancehall subject-matter, mired in the grim reality with which it deals, has offered no way out. At this time optimists hope that the appearance of 'conscious' music really does reflect a collective need in Jamaica to bid farewell to the world of bullets and cocaine. For the new 'conscious' culture appears to have wider implications: the extreme styles and attitudes of Jamaicans are emulated internationally by both inner-city and suburban youth, especially in the United States, from where 'Yard' drug posses support Kingston's ghetto economy.

The cutlass strokes slashed worldwide by Jamaica's cultural buccaneers have always been double-edged: on one side, dysfunctionally, dangerously wild; on the other, earth-shatteringly spiritual.

And like many rural Jamaicans possessed of pure faith, Luciano emanates positive energy. Moreover, in the Caribbean he has such a package of mythology working for him that he could have inspired an entire book section by Joseph Campbell, the collator and interpreter of global legends. Physically, he is the template of not one but two Jamaican heroic archetypes: Luciano's broad build and reddish-brown complexion recall the only known drawings of the legendary Cudjoe, the Maroon hero who brought the English redcoats to their knees; and Perry Henzell, the director of the classic film *The Harder They Come*, was so struck by the musician's resemblance to Marcus Garvey, also of Maroon origin, that he wanted to cast Luciano as the black prophet in a biographical musical. 'I have previously manifested in many forms,' Luciano claims, suitably matter-of-fact and mysterious.

This prevailing mood in Jamaican music in the late 1990s sets off an important re-evaluation of its purpose. Although one of the most popular acts of the previous two years, Bounti Killa, was still adhering to the old thoughts and mores, it couldn't be long before he too was hymning praises to Jah.

Beenie Man, for example, his closest contemporary rival for hottest Jamaican deejay, does precisely that, wearing his soul on his red, gold and green sleeve; despite superb paeans to downtown life like the anthemic 'Slam', tunes like his powerful reality song 'Freedom' and 'Blessed', the title track of his invigorating LP tribute to Haile Selassie, are dedicated as much to the creator. A man of the ghetto as much as Luciano is a man of the hills, Beenie is a consummate professional: at twenty-one he already had been performing for fifteen years – at the age of six he was guesting on records as Boy Wonder. At the beginning of the nineties he could be seen at sound-system events like the celebrated House of Leo, dancing on his own, a one-man posse – though at that stage Beenie Man had less recognition than he had had almost a decade earlier.

'Mi nuh jump 'pon no bandwagon t'ing,' insists Beenie Man. 'Yuh just have to deal with life like yuh supposed to, seen? 'Cause some youth nuh really understand the concept of Rasta. They just a sell Rasta, put on some locks and jump up and down saying "Selassie I". I'm not into all that: it no really mek sense. Yuh have to be creative, love original stuff at all times.'

In Jamaica there is a wealth of talented new conscious deejays, especially Anthony B, nominated as the best new act of 1995.

A twenty-six-year-old from Portmore, a Kingston dormitory town now nearly as large as the capital itself, Anthony B began his career seven or eight years ago by simply beating pans on the street. At the African Star outdoor nightclub in Halfway Tree, where he is shooting an onstage performance for the film *Dancehall Queen*, Anthony traces the almost archetypal career progress that has led to the extreme success of his song 'Fire Pon Rome' – and a reputation for songs that deal with matters of social concern. When he left school at the age of seventeen, he began to hang out with the Black Scorpion sound-system posse, grabbing the mike whenever the opportunity came his way. After an unsuccessful first record, 'Just Sniff Coke', he was inspired by Rastafari, and as 1993 turned to 1994, his songs 'One Thing' and 'Hurt The Heart' put him in the eyes of the public. 'Consciousness is truth,' Anthony emphasizes. 'A people of the world like truth.' It is Luciano, he insists, who is his main contemporary inspiration – 'a man with a work'.

★

But some of the most exemplary Jamaican music of the decade has been produced by older dancehall acts who have experienced biblical-style conversions to 'consciousness'. None is more remarkable than Buju Banton, once the personification of Jamaican homophobia – his 'Boom Bye Bye' tune virtually pronounced a death sentence on gays. Then, however, he 'locksed' (grew dreadlocks), and produced the finest reggae album of the 1990s, *Til Shiloh*, a work of mature spirituality. Where did the record's title come from? I ask this histrionic character at a rehearsal studio in downtown Kingston.

'I started reading the Scriptures where it said, 'The sceptre shall not depart from the tribe of Judah till Shiloh come.' I penetrated the word Shiloh and fell in love with it. I found it an infinite word. It not only means for ever, but it also means the heavenly, mystical presence of the glory of the Holy Spirit of Truth.'

And how did this extraordinary shift in lyrical subject-matter come about? 'Inside me, there was a musical rage to let out. I went out and gave Jah thanks and praise, because the inspiration was so strong, so much so that I and I even shed tears as the words came together. It was even more than I could imagine – that I and I look 'pon myself and say, "Boy, God really love me." I was in a pensive mood, looking at the situation we're living in.'

Almost as surprising is Capleton, a newly dreadlocked raucous dancehall deejay. Early tunes, like 'Bumba Red', were not particularly politically correct. But Capleton's later songs, like 'Babylon Judgement' and 'Chant', are conscious anthems. Even the dancehall queen Lady Saw, whose legendary stage shows are both raunchy and extremely funny – there is a constant central theme of self-mockery – straddles the ostensibly contradictory themes of consciousness and dancehall.

From Port Maria on the north coast, Lady Saw soon tired of work in the area's free-trade zone and took off for Kingston. Named after her biggest original influence, the great Tenor Saw, she scored her first hit with 'Find A Good Man', although her initial reputation spread with the self-explanatory 'Stab Up Mi Meat'. 'I saw other guys doing X-rated stuff and getting away with it,' she says, 'and I tried it, and it worked. Now I just go onstage and whatever happens in my mind, I go with it.'

In Lady Saw's stage performances, which are remarkable for the undiluted sexuality on display, she has been known to grab the hands of members of the audience and rub them between her legs. But all this is done with a humour that moves such actions to a higher plane. In her song 'What Is Slackness', Lady Saw responds to critics: she suggests that the real 'slackness' is public utilities and facilities that don't work in the manner in which they were intended.

As a pointer in this direction, her AIDS-awareness song 'Condom' has been a number-one single in Jamaica. The feisty Lady Saw also has had a number-one single on the New York reggae charts with 'Give Mi A Reason', a beautiful country-tinged love song. 'What is consciousness?' she asks. 'Is it conscious that they ban my shows in Montego Bay, yet can't even repair the roads for the people to travel on or give them a decent transportation system?'

Among male artists the recent 'locksing' is a significant detail. The rhythm of conscious reggae is the kete drum, the basis of the 'nyabinghi' music performed by devout Rastafarians: this is the beat of, for example, Beenie Man's song 'Freedom'. As we move apace into the new millennium, the apocalyptic predictions of Rastafari seem daily more relevant.

'Rastafari has come back, even with the youngsters,' Luciano asserts. 'They feel as I do. I decided to look below the glittering surface and find the truth: and I realized all you need is a love of God and you feel clean and comfortable.'

How can you think of Rastafarianism without hearing the name Bob Marley? What happened in Jamaica to his words of warning? Were the lessons of the prophet of the Third World no longer being heeded in his homeland? Somewhere in the nation's collective psyche it must have seemed time to return to the grace once bestowed on Jamaica by Marley's music and presence. 'I thank God every day for this return to consciousness,' Rita Marley tells me. 'All respect to Bob in setting the pace. This kete rhythm has allowed cleaner lyrics: they lick the drum and the heartbeat feels like one.'

In fact, since the great musical artist's death in 1981 there has been an embarrassing number of not-the-next-Bob-Marleys. With one exception: the only Jamaican artist for whom such comparisons were never risible was Garnett Silk. Thanks to superb albums like *It's Growing* and a classic high soul voice, Silk was recognized as the finest new Jamaican singer of the 1990s. But he was also a devout follower of Rastafari who recorded songs of coruscating social criticism, with the result that he became the first prophet of the new 'consciousness'. Hinting at that curious sense of paradox with which Jamaica seems forever riven, however, it was the gun that brought about his end: in December 1994 a loose shot hit a gas cylinder outside his house, killing him. His tragic end seemed to be felt by all Jamaica.

'Garnett Silk bring it all back,' says Jah Stitch, a celebrated deejay of the 1970s.

Bob was dealing with something original, but it was music to personally experience rather than dance all night in a club to. But Garnett Silk brought consciousness into dancehall music: he used the rhythm of dancehall with cultural lyrics that were very deep. Right now, it can't turn back. Everybody just have to follow the trail. He gets the message across through dancehall – him a great teacher.

The king of consciousness remains the redoubtable Luciano, the man who picked up the mantle cast down by Garnett Silk's tragic death. In Jamaica in the 1990s it was Luciano-mania. Everywhere from darkest downtown to the highest hills, his addictive songs of devotion were adored by the local population; you could hardly turn on a radio without hearing the sweet, lilting tunes that make up *Where There is Life*, his album on which every song is a celebration of God – 'It's Me Again Jah',

'Lord Give Me Strength' and 'He Is My Friend' are just three of the titles. It came as no surprise that in 1996 Luciano was named vocalist of the year at Kingston's annual Rockers Awards.

A humble poet at heart, Luciano has a clear view of both the reason for his popularity and the source of his inspiration. 'This system requires a lack of love and understanding to work,' he insists to me.

Mankind is still living like hooligans: if the wealth of the earth is not fairly distributed, there will inevitably be chaos. Those nations that take wealth to their countries alone cause an imbalance. And so we have earthquakes, cyclones and hurricanes.

I'm happy to be part of this musical renaissance. There was a decadence in the music, part of the global thing of materialism taking over mankind. And in the same way that the music has changed, so there will also be a breaking-down of this present world order. Even world leaders know this current system is collapsing. Any system that isn't based on equality and justice simply cannot last.

In a neat poetic twist, one of the cameramen at Luciano's Treasure Beach video shoot is a Bobbadread by the name of Sizzler (or Sizzla). Two years later he is one of the biggest new stars of Jamaican music, intoning musically frenetic and religiously fundamentalist tunes like 'Black Woman And Child' to great commercial and artistic effect. Managed by Fattis Burrell, a lovable giant bear of a man, he has set up home in August Town, St Andrew, in the shadow of Dallas Mountain, where he lives with a community of Bobbadreads. When Don Letts, Rick Elgood and I go to film an interview with him there, we find ourselves almost making a fatal error by asking the simple question, 'Shall we shoot you now?' Considering Sizzler/Sizzla's former occupation, we are surprised by the consternation that this sets off.

Now Peter is being led away. I don't know where they are taking him, and I fear the worst.

Then one of the gunmen tells me to get up and come with them. With difficulty I get to my feet. It is vital that they continue to believe that my hands are tied tight, although I have covertly loosened my bonds. Near the door is the guy with the very dark complexion.

'So you are about to meet your end. Which do you think you are going to? Heaven or hell?' He smiles, almost sweetly.

'Whichever is chosen for me,' I reply, not really knowing what else to say.

'Well, you are going to hell,' he bellows at me, with a vile and evil expression.

'If that's how it has to be,' I respond as calmly as I can, praying I'm calling his bluff.

1996–1997

It is Ash Wednesday 1996, a national holiday in Jamaica. Don Letts is into his second week of directing the shooting of *Dancehall Queen*.

Today the location is the small street market opposite the Carib cinema at Crossroads in downtown Kingston. The opening shot of the movie is being filmed; it employs a dolly railtrack that takes the cinematographer's camera in the opposite direction to the street vendor's cart pushed by Marcia, played by Audrey Reid, as she arrives at her pitch. There she discovers that her regular spot has been usurped by Priest, played by the fine local method actor Paul Campbell.

Both actors are impressive. Audrey's ghetto-gal accent is spot-on; Paul has an edgy tension about him. He is wearing green contact lenses that give his eyes a dead look and has dyed his hair a sort of gingery orange, a style both cuddly and sinister, favoured, I have noticed, by the sort of chaps who look like deportees. One scene has to be interrupted as he remembers to replace his fake gold tooth.

The sun is searingly hot. But during the lunch break, when factor 21 is applied liberally by all participants, the sky suddenly clouds up. Then it is a case of snatching scenes in between clouds and worrying about problems with continuity.

There is a further continuity problem. An integral part of this first scene in the film is a pothole in the road, in which a wheel of Audrey's cart gets stuck. But when he comes back from lunch, Don Letts discovers three men from the public-works department filling in the hole with wet cement.

★

In one of the closing scenes of *Dancehall Queen*, Olivine, the reigning monarch who is about to be deposed, puts on a display of near-masturbation masquerading as dance. Anywhere else in the world it might lead to a spell in prison, but in Jamaica it could be an act in any weekly contest. When the movie was released in 1997 it became the most popular picture in Jamaica up to that time (eclipsing even *Home Alone 2*). Its success is a reflection of what these contests offer: an escape for women from ghetto poverty and a route to a new life. It is Marcia the street vendor who succeeds in toppling Olivine, in the film's classic scenario. 'I know it seems like a Cinderella story, but it's also the truth of what happens,' said Suzanne Fenn, the film's co-writer. 'The whole point about the idea of becoming a dancehall queen offers hope, even if it's only an idea of a way out.' Carlene the Dancehall Queen was a central inspiration for the film.

Dancehall dancing manages by turn to be undilutedly sensual and warmingly funny – as good sex should be, of course. 'A night out at a dancehall club can be absolutely hilarious,' said the film's co-director Don Letts.

'None of these girls are regarding themselves totally seriously. Or at least the ones who win aren't. It's all very much tongue-in-cheek – or wherever,' added his directing partner Rick Elgood.

In the very concept of the dancehall queen can be read a typically Jamaican twist on female empowerment, replete with the number of paradoxes that seems requisite for most matters on the island: distinguished academics like Carolyn Cooper of the University of West Indies, for example, trace the line from Nanny, the female Maroon chief, to dancehall queen; but others see this heritage as going back no further than to the influence of the island's raunchy go-go clubs in which tomorrow's dancehall moves (and often much, much more) may be seen today, and the favours of the dancers are frequently for sale.

My first encounter with the uniquely Jamaican experience that is a go-go bar occurs when I stop with my mate Peter (a few days before the hold-up) at what we assume is an ordinary roadside rum joint in Annotto Bay, on the St Mary–Portland border between Port Maria and Buff Bay. Finding the tiny front room packed by the four or five people already there, we take our rum and Pepsis through to another room at the back. Pulling ourselves up on a pair of stools at the bar, we proceed, to the rhythm of the dancehall soundtrack, to discuss the issues of the day.

We are the sole occupants of this back room, until a not unattractive young lady, whose legs bear the characteristic welts and machete scars of ghetto gals, steps in behind the bar. We continue our discourse. Before long we register that this young lady has mounted the bar, shed half of her clothing, and is proceeding to gyrate to the music around our drinks. Soon she has removed her underwear and is providing us with a decidedly gynaecological inspection of her nether regions, pink, gaping and glowing as they are thrust in our faces at a distance of some six inches. Rather than being turned on, we are simply puzzled, possibly in a state of minor cultural shock. We are obliged to curtail our conversation. Finishing our drinks, we depart to continue on our journey, somewhat fazed by the absurdity of this cultural experience. (Other go-go clubs, however, are more sophisticated, with gorgeous girls, and can be jolly good fun.)

'There are links between dancehall fashion and go-go,' says one dancehall-queen contest winner.

It's the same thing: it's all dancing to Jamaican music. So it comes under the same line. Go-go dancing is something that's been in Jamaica for years, long before my time. And I think will always be here, even when dancehall is gone. Go-go is not degrading to me because I can accept people for doing what is an honest job. There is little difference between dancehall and go-go: you're just not paid in a dancehall. We're both representing reggae music and sexiness.

Although dancehall-queen contests were happening long before *Dancehall Queen* hit the cinema screens, the success of the film has given a new impetus and urgency to the regular competitions. In the audience at one such contest in Montego Bay is the international heavyweight boxing champion Lennox Lewis, there to view a bevy of dancers anxious to let the audience see how long they have spent on their nails, hairstyles and costumes.

'At that contest,' remembers Rick Elgood,

there was some absolutely outrageous dancing – some of them just wound and ground and flashed their pumpums and some of them wore very revealing costumes. But the ones that won weren't like that. In fact, some of them were very good dancers. There were about twenty contestants that were cut down to ten and then to four. The girl that won, a local girl, went on to win another competition, when they had a music convention in Montego Bay. The event itself was very long-winded, starting off with a fashion show, with Stone Love sound system in charge of the music.

When the girl was crowned it was a major event going on for about half an hour. It was done by an enormous woman who stood in the way with her massive bulk, stopping anyone in the audience seeing what was going on. The girl was in tears, she won something like a thousand US dollars. There was a very big crowd, and the event went on too long. I noticed a lot of grabbing of girls backstage.

Any dancehall night at Cactus, Mirage or Asylum will see an army of wannabe queens, gangs of girls from all over Kingston and beyond letting it all hang out, courtesy of such dancehall designers as Ouch! – run by a pair of female Jamericans (Jamaican-Americans) whose previous employment had been as members of the US Marines – and Lexxus. Lexxus, a fey character with dyed blond hair, plies his designer and tailoring trade from small upstairs premises by Skateland in midtown Kingston's Halfway Tree. His styles are highly popular with visiting Japanese tourists. 'Dancehall fashion comes from an African thing,' he says, as a bra-less model demonstrates a dress made of see-through vinyl, the perspiration on her back soon fogging up the fabric. 'And things have gone so far with exposing parts of the body that the next fashion is bound to be pure nakedness.'

At any of these clubs you may sometimes find the one and only original dancehall queen herself, the self-titled Carlene the Dancehall Queen. Some – especially Carlene – will claim that this very Jamaican cultural phenomenon is all her fault, for it turns out that Carlene's regal position was not bestowed on her, but created by this woman-who-would-be-queen.

In 1986, when Carlene was only fifteen, she wore a three-inch mini-skirt while out in Kingston, causing traffic chaos in Halfway Tree Road; the phenomenon was even reported on the radio. 'I always had it in me to wear little of whatever. I didn't think of it as rude. I just thought of it as what I liked for me.'

But Carlene's reign did not begin until February 1992. That month, at a 'Fashion Clash' at Cactus, Carlene's crew faced a team of four of Jamaica's top models, including the reigning Miss Jamaica, all clad in swish evening dress – in contrast to the dancehall styles sported by Carlene and company.

The next day headlines in the press bestowed on her the tag of Carlene the Undisputed Dancehall Queen. 'All this came because of my unique designs. It was never a dancehall clash that made me dancehall queen. It was a fashion clash.'

When I call on her at her modern house in Portmore to film an interview, Carlene the (Undisputed) Dancehall Queen is in character, wearing a one-piece fishnet outfit over a vinyl bra-and-panties set, and thigh-length boots: as she talks she reclines on a fake zebra skin that covers her bed. A Bible lies open by the side of it. Downstairs is the dancehall superstar Beenie Man, with whom she has had a long, well-documented romance, and some of his crew, drinking Moët et Chandon and Johnny Walker Black Label and burning herb – lifestyles of the (reasonably) rich and famous, JA-style.

A surprisingly hefty, big-boned girl, Carlene looks as though she might pack quite a punch. From an uptown background, with a Lebanese father, Carlene started out with a beauty salon in Negril aimed at the tourist trade before graduating to become a designer of dancehall clothes. Needless to say, in relentlessly, troublingly colour-conscious Jamaica her light complexion has led to suggestions that that is the main secret of her success. 'I am half-white, half-black, but I'm still Jamaican and I consider myself very black, even though I am so *clear*,' she says, employing the habitual Jamaican euphemism for having light skin – though the word 'clear' itself is a troubling reduction of thought. 'Wearing a blonde hair is something that I consider sexy. A lot of people said I reigned and got accepted because I am upper-class, very clear-complexioned and my nose is straight,' she says with more than a hint of pride.

That's the advantage they think you have over a black girl. Kind of, yes. But I worked hard for where I am. I worked hard for what I wanted said and done. If a girl is so clear, she doesn't usually have the body I have: she'll look more flat-chested, with no bottom.

I've never gone nude. I've never exposed my private parts. My buns has been there – that's part of my assets, my breasts and my bottom. In Jamaica men like that.

Whatever the complexities of colour, Carlene picked up her royal title and ran with it.

Dancehall Queen has become a full-time job for me, because I made it that. I sat and I thought of what I was doing, what I wanted to do. How far I wanted to go, exactly what limit I wanted to reach – all of this.

People think, 'Oh, she's lucky!' No, it wasn't luck. I had fight from the media, from church people, everybody. I decided I was going to fight back. This is why what I'm doing is still alive. I love that people are taking my image and utilizing what I do today. It's been five years that I'm dancehall queen.

Why did Carlene want this job? What was in it for her, apart from ephemeral stardom? She seems to understand her position as an archetype:

I had to put aside a lot of things that I wanted to do. Because I am living for a lot of people. A lot of people out there have put down dancehall as gun and violence – and it's not so. For the kids who look up to me as a role model I want to always let them know that what I do onstage is a job. And that offstage I'm a normal person and that the media has done a lot of injustice. I didn't know all this was to come with the title Dancehall Queen.

Stories about dancehall are rarely absent from Jamaica's press, and are often far more favourable than suggested by Carlene's remarks. The genre has even spawned its own publications, specifically a pair of weekly tabloids, *X News* and *Hardcore*, both filled with scantily clad girls and newsbite stories. ('Them seh 'im 'ave a gun, but 'im jus' 'ave a bun 'n' cheese!' was a pull-out quote that especially caught my eye in an *X News* article about a man being shot by the police.) 'There is something about Carlene that defies explanation,' says Milton Williams, publisher of *Hardcore*. 'She has been around for a long time: in dancehall to have any longevity is quite unusual. But she has a certain degree of class and attitude in the way she portrays herself that keeps her popular.'

Needless to say, dancehall's in-your-face X-rated sexuality hardly conforms to the view of womanhood as perceived by feminism. Carlene comments:

I say to those people who think what I am doing is sexist, enjoy life for what it is and what you can make life to be. Do not let other people's happiness be sadness for you. A lot of people look at what I do for encouragement. I know this for sure, especially the ghetto society: I have made girls who would have probably had three or four babies think, 'Well, I can dance, so I can make something of my life. I don't have to wait on a man, or think if I don't have a baby, that's it for me.' Dancehall dancing has gone to the highest level: you have Janet Jackson dancing the Butterfly.

But isn't it sexist to simply consider the role of women in dancehall? What about men? 'Men are outdoing us sometimes now: men now go out of their way to look good,' said Carlene. 'The women of Jamaica also want the men to look good. Jamaican men have become much more fashion-conscious than ever before. They're going to the gym, they're bleaching their skin to look cool.'

And how long does Carlene intend to reign for?

People have tried to dethrone me. I have never had a real challenge to say, 'Give me this title!' Because there is no real dancehall queen. I planned this, I started it. When I'm through making this statement I want to make, I will have to give up my title. But I'll be Carlene the Dancehall Queen for life. I think I'm going to go down in history as the Dancehall Queen: there is no competition there.

At this time Carlene is also endorsing one of Jamaica's newest products, Slam condoms ('fe the Wickedest Slam!'). 'They're studded, like Rough Riders, but don't have that rubbery smell,' she explains thoughtfully; on the television advertisements for Slam, Carlene breathily intones the tag line, 'Feel the rhythm, feel the ride.' You feel this could almost be a high-concept one-line summation of the life of Carlene the (Undisputed) Dancehall Queen.

When I finish talking to Carlene, I leave her house but realize I have forgotten something as I am getting into the car. Climbing the stairs again, I find that Beenie Man is with Carlene in the bathroom; I can't imagine what they seem to be doing to one another.

October 1997

The morning after I have been at Carlene's house I again find myself driving into Portmore. A once uninhabited scrub headland, it was established as a commuter dormitory town for the capital in the 1960s and now has a population of 80,000, rapidly rising with the development of the Hellshire Hills. I head out of Kingston down the grandly titled, often partially flooded Marcus Garvey Drive, past the Tuff Gong record company headquarters over on the left, behind high, tough link-fencing, in the midst of another set of breeze-block buildings that look like trading estates. A few hundred yards further down on the left-hand side I pass the gantry cranes that dominate the trading port of Newport West, a commercial and shipping area which was an Edward Seaga project – accordingly it is said to give plentiful employment to his JLP supporters.

Then over the causeway bridge across the west of the harbour to the Portmore sprawl. The bridge, built only in the late Sixties, becomes a one-way route during the morning and evening rush hours. Until just a few minutes ago, both lanes were hurtling traffic over it into Kingston's endless gridlock.

Directly on the other side of the bridge are an adjacent pair of narrow spits of land. On one of them is the road I am driving along, flanked by rows of rickety roadside shacks run by fishermen's wives and fronted by ice coolers crammed with that morning's catch. To the rear of the fishing huts is a harbour-polluted, soiled strip of beach so narrow it is almost nonexistent. Here, in 1986, were found the chopped remains of the three alleged perpetrators of the pillaging of a new eye clinic a friend of mine had set up. Vigilante justice is common in Jamaica – of course you always hope they get the right people. In a case outside Mandeville, six police watched as angry residents hacked to death ('Is my turn: give me a lick!') a gang of robbers, already slowed down by their wounds from the cops' bullets. It is out this way as well that at least one of the gunmen who attacked Bob Marley in the assassination attempt at 56 Hope

Road was alleged to have been hanged from a tree by some of his ghetto brethren.

The other spit of land, which seems like no more than an oversized sandbar jutting out into the ocean, is home to the grim, imposing spectre of Fort Augustus, constructed in the mid-eighteenth century as the major fortification of the western side of the harbour, and now the women's prison.

I skirt around the edge of Portmore and past the Cactus Club on the way to the Hellshire beaches, the long stretch of white sand dunes that are the nearest large seaside playgrounds to the Jamaican capital. The beaches, a series of coves of varying sizes, are reached through the raw rock ranges of a cactus-strewn set of low hills – the Hellshire Hills – far drier than you would expect in the tropics.

There are two main beaches, roughly adjacent to each other. The first is Fort Clarence, the recently developed area with its holiday 'bashments'. The funkiest of the two beaches, however, the one with the rootsiest and most cultural vibes, is a couple of miles further on. Popularly known as Hellshire Beach, it is actually the fishermen's beach at Naggo Head. Naggo Head is named after the Naggo people, the original settlers. I had for long assumed this to be the name of, say, an obscure African tribe. Then I learned the truth, which has its own inevitable Jamaican simplicity. The Naggo people were displaced plantation labourers who were moved to the area from their original homes after slavery was abolished, protesting loudly, 'Wi nah go!'

Today much of this beach is lined with rows of bamboo huts in which all species of local fish are cooked for sale. One of my favourite experiences in the world is sitting barefoot, with the cool sand between my toes, and devouring a parrot fish or grunt or snapper at Joy's One-Stop, my favourite of these shacks, tucked away almost in the dunes. Joy, solidly built but without a hint of excess fat, is charming, sexy and efficient, and runs her yard with a rod of iron.

On this visit she even gives me a lesson in fish-cooking, JA-style. 'The taste is in your finger,' advises Joy, who has poured herself into a figure-hugging leopard-skin-print catsuit. 'Depends on 'ow yuh season yuh fish. Before yuh put it in the oil to fry yuh 'ave to season the fish with a lickle black pepper and a lickle salt, and let it soak for a t'ree minutes.'

Hellshire fish is served either with 'bammy', the flat cassava cake that was native to the Tainos, or more usually with 'festival'. 'Hellshire-style Festival' is a selling feature on the painted wooden signs announcing fish 'one-stops' all over the island: a sausage-shaped bread, it is made from flour, baking powder, salt, water and sugar – lots of sugar. As though making best use of one of the island's greatest natural resources, Jamaica has one of the sweetest collective national tongues I have encountered: the consequences in terms of tooth decay are omnipresent, a boon to purveyors of gold teeth.

Joy insists that her restaurant was the first one on the beach, and has been there for around twenty-five years, since her mother started it up. In those days both Countryman, the dread superhero of Dickie Jobson's film of the same name, and Ijahman Levi were living nearby. ('The Van Morrison of reggae' is how the latter was sold when his epochal suite-like *Haile I Hymn* was released on Island Records in 1978. In an earlier incarnation, while living in Harlesden in northwest London, he recorded a reggae version of 'White Christmas' as Nyah and the Snowflakes.) 'It was kinda rough, but it was peaceful,' Joy remembers that time. 'Better than now. Now we have a lot of war and t'ing like that.' Like people the world over, Jamaicans do a lot of remembering of the good old days.

Inevitably there are a host of interesting stories of Countryman's era at Hellshire, back in the time when Michael Thomas came from the United States in 1972 to write a classic piece about roots and Rasta culture for *Rolling Stone*. Thomas described how, when the pressure got to him, Countryman would swim out to sea beyond the reef until he could swim no more – and then would try to swim back.

Anyway, according to one no doubt apocryphal tale, Countryman's woman was vexed with him that they didn't have a radio with which to brighten up the evenings they spent in their one-room shack. Then she went away for a few days. When she returned, 'Country' showed her how much he cared for her by producing the radio he had bought. But then he had to explain to her that in order to buy the radio he had first sold their home.

On Sundays and public holidays Hellshire Beach is as packed as Coney Island. Bare-chested men stroll the length of it, waving lobsters in your face, ready to cook them up on fires behind the shacks. Small children sell lighters. A horse is led back and forth, providing children with rides – 'What is the name of your horse?' 'Investment.' But on this occasion, a Friday morning, there is hardly anyone around. Before the hour-long drive back to Kingston, I decide to take one of those invigorating, cleansing swims out to the reef. It is about a fifteen-minute stretch there and back (but watch out for those kamikaze fishing boats hurtling back in), though you can make it longer by hanging out on the reef for a while.

As I step into the warm Caribbean water, four late-teenage girls, who are by no means unattractive, run giggling into the sea past me; one of them appearing to pat me on my behind. I swim a few yards underwater. When I surface, the girls are standing close by, the sea just below their shoulders. 'Where yuh fram? Where yuh stay?' enquires one of them. I make small talk with her, ignoring a remark by another of them: 'She wan' fook yuh.' Playful banter, I assume.

Then the girl to whom I am talking comes more closely in front of me, as though she has had an idea. 'So yuh wan' fook mi oonderwahter?' she suddenly enquires, showing me that beneath the surface of the clear water she is standing with her not unshapely legs wide apart.

What? I beg your pardon!

Ummm . . . I try to be as polite and gentlemanly as possible, feeling it would be something of a loss of face to admit to being utterly flabbergasted by this suggestion. 'Well, it's a jolly nice idea. Thank you. But unfortunately I don't have a condom on me.'

198

'So yuh nah fook gal wi'out boot?' My potential paramour looks contemptuously at me.

'Umm. I just don't think it's a terribly good idea, do you?' I nervously respond, making my excuses and swimming out to the reef, where I am able to speculate on how many other men she has put this potentially germ-infested but not unappealing proposition.

November 1995

It is around five in the afternoon, late in November 1995. I am sitting in my cottage at Strawberry Hill, the hotel in which I am staying in Irish Town, 3000 feet above Kingston. Outside the rain is torrential, batting down and bouncing off the woodwork of the building. There is 100 per cent cloud cover. Nothing is visible beyond the mango tree a yard from the verandah. In this magic elixir of a tropical rainstorm, waterfalls pour from the sky; it is aquatic poetry, natural art of the highest form, in which time hangs like the thick tropical air.

All of a sudden there is a break in the thick swathes of cloud and a rainbow is heading almost vertically down into the valley below, right opposite my cottage. Then I notice that, rather unusually, the rainbow appears to have only three colours - thick bands of red, gold and green, a rainbow of Rastafari. Through the dense blue-grey cloud appears a white and yellow building, around which the mist swirls like a halo. It is the small church on the hillock opposite the house, on the far side of a deep valley. For a few minutes only the rainbow and this beautiful place of Christian worship are visible, alone together, an oasis in the unending cloud desert. The sky brightens into a silvery, satiny canopy illuminated by the panelled light of the late sun; the rain stops.

Such elemental shamanism electrically comes upon you everywhere in Jamaica, all the time. The island resonates with primal power and energy. This is a country in which something else, something of the spirit rather than matter, seems to be forever the defining principle.

Any Sunday morning, for example, the most remote Jamaican rural roads will be dotted with families of descendants of African slaves, the smallest children and the most elderly, wrinkled grandparents immaculately turned out in attire that is extraordinarily formal. Slowly they wend their way up and down absurdly steep hillsides (a walk in the Jamaican countryside always proves beneficial to the calf muscles), copies of the Bible and shiny white handbags grasped firmly in their hands. Sometimes they pull themselves up into the rear of trucks or buses that grind slowly up the grades.

They are, of course, going to church. Allegedly there are more churches per square mile in Jamaica than anywhere else in the world. Certainly Christianity is the country's predominant religion, but it can take on some rather unusual forms. As in other parts of the Caribbean and South America, pagan elements have become fused together with Christianity in Jamaica: specifically, the worship of African animist ancestral spirits. (The word 'animist' suggests animal worship but in fact comes from *anima*, Latin for 'soul' – it is an intellectually rigorous doctrine in which life is believed to derive from the spirit, as in Christianity.)

Lest anyone suspect that animism is a lesser form of religion than Christianity, it is worth considering these words of John S. Mbiti in his work *Concepts of God in Africa*:

Because traditional religions permeate all the departments of life, there is no formal distinction between the sacred and the secular, between the religious and non-religious, between the spiritual and the material areas of life. Wherever the African is, there is the religion: he carries it to the fields where he is sowing seeds or harvesting a new crop; he takes it with him to the beer party or to attend a funeral ceremony;

and if he is educated, he takes religion with him to the examination room at school or in the University; if he is a politician, he takes it to parliament.

Traditional religions are not primarily for the individual, but for the community of which he is part. Chapters of African religions are written everywhere in the life of the community, and in traditional society there are no irreligious people ... A person cannot detach himself from the religion of his group, for to do so is to be severed from his roots, his foundation, his context of security, his kinship and the entire group of those who make him aware of his own existence ... to be without religion amounts to a self-excommunication from the entire society, and African peoples do not know how to exist without religion.

In Jamaica there are three main subdivisions of Christianity that are specific to the island and its African heritage: Pocomania, Kumina (a.k.a. 'African') and Revivalism – a trio of cults with their origins in Africa. As a matter of course each of them employs what commonly has become known as obeah or 'science', the colloquial Jamaican term for this practice of magic – or, depending on your point of view, of metaphysics (of an especially histrionic nature in this setting). It hardly surprises me when a rather agreeable man who is at Treasure Beach for a weekend with Mitzi Seaga, the ex-wife of the former prime minister, advises me, 'This is a country in which everyone believes in voodoo.' Voodoo and obeah are the same thing, and an obeahwoman may be known as a 'Frenchwoman', referring to the widespread practice of the art in nearby French-speaking Haiti. At one time obeah was considered a dark practice and 'myal', or white magic, was considered to be its counterpoint. Now, however, these opposing forces seem to have become fused together.

In 1774 Edward Long, the British author of *History of Jamaica*, wrote:

Not long since, some of these execrable wretches in Jamaica introduced what they called the myal dance, and established a kind of society into which they invited all they could. The lure hung out was that every Negroe initiated into the myal society would be invulnerable by the white men; and although they might in appearance be slain, the obeahman could at his pleasure restore the body to life.

Akan magic, which is essentially the origin of both Pocomania and obeah, had a great appeal to followers of other African religions. The Akan religion was dominant in Jamaica. Akan is from the region of what is now Ghana and was spoken all over the ancient kingdom of Ashanti. The supreme Akan god is Onyame or Nyame, which may have originally simply meant 'sky'.

The ostensibly eccentric practice of obeah reflects the origins of Jamaica, a combination of the sensibilities of the Taino nation, the Spanish, the African and the English. Today it is the last two that are the most visible. Yet as it was the Spanish who first ruled Jamaica as colonists and brought slaves to the island, so it was the high church of Catholicism to which at first were welded the rituals and structures of African animism. The swinging of incense, chanting, and plaster and stone statues bore some resemblance to the forms of African religion, although the specifics of the religion brought by the slaves added an even headier potency. It was this blend that led to Pocomania, whose ceremonies persist to this day, undeterred by the swing to Protestantism after the English invasion of 1655. '*Te deums* without tedium,' as the excellent *Insight Guide to Jamaica* describes them.

But when it arrived in Jamaica, and especially after the abolition of the slave trade led to a cessation of contact with Africa, Akan began to evolve and mutate. For example, in the form of Akan in Africa, Asaase was the female counterpart of the deity. Yet in Jamaica Asaase seemed to have become a male. An explanation of this is that there is often no clear distinction in Jamaican speech between male, female and inanimate object. Isolated by circumstance, the Maroons clung closely to the

202

original African Akan religious heritage and believed that Accompong was God of heaven, creator of all things and deity of infinite goodness.

After an act passed in the Jamaican parliament in 1696, slaves were forbidden to meet in large numbers on Sundays and holidays. This meant they could no longer openly celebrate their religion. From now on this had to be carried out with considerable stealth, the priest becoming the secretive, lone operator of the obeahman. Inevitably this only cemented it more firmly in the psyche of slave underground culture. Soon the British began to see that obeah and slave rebellions were virtually synonymous. So concerned, indeed, were the ruling powers that in 1781 an act banning obeah altogether was passed:

And in order to prevent the many mischiefs that may hereafter arise from the wicked art of Negroes going under the appellation of Obeah-men and women, pretending communication with the devil and other evil spirits, whereby the weak and superstitious are deluded into a belief of their having full power to exempt them whilst under protection from any evils that might otherwise happen: Be it therefore enacted by the authority aforesaid, that from and after the first day of January, aforesaid, any Negro or other slave who shall pretend to any supernatural power, and be detected in making use of any blood, feathers, parrot beaks, dog's teeth, alligator's teeth, grave dirt, rum, eggshells, or any other materials relative to the practice of obeah or witchcraft . . .

Yet should the white rulers have been surprised at such practices? The souls of the slaves were given no outlet whatsoever: as the plantocracy was insistent that God had white skin, Christianity had been closed to Jamaica's slaves. Not being permitted an education, and therefore not being able to read the Bible even if they had been allowed to, they had no reason whatsoever not to fall back onto African religions and their assorted mutations.

It was slaves from the Akan kingdom, known as Cora-mantees, who generally were the most rebellious. According to Mervyn C. Alleyne, 'The rebellion of 1760 was ... led by Coromantees and was aided by the mysterious terrors of Obeah.' Among these obeahmen was Tacky, the rebellion's general in chief, who had already been a slave in west Africa. In April 1760 Tacky led around one hundred Coromantee slaves, who had recently been brought to Jamaica, to capture Fort Haldane at Port Maria, and destroy or set fire to various buildings on two plantations. This led to further outbreaks of rebellion in St Thomas, Westmoreland, Hanover and St James. Gardner wrote in 1873 that 'the negroes were greatly stimulated by their confidence in the powers of the Obeahmen'. (In Haiti the first act of Boukman's rebellion, in which the French were expelled from the island, was a religious ceremony.)

Kumina evolved from a Bantu religion, from southern Africa. Through drumming, dancing and singing, adherents of Kumina try to invoke ancestral spirits to come into them, at which point they may begin talking in tongues. White rum is sprinkled over drums by a priestess who also spits the alcohol over those taking part. Goats are sacrificed, their blood mingled with rum and drunk by participants. (In Jamaica, goats and chickens always seem to be being sacrificed for a bit of ritual blood-letting: you may feel inclined to question precisely how, if animism concerns 'the soul', the souls of slaughtered goats and chickens feel about this.)

Obeah is practised throughout the English-speaking Caribbean: in Trinidad, for example, where it is known as shango, the practitioners are often East Indians. Today in Jamaica obeah is commonplace in the lives of many individuals. In the south-west of the island lives an obeahwoman of such power and skill that some of Prime Minister P. J. Patterson's ministers are alleged to regularly consult her; such is her reputation that she frequently travels to Canada on three-month trips round the high-powered Jamaicans in that country. A Jamaican friend with a house in London was about to lose it through various legal shenanigans, and went to consult her: 'I didn't see how I could avoid losing my place. But she said that I shouldn't worry.

Then on the day of the court case to my amazement I heard that the other side had left their papers on the tube.'

Revivalism is a close relative of Pocomania. In this sect, however, the African elements are less prevalent, and it is strongly underpinned by Christian dogma. Significantly, it was started by Africans who arrived in Jamaica after slavery was abolished and who already had converted to Christianity in their homelands.

Revivalism's most extreme and visible manifestation was in Bedwardism, named after the self-proclaimed prophet Bedward. Bedward founded the Jamaica Baptist Free Church in 1894 in August Town, an area now part of northeast Kingston. Bedward would baptize his followers in the fast-flowing, freezing waters of the nearby Hope River, tumbling down from the Blue Mountains. The movement fell apart following Bedward's announcement in 1920 that he was God and would ascend to heaven on the last day of the year. Thousands of Bedward's followers from across the island flocked to make this journey with him, selling their possessions and giving him the money. After several cancellations of his scheduled journey to celestial regions, Bedward was locked up in Bellevue, Kingston's lunatic asylum.

To this day, August Town has a reputation for being a tricky semi-ghetto, riven with political strife. Its pretty, steeply undulating streets retain a reputation for religious radicalism; they are home to Bobbadread figureheads like Sizzla and Capleton and a favourite hangout of Luciano.

A side product of obeah is Jamaica's almost visible spirit world of ghostlike leprechaun characters known as 'duppies', who may have malevolent or benevolent characteristics. Duppy, according to one source, is a corruption of 'doorpeep' – and you recall the Burning Spear song that goes 'Doorpeep shall not enter'. But the origin is apparently just as likely to be African, probably from the language of Bude, which has the word *dupe*, meaning ghost: in Africa you will encounter the manner in which the duppylike jinn are interwoven into animism.

The belief in duppies and shadows (the latter being a principal tenet of the philosophy of Carl Jung) springs from what Cassidy refers to as 'the West African concept of the multiple soul: the soul within the body and the shadow outside it'. In many parts of Africa there are stories of people who cannot be killed because their souls are not in their bodies. 'Soul' and 'life' are regarded as concrete objects or substances – hence the Water of Life, contained in a small bottle, or the Bird of Life, a songbird on the wing. In mythological tales, this 'soul substance' will be hidden in a box or bird (in obeah, this often becomes a coffinlike box). When a person dies, his or her soul ascends to heaven, the shadow remaining near the body. Unless a suitable burial service takes place, the shadow becomes a duppy. Interwoven with the culture of duppies are all manner of myths: for example, one folk belief holds that if you take a black cat on a full moon and boil it down with a friend, you become invisible when you suck on one of its bones. Why do you need a friend? 'So 'im can tell yuh when yuh become invisible!'

The forms of Christianity on to which this most specifically African faith is welded may cause surprise, but is the consequence of a thorough logic. For the presence and obvious power of Methodists and Baptists in Jamaica is impossible to ignore, again for very specific, somewhat ennobling reasons: the followers of these two Low Church Protestant divisions were the leaders in England of the movement to abolish slavery. Jamaican planters and English anti-abolitionists would derisively refer to William Wilberforce and his followers as 'the Saints'. An early Jamaican source speaks of a runaway slave thus: 'He and his companions sit around the effigy of Saint Wilberforce, as they call it . . .' Methodist meetings in Jamaica became known as 'Wesleys', and congregations were called to them upon a Wesley horn. As can be attested to by anyone living in Britain or the United States who has near them a Baptist church frequented by Jamaicans, their perception of this branch of Protestantism hardly accords with that you might find in a Welsh valley or Scottish highland. Noisy celebrations of life-affirming joy in which trancelike states sometimes are induced are the norm.

In the 1790s the Bible came to African-Jamaicans, courtesy of a pair of freed slaves, George Lisle and Moses Baker, who had become Baptist preachers. Each rapidly built up congregations, Baker in western Jamaica and Lisle in Kingston. So large did their followings become that the two preachers appealed to the English Baptist Missionary Society for assistance. The slaves identified with the Jews who had lost their homeland and wandered the earth in search of it, a notion that persists today in, for example, the Rastafarian belief in being part of the Twelve Tribes of Israel. Soon white Baptist missionaries, fervent proselytizers for the abolition of slavery, began to come to Jamaica.

Not only did they bring the Christian religion to the slaves – who were not freed until 1838, although the slave trade had been abolished in 1807 – but through Sunday school they brought them education, with the Bible as the main text from which to learn to read. Everywhere you go in Jamaica, you still see people of all ages and classes poring over copies of the Bible, a direct throwback to the time when it was the only book most people on the island would read. Never have I come across a country where the Bible was so avidly debated. Stroll past a bus stop in the depths of the Blue Mountains and you are likely to hear a pair of elderly women heatedly discussing the true meaning of some obscure passage with which they are both thoroughly familiar.

October 1997

It was about sundown that Buck Lindo run into outlaws on his way to Zari Brisco in Zan – which is a Shefield Republic Cowboys Provence. Outlaw gang of 23 ride up to Buck and demonded him to hand over his socksbag of golddus – Buck Lindo said a sweting money is for an earnest person but envy is in the misions of crucks. Get out of my way – Then 2 men of the gang said: Make a fight of it. Buck fight with them and they get away with 60-thousand Shefield dalars out of a total of 10-000-milion – Later he met most of them in Red Patric Joint Then Buck opens a blazing gun casters and said Lets play guns for the last Roundup you are all wanted and will be arested. 18 men was gundown by Buck Lindo. He is an acting deputy. The rest of the gang is photographted in the newspaper. Wanted men.

Part of the attraction of the paintings of Ras Dizzy are the stories he scrawls in biro on the back of each of them. The one above, on the rear of a work entitled *Buck Lindo in Blazing Gun for the Last Roundup, JA, 1997*, is the familiar Dizzy mixture of themes, a set of cultural circumstances which dovetail with no great surprise into the spaghetti western world of Jamaica. I love Dizzy's work, his vivid, confident use of colour and the hilarious subject-matter. I also warm greatly to Dizzy when I meet the 'ageable' dread at a gallery on Hope Road where his work is frequently displayed. He tells me something of his background, which goes far to explaining the western themes of his work: how he was a soldier in the United Nations peace-keeping force in Palestine; how he was a Texas Ranger; his life in Sheffield in Yorkshire ... But it is when he begins to tell me of his career as the editor of the *Daily Mirror* in London that I start to believe that Dizzy exists in a rather separate reality than most people. Later I am told that he has no permanent home, and often lives rough, on the streets of Kingston, which may explain much.

Dizzy is part of a school of specifically Jamaican painters

known as the Intuitives, a descriptive term coined by David Boxer, himself a local artist of considerable repute and the curator of Kingston's impressive National Gallery of Jamaica. The work of the Intuitives tends to a heady blend of those Jamaican staples of mysticism, surrealism and an almost wilful eccentricity; it is the work of native artists who lack formal training. They are very separate from those who followed in the footsteps of the educated Edna Manley, the wife of Norman Manley and father of Michael, and a sculptor of considerable merit who is often considered the founder of modern Jamaican art.

The forefather of the Intuitives is John Dunkley, a barber whose colourfully decorated shop drew him in 1937 (the year that the English artist Augustus John came to the island to paint) to the attention of Delves Molesworth, then the English secretary of the Institute of Jamaica. 'Dunkley's easel paintings were of a very different order,' says Boxer. 'Dark, mystical landscapes, populated by strange creatures, jerboas, spiders, crabs, birds, they are paintings that would have delighted the Surrealists had they known of them.' John Dunkley's work has earned great acclaim. Edmund B. Gaither of Boston's Museum of Afro-American Art rates him 'at his best . . . a little short of Henri Rousseau in the alluring qualities of his pictures and the purity with which he presents them.' When requests were made to Dunkley by the Reverend Robert Verity that he join him and Edna Manley in the classes Verity was organising at the Institute of Jamaica, Dunkley made it clear that he knew his worth. 'Mr Verity,' he replied, 'I love yourself and Mrs Manley very much, but I don't think so. You see, I see things a little differently.'

Dunkley died in 1947. That year Mallica Reynolds painted a picture of a black Christ, sitting on the shores of Galilee. It was the first important painting of the man who became better known as Kapo for his work both as a sculptor and as a painter. 'The best intuitive art has the ability to animate us because it makes us see things as if we were looking at them for the first time,' wrote Edward Seaga, whose understanding of Jamaica's cultural heritage was a useful aid when he became Prime Minister. 'Between the artist and the medium there seem to be no inhibitions and the imagination is set free to relate what it sees with an immediacy which brings us to the heart of the artistic experience. Kapo's work is of this order.'

By the end of the 1980s, a further school of younger Intuitives had emerged, most of whom espoused Rastafari and included elements of the religion in their work. As well as Ras Dizzy, there was Errol McKenzie: whilst astral projecting he would experience visions whose images he would store in rocks, as though they were computers, for later use in his paintings. Allan 'Zion' Johnson presented often biblically-influenced naive visions of Jamaican life. Leonard Daley lives in Fidler Hill, St Catherine, past Spanish Town, where he paints auto-biographical paintings that grapple with concepts of good and evil and look as though they are dreamlike works that could be used to illustrate textbooks on the unconscious. Clearly complex and intelligent, he has a simple answer when I ask him about himself: 'I was born a fool.' 'Although Daley may seem to be a prototypical "outsider" artist,' writes Verle Poupeye in *Modern Jamaican Art*, 'his work readily compares with that of his neo-expressionist contemporaries (an observation that also applies to Ras Dizzy).'

One of the most interesting contemporary Jamaican Intuitive artists is Albert Artwell: his work springs directly from his belief in Rastafari, and his paintings frequently have the appearance of biblical parables. With Don Letts and Carl Bradshaw I set out to visit him at his home in rural Jamaica.

At seven in the morning on a bank holiday Monday we rise in Montego Bay and drive through the crush of traffic to the market square. There Albert Artwell is waiting for us.

It is something like an hour's journey to where he lives, up in the hills behind Mo Bay. Artwell, who is in his early sixties, is an imposing locksed and bearded figure exuding Rastafarian authoritative thoughtfulness with the requisite prophetic demeanour. He is clearly a very nice man; as we drive the undulating slopes that lead to his home, I think how much more rational are his replies to my questions than those of the other intuitive artists I have met.

We arrive at Albert's place. Like so many homes in Jamaica, it is built of breeze-blocks and is unfinished, metal guiding rods standing springily bare where they are intended to guide further blocks into place. He lives there with a wife, son and daughter, in a vaguely mystified adaptation to domesticity that seems common to many middle-aged men in Jamaica.

Perhaps it's just the ever-present stress of family life, but from this point on Albert does not seem so rational. Indeed, when I ask him a throwaway question about how he started painting, Albert's reply lasts for something in the region of twenty minutes. 'It was 'pon a Tuesday, on May 1973. I was in Constant Spring Road when the firmament was rent asunder and Jesus called to me from . . .'

The speech flows with such effortlessly purposeful relentlessness that it is impossible to interrupt. Everything else I ask Albert receives a similarly epic and palpably sincere response.

When we eventually leave, we ask Albert for the directions to Accompong, the Maroon headquarters in St Elizabeth. 'You a go a Accampang . . .' Albert, considering, repeats this French-sounding construction (try saying it) several times.

He advises us of a route to take. At a fork in the road some three miles to the east there is a small brown roadside bar. We ask further directions and a man with a bush-Jamaican-Asian appearance directs us up a hill.

The metalled road soon degenerates into a dirt track. The grass between the wheels grows higher and the earth and sharp rocks supporting it become deeper and more lethal. We drive more and more slowly, edging round perilous double-backed bends, reversing for almost half a mile when we meet a late-model 'deportee' four-wheel drive coming the other way. At one point we find ourselves passing through a pretty, abandoned township, complete with quaintly ornate railway station, once an important stop on the Kingston-to-Montego-Bay line, part of the now derelict rail network. Talks are taking place (talks are *always* taking place) about restoring this essential service, for which increasingly destructive hurricanes have sounded the death knell.

The inevitable happens. A thick clunk beneath our vehicle is the precursor of a grinding, scraping sound as we try to separate ourselves from the rock outcrop on which we have become impaled. When we begin slowly to grunt forward again, we do so only by paying the penalty of leaving behind a thick trail of oil. The sump has gone.

We are apparently miles from anywhere, stuck in the bush. Clearly, forward – at a pace even slower than we already have been travelling – is the only route to take. Eventually we come across a deserted tarmacked highway that resembles the kind of undulating, looping B road you might come across in the middle of the north Yorkshire moors.

Gingerly we drive along it, turning off the engine and coasting downhill whenever possible, pushing the van uphill from time to time.

Eventually we arrive at a small hamlet, signalled by the inevitable single-storey brown-painted roadside bar. Lunchtime drinkers sit outside, idly gazing up and down the tarmac as they stretch out a bottle of Red Stripe beer to last several hours. Bunting announces a bank-holiday sound system later on.

We pull up outside the bar. Within minutes a mechanic has appeared. Within no more than another quarter of an hour half the village seems to have been enlisted in repairing the vehicle. A jack has appeared, and an oil sump salvaged from some vaguely related vehicle is being stuffed into the fittings on our van. By now it is the middle of the day, growing hotter by the second. Almost the only shade is to be found under the awning of the bar.

I am starving hungry. We left Mo Bay before breakfast and haven't managed to find anything to eat: at one place we stopped at, I tried to buy food and somehow ended up with a large bag of overdry herb that I didn't want. But this bar doesn't even have the traditional Jamaican staple of a packet of crackers. Nor is there anything to drink that is nonalcoholic and doesn't contain an acidic rush of stomach-stinging bubbles. The cold Red Stripe I gratefully swill down goes straight to my head.

All the same, I soon find myself in conversation with a muscular man in his mid-thirties who, when he stands up, reveals himself to be exaggeratedly short. His name, inevitably, is Rambo, and he is the second-in-command of the local don wannabe. This character, who is well over six foot tall, providing a fetching contrast with Rambo, tells me that he runs a flower-export business in Montego Bay. He is swigging mouthfuls from a bottle of overproof, and his rum breath hangs like globs of jelly in the still air around him. Then he demands that we buy further drinks for him and his crew. We ignore him, passing the buck to other members of our party. When he realises no one is treating him as seriously as he expects, he orders the mechanic and his helpers to down tools. 'Stop work!' he bellows. 'STOP-WORK-STOP-WORK-STOP-WORK!' The mechanic and his helpers also ignore him. The don wannabe stomps off in a huff.

His second-in-command draws heavily on his spliff; Rambo's slightly distanced perma-smile remains intact. Passing teenage girls stop and feel the muscle on his arms, dangling out of his 'merino', the name given to the ubiquitous Jamaican fashion of string vests. His size and bearing remind me of Cudjoe, the great Maroon leader, who was short but colossally broad and agile. I tell Rambo this.

It turns out that he too is a Maroon, as are many people in this hamlet. Over a 'hot' (i.e. not out of the icebox) Red Stripe or two, sitting there frozen in time, he tells me of some suitably rebellious Maroon-like exploits in the ganja trade. Once, he remembers, he was with some brethren harvesting a herb crop when an army helicopter appeared on the horizon, heading for them.

Army and US Drug Enforcement Agency helicopters are

the scourge of the ganja-grower and this part of Jamaica is prime herb land. There are those who argue that ganja cultivation is a social necessity. 'What happened,' said a friend of a friend who lives up in the hills nearby, in a house once owned by Alex Haley, the author of *Roots*,

is that during the 1970s standards of education fell dramatically after Manley kicked out all the foreign teachers. So the kids who grew up then received almost no education. So what else is there for them to do but make money from ganja?

But what happens now is that the army helicopter will land and have to be paid off. Then a couple of days later an army or police jeep will arrive, who will also have to be paid off, and they will tell the growers where the ganja has to be taken when it's harvesting time. So they will take their crop to whichever Mr Big they've been directed to. And he will take it and then simply refuse to pay them.

And the result is that a lot of these guys are therefore virtually destitute. They are very angry and ready for any sort of violent redressing of their wrongs.

As the chopper drew above them, dropping downwards, Rambo enacted an age-old ruse and started running across the field. The helicopter headed after him, letting his fellow harvesters slip away into the bush with the gathered herb. As the chopper descended towards him, Rambo dove into one of the sinkholes that dot the limestone escarpments of Cockpit country, into which Cudjoe's troops would disappear at the approach of the redcoats. The helicopter sputtered above him for some twenty minutes: only when he heard the sound of its engine wheeling away and waning in the distance did Rambo emerge from his hiding place – with trepidation, in case some troops had been dropped off to ambush and capture him.

Later, seemingly apropos of nothing, perhaps as a warning, Rambo volunteers that 'there is no evil I have not known or experienced'.

With the truck fixed, cash changes hands and we head on

our way to Accompong. Rambo is sitting silently next to me, the distanced perma-smile firmly in place, having decided that he will become our guide. He directs us along our way.

Accompong sprawls over the summit of what appears to be the highest hill in the region with ample views of all surrounding approaches. It has been hard enough for us to get there in a motorized vehicle. What can it have been like for redcoat armies trying to bring the Maroons to heel?

Apart from the view, Accompong is a disappointment. The colonel is down on the coast. There is an adequate museum and the expected throng of middle-aged and elderly dreads, eager to bend our ears with raps about Rastafari and requests for Red Stripe or money. We head on our way to Negril, Rambo still accompanying us, until an executive decision is made to drop him off at a road junction.

We hit the coast road on the south side of the island, not far from Bluefields, a gorgeous, wide, curving bay to the east of Savannah-La-Mar, from which Henry Morgan sailed to sack Panama in 1670.

Someone I know lives here, a pony-tailed English painter called Willie Fielding. He lives in the former great house of Oristan, itself built on the foundations set by Columbus's son in the early sixteenth century. On the lawn grows a breadfruit tree that is reputed to be the oldest in Jamaica, planted in 1793 when Captain Bligh is said to have anchored his ship *Providence* in Bluefields Bay. On his balcony, overlooking the breathtaking flat blue bay, he sits and paints. The A2 coast road runs along the edge of the sea below his home.

Willie is a man with a sophisticated view of life. 'Jamaica is like *Mondo Cane*,' he says. 'It's great for danger junkies.' One of his best accounts of surreal adventure tourism JA-style concerned a busload of tourists outside Negril whom he spotted gaping at a dead cow in the middle of the road, all four legs rising up vertically into the air. Then they gaped some more: on the other side of it stood a naked man, leaning down to grab the animal's entrails and then holding them aloft like some ancient diviner.

Willie once had chanced upon his local fish-and-bammy corner to find a car, furiously ablaze, upside down by the side of the road where it had evidently ended up after failing to make the turn. 'Is anyone in it?' he anxiously asked a girl of about eleven years who was standing watching. 'Mi nuh think so, suh,' she replied, ''cause usually yuh can smell de flesh burn.'

All that is burning when we arrive there, however, is roasting fish. As the sun sets over the sea, I eat my first food of the day. Two hours later, just after we have reached Negril, I have violent stomach cramps and diarrhoea and spend the evening and next day in bed.

The following evening I am feeling much better. If Jamaica is like the last outpost of the wild west, Negril is its furthest extreme. Stuck away at the far western end of the island, Negril has always been somewhat outside the focus of the Jamaican authorities. Accordingly, the resort has several unique selling points.

Hoping that a journey to a higher plane may prove healing, as well as being anxious to bind my insides, I drink a glass of mushroom tea, a local speciality, with Rick. Psilocybin mushrooms of varying strengths are openly on sale in Negril. The benign effects they bestow upon you have become part of the town's hippy tradition. Though a friend swears that the best way to consume them is to fry them and eat them on toast, I have always found the tea is the most effective method of digestion. This tea is best purchased at Miss Brown's on the way out of Negril on the road to Savannah-la-Mar. Just to add to the confusion, there are two Miss Brown's, next door to each other. I could never understand the explanation of what had gone on here – they seem to be relatives – but I generally stop at the first one. The mushroom tea comes in three strengths – mild, medium and strong – and is sold in old rum bottles. It's not especially cheap; a bottle comes in at around US$45, the cost these days, I imagine, of a couple of tabs of dodgy E.

For that cosmos-shifting experience I have always preferred the strongest. Do not be fooled when you think it's not working. Settle back into yourself somewhere and let the mushrooms impart their ancient knowledge. One night when Adrian Boot and I had downed a couple of glasses of Miss Brown's finest, I found myself pacing around edgily as I waited for the mushrooms to kick in. 'Just let the mushrooms take you with them,' he advised, 'get to that point where time stands still – that way you'll get better value for money.' Finally finding myself in the spirit of things, I observed how the air, which I had always assumed to be essentially clear, was like a cosmic soup, filled with creatures and movement. Moving from the micro to the macrocosm, I then studied in detail the transport systems clearly visible between the planets above us. Soon the sun was coming up.

There are the usual number of unsavoury tales associated with the mushroom trade. In one of the most memorable, and no doubt apocryphal, the local police for some reason became irritated with a street mushroom dealer. Taking him to the station, they forced the man to eat his entire stock. He is still occasionally sighted on the lanes of Negril, it is said, rambling like the madman he now is.

Anyway, I down the mushroom tea with Rick. Then we go out: Hey, let's rock 'n' roll! By the time we reach Alfred's reggae bar, the tea is starting to kick in. The bar is filled with the usual mixture of American tourists (Bo Derek-like hair from beach braiders adorns many of the females), and locals, many of whom are on some sort of hustle, especially the hookers, with their leopardlike prowling zeal. A group is playing a mix of early reggae and mento, its calypso-influenced precursor. Rick and I sit on the beach at the edge of these proceedings, investigating the molecules in each grain of sand, feeling profoundly at one with the universe, managing largely to avoid the predatory attentions of the working girls. Only twice do I need to remove hands from the pockets of my shorts.

But it is disheartening when we move to sit down at one of the bar's beach tables. Two men, one older, one younger, also sit at it. We nonchalantly exchange information. They're American, father and son. I apologize for our somewhat laid-back state, explaining its origin. 'That's OK,' says the father, 'we're on smack.'

As they say, everything can be bought in Negril. But the presence of heroin in such a blissful, formerly innocent scene is deeply depressing, only emphasized by the father-and-son relationship of these smackheads.

Depending on your resilience, Negril is either a wonderful and profound major experience or a complete drag. It is more expensive than much of Jamaica. If someone is trying to hustle a Red Stripe out of you and you give them forty dollars, they will complain that it is not enough. I remember in the early 1990s being amazed when a Negril roadside vendor tried to charge me the equivalent of five pounds for a glass of Irish Moss. In fact, nowhere is the adage truer that whatever amount of money you take out with you in Jamaica will have been hustled away by the time you get home. It's all there on the beach: a stroll along a few of the resort's seven miles of white sandy beach can be like running a gauntlet of hustlers: drug-dealers ('Ganja-coke-crack-mushrooms' is the familiar refrain); hair-braiders and anointers of aloe vera – a good cure for sunburnt skin; T-shirt shacks; and the simple question, 'Yuh wan' fuck mi?' (As an add-on to that last 'product', you will also find for sale the popular aphrodisiacs of 'Chinee' brush, Spanish fly and 'stone'.)

Beachfront prostitution, by day relatively discreet, is by night a hassle. Once upon a time, committed working girls were rivalled in numbers by what seemed to be enthusiastic amateurs. Now, however, there seems to be thorough career devotion. Don Letts recalls talking to a pretty girl who attached herself to his table while he was eating breakfast one morning. Suddenly she produced a nude Polaroid of herself, shot with the emphasis on her stretched-apart vagina. 'You wan' some?' he was asked.

At least such a scene sets an appropriate tone. One detects in many Negril hookers a sense of resigned irony, allied to the spunky cheekiness that is such a national characteristic. Many of these girls, who congregate by the beach-front bars in the evenings, are quite beautiful – you might not always realize what their job is and, ego-driven, simply feel pleased with yourself that you have struck lucky. Until you are in bed with the girl and she suddenly coldly announces, 'Yuh wan' fuck mi, it gwan cost yuh one hundred dollar US.'

You can see women who have done this job too long. Battered by a combination of time and life's miseries, pain etched on their faces, such women resort to more and more revealing clothes and their patter holds a palpable desperation. Uncharitably, you worry that even by speaking with them you might end up with a life-threatening disease. You also fear for the health of the young Americans who pour into Negril over their spring break for a few days' hedonism.

Unfortunately, as in so many parts of the Third World, sex tourism is an integral aspect of the appeal. Men come to have sex with women; women come to have sex with 'rental dreads'; some men come to have sex with other men, and some women come to have sex with other women; and – the most disturbing – some men come to have sex with children. As is justly the case anywhere, such individuals risk their lives. Buju was aghast when he learned that a Canadian 'batty-man' had attempted to touch up his fourteen-year-old brother in a beachfront house. Storming down to the property with his machete, the man leapt from a first-floor window when he saw Buju heading up the stairs towards him. He was last seen running up the beach, limping. What would Buju have done if he'd caught him? 'Mi dead 'im. Batty-man mess with children have fe dead him.'

In Jamaica I have often been based at Strawberry Hill, a hotel in the Blue Mountains ten miles and 3000 feet above Kingston. Set amid a 28-acre garden that crowns the hill with riotous bougainvillea and banana plants, 'Strawberry' consists of twelve pure-white cottages, some on the edge of sheer mountain drops. When I first came to Jamaica in 1978 there was only one reason why I had heard of this small hotel: it was where the wounded Bob Marley had fled after the political assassination attempt in 1976.

I am always very pleased to be staying there: to me Strawberry Hill is probably the most beautiful place in the world. From the verandah of my cottage I have a view of much of the south of Jamaica. Ten miles below, half an hour's switchback drive down the mountain, the grid plan of Kingston is laid out like a relief map, even the shantytown of Riverton City, from whose ceaselessly burning city dump a plume of smoke spirals. To the left, beyond Dallas Mountain (the original home of the British colonial who founded the Texan city), is the narrow isthmus where planes land at Norman Manley airport; at the western end of this strip of land is the small town of Port Royal, all that remains of the island's first capital under English rule, the successor to Spanish Town, Jamaica's first colonial capital. Beyond Kingston, over the causeway, beyond the women's prison of Fort Augustus, is the dormitory town of Portmore. And beyond Portmore, with the Cactus Club at their base, stand the baking dry, cactus-strewn Hellshire Hills, gateway to Hellshire Beach, the Sunday destination of many Kingstonians.

To the right of Kingston, at the other end of Nelson Mandela Highway, is Spanish Town. The original capital when the island was ruled by Spain, from 1520 to 1655, Spanish Town is like a no-man's-land between Kingston and 'country'. To the north is the sumptuously picturesque drive through Bog Walk and Fern Gully to Ocho Rios and the north coast, one apparently used by the most dangerous drivers in the world. To the west is Old Harbour, May Penn and Mandeville, all easily made out on a clear day. Beyond them are the south-coast towns of Treasure Beach and Black River, and to the west Savannah La Mar and Negril.

Stunning though the view over Kingston may be, it is the almost vertical mountains behind the hotel that give it the finest views anywhere in the world: angular ranks of sedimental mountains fold in on each other, peeling apart to reveal deep, plunging valleys, or small hamlets like Redlight, the brothel town for the nineteenth-century British army base at New-castle, visible 2000 feet above Strawberry Hill. Lying in a hammock on the wraparound verandah of one of the cottages, sipping a rum punch and meditating on this view, I can think of few better things in life. Once I watched a cloud drift in through one door and out another.

This visual paradise is moreover reflected in the visitor's inner world, through magical dreamscapes that seem to enter the sleep of anyone who stays there. Jamaica's Blue Mountains are like the defining principle of the island; they are its soul, the repository of the national collective unconscious, where the extent of the synchronicity you're experiencing seems like a gauge of your spiritual progress. Here, even more than elsewhere in Jamaica, nothing is planned, everything is of the moment.

The afternoon before the 'stick-up', as such home invasions are matter-of-factly referred to in Jamaica, I had driven my rented Toyota Corolla up the mountain, away from Kingston. Risking the vehicle's suspension along a road that is more like a permanent pothole, I had decided to bask in the spectacular, breathtaking beauty of the long route to the north coast over the mountains. The road winds up from Irish Town through the Jamaica Defence Force headquarters at Newcastle, past the national park that straddles its peak, before it turns downwards for the two-hour winding journey to Bull Bay on the north coast.

In 1999 I retraced my route along that fabulous journey, and this time the road was even rougher than I remembered it: over time the regular tropical deluges pound away all road-repair work. For chunks of the route, the metalled road proves perfectly adequate. Then you'll round a bend and come across a mile or so that is completely washed out, sheer rubble with deep wheel-sized ruts. Luckily my car, whose brakes were firm, could cope easily. The altitude and poor road conditions gave no guarantee that I wouldn't suddenly find a tinted-windowed, plastic-gold-encrusted car of indeterminate Asian origin hurtling towards me, music blaring loudly enough to cause landslides. Or one of Jamaica's ubiquitous herds of goats hanging out in the middle of the road. On every corner I honked my horn. Amid the bamboo, pines began to appear as I climbed the Blue Mountains, the topmost peak invisible in the clouds to the northeast, 7402 feet above the Caribbean. More than half of Jamaica is over 1000 feet above sea level.

What I didn't expect to see, along a straight stretch of road whose surface cracks seemed ancient, was a woman pacing towards me along the thick, darkly mottled moss between the wheel tracks. Her face, in its early thirties, was so contorted into a grimacing rictus that I did not immediately register that she was not wearing a stitch of clothing. Perhaps, I thought for a moment when I did notice this, she was simply hurrying for a wash in a nearby waterfall: after all, this undulating, upward road is generally empty of traffic. It was only when I saw the two men trekking along behind her that it dawned on me that I was witnessing an example of Jamaican care-in-the-community, a cost-cutting exercise upon which the government had recently embarked. Or at least I hoped I was.

I stopped and ate at the Gap, the only restaurant on the road. Rather unexpectedly for Jamaica, it is somewhat slow of service. As Abba's 'Dancing Queen' played in the background, I found myself in conversation with one of the Canadian administrators of Alcan, the mining conglomerate that digs up the island's bauxite-rich red soil to turn it into aluminium. 'Despite all its economic problems,' he mused, 'Jamaica is just one step away from being a First World country. One push and it will be there.'

These positive words ringing in my ears, I set off again on my journey. Reaching the peak of the road after about a mile, I passed the prehistoric ferns – on which dinosaurs once snacked – of Holywell Park and headed downwards. Following the Buff Bay River valley, I found stretches where the road was thickly lined with ginger, brushing against the car on each side and parting to reveal plunging drops. It was a lush, full-blast tropical experience: endless canopied corridors of trees, breathtaking waterfalls, bridges over foaming torrents, vistas opening up of steep-sided coffee plantations, rumpled settlements suddenly appearing in the far distance. And everything very, *very* green.

After an hour or so I crossed a bridge from the west to the east bank of the river and pulled up at a small single-storey general-provisions store, its wood painted the customary deep brown. Attached to it was a small bar. I went inside, and asked for a Ting, the ubiquitous, highly carbonated Jamaican grapefruit drink, guaranteed to swell up your belly until it is like an inflated football. But no: Ting 'finish', which would seem to say a lot about the rural economy.

Dropping ever further down, I drove past a clear character judgement roughly painted on a wall: 'Only a dog would piss here!' Then I was rolling more gently until the road levelled off and I was on the flat, dodging dogs, goats and bicycles that veered across my path with inches to spare. And then I was just inside the parish of Portland in the small coastal town of Buff Bay, which seemed positively bustling after the absolute quiet of the drive.

Hitting the better-surfaced coast road, I turned right, heading for Port Antonio, palm-fringed deserted roadside beaches and the blue-green Caribbean on my left. After forty-five minutes I was in Port Antonio, capital of the parish of Portland. In 1720 the first Duke of Portland (to whom the

Queen Mother is related) was sent here to run the area, and the parish was later given his name. The Duke had seven children and died here, leaving the town's Titchfield Hill area for 'poor whites'. On the island in Port Antonio harbour, a naval hospital was established and it became known as Navy Island.

Stuck away on the northeastern corner of Jamaica, Port Antonio has always been isolated from the rest of the island. This is part of its charm. In the late 1970s, when I first came here, only the hardiest of tourists made the difficult trip to what was pretty much a quaint one-horse town, seemingly frozen in the attitudes and mores of Jamaica in the 1940s and 1950s, although a lot less affluent than it had been. Portland also has the wettest weather in Jamaica, at least a hundred inches plummeting down a year, sometimes ten inches at one time. Now there are a few more Italian holiday-makers – Italians and Jamaicans seem to bond with great facility: behind one of the upstairs gingerbread balconies in the main street you can even find a small, inexpensive Italian restaurant. A garish modern shopping complex has been built on the site of the Delmar cinema at the base of Titchfield Hill. A different three-film programme used to show there every night on the bullet-holed screen, and you could always persuade the projectionist to start the film again from the beginning if you'd missed the first ten minutes.

In the 1870s bananas had replaced sugar cane as the principal crop of the island, and Port Antonio had become the trade's main port in Jamaica. Captain Lorenzo Dow Baker, who took the first boatload to the USA and formed the Boston Fruit Company (later taken over by the perpetually worrying United Fruit Company), had a two-fold impact on the economy of the island: during the cold winter of the northeastern United States he began to fill the passenger accommodation of his banana boats with vacationers, thus sparking off Port Antonio's tourist trade.

In the immediate aftermath of World War II, Port Antonio

had some prominence, even a certain cachet, and soon the town became a place of residence and a watering hole for American and European high society. The pioneer of this was the swashbuckling movie star Errol Flynn, who bought property in the environs of Port Antonio, including the miniature tropical paradise of Navy Island. Flynn, who had been washed up on the shores of Jamaica in his yacht during a hurricane in 1947, was as immediately taken with the island as I was. 'Never had I seen a land so beautiful. Now I know where the writers of the Bible had got their descriptions of Paradise. They had come here to Jamaica,' he wrote in 1959 in *My Wicked, Wicked Ways*, his autobiography. By the time he brought Patrice Wymore, the Hollywood actress who became Mrs Errol Flynn, to Jamaica in 1951 he had also purchased a 2000-acre cattle ranch and had his yacht permanently berthed off Navy Island. An elegant woman whose gliding walk is a testament to Jack Warner's deportment school, Patrice Wymore-Flynn still lives near Port Antonio, running the ranch on which coconuts are also farmed.

'So I walked into paradise,' she told me.

And Errol said, 'This is our retirement home.' I was so much younger than my husband: that word wasn't even in my vocabulary. But this is what he intended it to be, and time ran out for him when he was fifty. I found out later that doctors had told him that he was in trouble with his heart. But he chose to ignore them and not admit it to anyone. These days with bypass operations, it could have been averted or avoided. Something could have been done.

The broad Rio Grande, which flows from 3000 feet up in the Blue Mountains to the sea a few miles to the west of Port Antonio, was once the principal route for transporting banana crops, loaded onto bamboo rafts, down to the town. Flynn rounded up the likes of Noël Coward for excursions riding down the Rio Grande by both day and night, when the rafts would be lit by torches and the raft-riders fuelled by the contents of the hampers taken on board. 'It was always there as a means of transport,' remembered Patrice, 'but Errol saw it as a way to have a good day out on a river. He started to popularize it by bringing friends over, and he started to have rafting races. It started to take off as a tourist attraction.' As a generally fabulous experience, the leisurely five-hour ride down the river takes some beating.

Other celebrities followed Flynn into the area: Ginger Rogers, Clara Bow and Bette Davis, for example. Members of the German Thyssen steel dynasty were also taken by Portland's lush beauty, purchasing a substantial estate to the east of the town; it is still a favourite of Francesca Thyssen, now married to the Crown Prince of Austria.

On this far side of Port Antonio, on the road to Boston Bay with its locally celebrated 'jerk' kitchens, have been built some of the most extraordinary luxury hotels in the world. The moody Trident, to which convalescing high-level British politicians have been dispatched (both the former prime minister Anthony Eden and Barbara Castle, Labour minister of transport in Harold Wilson's first government), was the most formal; until recently jacket and tie was required for dinner.

Set on a rocky headland, the Trident seems like a 1930s Hollywood notion of England. For miles around there are gorgeous beaches. From the Trident you can fall out of bed into the clear, calm ocean. Here there's only a small, artificial stretch of sand, and a thundering sea whose spray lashes the windows of your cottage as it smashes against the jagged rock coastline. (When I arrived at my cottage, the ageing bellhop showed me how to lock the doors to the sea-soaked verandah: 'So no one can get in now,' he said in a tone of what was no doubt meant to be reassurance, chillingly suggesting something that hadn't even crossed my mind.) Perhaps the hotel was designed for English people who only feel comfortable with adverse conditions that can make them feel they are in Cornwall.

Over a 'Tridentburger' in the hotel's terraced dining area, Patrice Wymore recalled a more exotic meal at Navy Island with Noël Coward and her husband.

We had drinks on board the boat, and then I had the dinner prepared on the shore. The tablecloth was made of banana leaves. Dinner was served amidst the light of the torches on the beach. It was quite dramatic. For the old names, this area with all its gracefulness of old Jamaica was *the* place to be.

In the sixties, when Frenchman's Cove was at its height, people who came there to stay decided that they loved this part of the island so much that they built homes. There were about fifty homes of winter residence. It was very active: endless cocktail parties and luncheon parties and dinner parties. Then the people who had these retirement homes either died or got too old to cope. And a second group moved in. And I've been here so long that a second group has moved out.

It was very old Canadian and New York society. Very wealthy but you would never know it. I used to call it the very elegant bathrobe society. And then in summer the Kingstonians would bring their families over, to get out of the heat of Kingston. So there was a summer season, which was even more hectic than the winter season. Jamaicans like to play.

The gardens of the Trident, all exaggerated topiary and magically springy moorland-like soyzia grass, seem like a cross between Newport, Rhode Island, and Frinton-on-Sea, Essex. Meanwhile, contented peacocks with little to do other than eye each other up mate by the croquet mallets in front of the breakfasting guests, of whom there rarely seem to be more than half a dozen.

In the tradition of the Fawlty Towers-like English seaside hotel, lent a surreal edge by traditional Jamaican anarchy, the Trident offers a character-building sense of making life a little difficult for the guest. Possibly because it's so near Cuba, it seems to have adopted the great Soviet tradition of not supplying a bathroom plug, for example. Dining is tricky, a choice of a rudimentary meat or a fish dish. You are asked if you want some dessert. You decline. Then, as though the question was only a formality, you find it placed in front of you anyway. (Ten years ago I would occasionally visit the Trident in the afternoon for cucumber sandwiches and Earl Grey tea – a pleasant, vaguely Hitchcock-like diversion when I tired of eating fire-roasted breadfruit at a beach house on the other side of town. Now I'm inclined to think that my bush-cooking far outdid anything the Trident's kitchens currently serve up.)

The hotel has plenty of traditional Jamaican character: only one phone line out that is working, an occasional peeling patch of wallpaper. Here it seems like that aristocratic affectation of frayed shirt cuffs and collars.

Amid its plastic plants and thrift-store art are a set of testimonial photographs from Glenn Close, Racquel Welch, Whoopi Goldberg and Tom Cruise, all of whom have made films nearby. Jackie Onassis, who also visited, seems to have declined to provide a picture, as has Johnny Depp, who stayed at the neighbouring Trident Castle at Peg Point, built in 1980. The cannon by what is now the castle's pool was sited there so that warning could be sent to Port Antonio of approaching French ships.

What says most about the eccentric spirit behind the Trident are the originals of a set of paintings by Jonathan Routh, the star of the 1960s television programme *Candid Camera*, who moved to Jamaica to live. The subject of these hilarious paintings is the mythical visit to Jamaica of Queen Victoria to 'reason' with the Rastamen – a legend that has long grown in this island where, as Chris Blackwell says, 'there are no facts'.

The couple of miles distance between the Trident and Frenchman's Cove to the east does not necessarily mean a smooth drive. Oh, look, on that bend by the Trident castle there's a man sitting in his parked truck wiping his forehead and arm with a red bandanna: he must be hot. Oh, look, he seems to be waving it at me very vigorously. Oh, he's showing me that just around the bend my side of the road has been dug up completely and I've got about three feet to slither to a halt.

The grounds of Frenchman's Cove are so perfect and exact that it can look like a Walt Disney version of Jamaica, like a backdrop to the Pirates of the Caribbean ride at Disneyland – this was what the Disney dangling liana vines and sumptuous lagoons might have first been based on.

With a freshwater river that meanders into a small lagoon, Frenchman's Cove has one of the best beaches in the world. Even on the perfect day when I visited, it had no more than a score of guests on it. 'A lot of people can't handle the idea of Jamaica: they don't know what they're missing,' said Melissa, a twenty-eight-year-old San Franciscan banker who has been coming to the island all her life, staying at her grandparents' house in San San Villas, the luxury development on the hill above Frenchman's Cove. San San Villas has its own police station, a clear mark of status and wealth. Relatives of the heirs to the Woolworth estate have one of the properties and my friends Jon and Ziggi Baker have built a recording studio with guest cottages in the grounds of their house.

Just the other side of Frenchman's is the gorgeous monkey-free Monkey Island in San San Bay, another archetypal Caribbean sight. The Aga Khan bought Monkey Island and gave it to his wife, who wanted to turn it into a bird sanctuary. He also bought a house for her called Tiamo, on the way to Goblin Hill, just behind the coast.

The sumptuous residences that line the edge of the sea in San San Bay rent for around US$10,000 per week. For that kind of money you get employees in the sea in front of the houses, scraping sea urchins from the rocks, a task that never ends.

At the edge of San San Bay is the Blue Lagoon – or Blue Hole, as it is more familiarly known in Jamaica – a shipment point for bananas on to Port Antonio at the end of the nineteenth century. Now owned by a local called Valerie Marsouca, it belonged in the 1970s to the writer Robin Moore, who wrote the novels there from which the films *The French Connection* and *Green Berets* were made. But by 1978, when I first went there, Jamaica's political instability had moved him to leave the island: the Blue Hole was being run by a Jamaican who had returned from London. I have vivid memories of waterskiing on the lagoon and out to sea, and having long, understandably bitter discussions with this manager about the 'bad men' who had hacked off his arm with a machete in a hold-up. 'Oh, I call him the one-arm bandit,' said Ms Marsouca, with a typical Jamaican verbal twist. 'It wasn't his property – he'd simply "captured" it for a time, like people do here.'

The Blue Lagoon's thick natural colour is a consequence of its depth – 'bottomless', according to local myth; 210 feet, according to the *Insight Guide* – and the overhanging greenery that is reflected in it. Since Valerie Marsouca brought an end to the one-armed bandit's oil-slick-inducing waterskiing business, manatees, dolphins, leopard rays and 'long-jaws' have returned to the lagoon, into which flow at least six freshwater streams. She has built a fine restaurant, bar and gift shop of the unobtrusive, classy standard you might find in California. A couple of rafts float in the lagoon, almost invariably with a pair of blond German girls sprawled on them, dipping from time to time into the chilly water that has poured down into the lagoon from the Blue Mountains.

Leaving the Blue Lagoon, I climb into the car and head for Ocho Rios. Some fifty yards before Norwich beach I drive past a small turn-off and hit a rainwater-filled pothole. A couple of men in their early twenties are standing by the side of it, and they must step back to avoid being splashed. They are not at all pleased. 'Motherfucker: fuck off, asshole,' they scream at me. This is the only hint of a bad vibe on this entire trip.

On the winding drive from Port Antonio there is plenty of Sunday beach traffic. I find myself stuck behind a blue Toyota pick-up truck, in the back of which sit a trio of girls in their early twenties, all clad in swimsuits, all quite attractive. As one of them tosses a cigarette packet into the roadside bushes, I wag a disapproving finger at her act of ecological vandalism. All the girls start to wave at me and smile. Then, in case I haven't got the point, one of them suddenly drops the right side of her swimsuit top, revealing an ample breast. Which, to the great mirth of her two companions, she proceeds to fondle and wave at me. I wave back. Then all sorts of notions flash through my mind, the last being probably the least driven by libido: that one of the two men in the cab of the vehicle may be her boyfriend and at any moment he might pull the vehicle to a halt and get out with a machete to give me a 'chopping'. I avert my eyes and overtake.

Once past Port Maria, the journey takes us beneath Firefly, Noël Coward's hilltop home, open now as a museum, and on the five miles to the small town of Oracabessa and the Goldeneye estate where Ian Fleming wrote the James Bond books. Now owned by Chris Blackwell, this once spartan bungalow has been transformed into a luxurious holiday home. In the property's considerable grounds has been built Goldeneye village, offering a further ten bedrooms. Any doubts I might have about Goldeneye becoming a business are assuaged by the subtle way that the wooden buildings, designed by the architect of Strawberry Hill, Anne Hodges, blend into the lush grounds. They are so unobtrusive that they are sometimes hard to find.

When I drop in on the property, the family of the hip New York video director Hype Williams is staying in the main house; Jeremy Thomas, a British film producer, is with his family in the village; and the actor Dennis Hopper is arriving at the weekend. Next weekend the Francis Ford Coppola clan have the entire property block-booked for $50,000. I stop for photographs and some vigorous jet-skiing.

Eighteen miles past Oracabessa is Ocho Rios, a bustling tourist town midway along the north coast with little charm and a surfeit of street hustlers. Chris Blackwell explains what went wrong: 'In the 1950s Ocho Rios was a fishing village with beautiful houses. The area in Ocho Rios around the port was reclaimed from the sea in the 1960s, and set the town's character as urban sprawl. Ocho Rios used to have a tremendous amount of well-heeled social people that simply don't go there any more.'

Today the Jamaica Inn, which you hit on the eastern perimeter of 'Ochie', a couple of miles out of town, is almost all that remains there of that elevatedly upscale world. The pet project of a Texan newspaper publisher, the hotel was constructed in 1950 by the Maffesantis, a local Italian building family. And Jamaica Inn conveys a feeling of southern Italy and the Amalfi coast. Set at 35 degrees to the beach, so that all rooms get sea, land and mountain views, the hotel has a soft, subtle ambience and almost cloistered atmosphere, the consequence of this natural setting and the Italian flavour of its architectural detail – its pillars and romantic dining terrace, its landscaped gardens and broad sweep of sifted sand. Quintessentially elegant, the hotel is enhanced by what Peter Morrow, its barefooted owner, describes as 'the worn English look'.

In the large piles of *Country Life* placed around the property is a clue to the clientele of Jamaica Inn: the hotel is the territory of those double-breasted blazer-wearing *Times* readers on your flight whom until now you had trouble picturing in Jamaica. You are not surprised to learn that the Jamaica Inn still demands that a jacket is worn at dinner, the last hotel in the Caribbean to insist on this.

Winston Churchill stayed in the White Suite when the hotel was newly completed, declaring it to be his favourite in the world. Princess Margaret would arrive with such bush-jacketed companions as Colin Tennant, and Roald Dahl would regale fellow drinkers at the bar over rum sours. Today the likes of Lord and Lady Sainsbury arrive for Christmas along with Sir Bryan Goswell and Albert Finney. When he was prime minister, John Major used the hotel as his base from which to watch the test match in Kingston in 1997; unfortunately the cricket was cancelled because of the state of the pitch, which suggests separate metaphors for both JA and JM. In keeping with a hotel much of whose market is the elderly uppercrust, many a night has been spent in the bar by Keith Richards, who has a house nearby.

At 6.30 in the morning, as the sun is rising and a pinky-gold light reflects off the wild sea, which bashes the rocks beneath the structure of my terrace, the view from it is so wonderful as to be exciting. My terrace itself is like a little cottage by the sea, a large stone-floored living room that happens to have one wall open. It has its own formal colonial writing table against one blue wall and a wood-framed couch you can sink into against the other. I don't know if it's the salt from the sea breeze or the timeless view of the mountains behind the bay, but as I sprinkle lime on my paw-paw at the beginning of my breakfast, sitting at the small wooden table, I know what Noël Coward meant by the 'complete peace' he referred to again and again when considering Jamaica.

'The Jamaica Inn is an energy point,' says Peter Morrow, who is sipping Blue Mountain coffee on the terrace.

On the beach Leroy the boatman, lounging on one of his vessels, give his view of why Jamaica Inn's clientele tends to be of a pensionable age: 'Dem nah get nuh young people 'ca dem nah have nuh disco!'

Arriving at Round Hill, nine miles west of Montego Bay, I adjourn to the bar for a refreshing rum punch. I am greeted by the sight of blond American teenage girls with braided hair chatting up the barmen. This seems not especially auspicious, not what I had expected of the hotel that for so long has been a magnet for the world's exceptionally chic or well-heeled.

Would this have happened in the days when Oscar Hammerstein would adjourn here for rest and recreation? When Leonard Bernstein would try his latest compositions on the lounge piano? Very probably, as a matter of fact.

In 1953 a local man called John Pringle set about raising the money for what he described to me as 'the first of all the cottage colonies for the very rich or beautiful'. Seeking further funds for the $1 million cost of building the property, Pringle decided to fly to New York – and found himself sitting beside Noël Coward. Pringle immediately went into salesman mode, showing photographs of the site to this superman-of-all-arts.

And with his hand tightly clasping my knee, he said, 'If you stop boring me, I'll buy one of your fucking cottages!' And that really was the beginning of Round Hill, because through him I met Adele Astaire, and she bought a cottage, and then they introduced me to other people and through his introductions – he wrote letters to people – I got about five or six people to buy cottages. And that's how Round Hill started really.

When the hotel opened in 1954, the party included a two-hour concert by Coward.

He gave the opening party at Round Hill. Four hundred people. He performed for two and a half hours. He performed with his accompanist: he flew him out from London. It was on the terrace. In those days Noël was getting £50,000 a week in Las Vegas. They flew in from London, they flew in from Paris.

I'll never forget the opening night: nothing worked at the hotel. The governor was Hugh Foot, who I adored. Great friend of mine. I was wildly left-wing. Still am a little. Strange to have a place like Round Hill. I used to get into terrible fights. Well, if you could fuck the rich – my God! – what better occupation. On the opening night Hugh Foot arrived with Sylvia, his wife. She said, 'I want to have a pee.' Right at the entrance there was a powder room. I was waiting outside for her to come out and there was suddenly a blood-curdling scream. And she came out half-dressed. When she flushed the toilet, the lights went out and boiling steam came out of the toilet, scalding her bottom. Nothing worked in the place. After Coward's party, when people started leaving at about three thirty or four in the morning, we had no water in the kitchens. So my wonderful staff and I spent the whole fucking night with seawater and buckets washing up for the next morning's breakfast.

In a sort of posh version of time-sharing, the owners of the cottages were obliged to rent out their properties when they were not there themselves, and a number of hotel rooms were built. Over the next few years Round Hill became a focus of the 'winter season'. Noël Coward, according to Pringle, 'sent all his friends to Round Hill – those that he didn't want to stay with him'. The list of people who holidayed and partied at Round Hill reads like a Who's Who of the postwar years. Princess Margaret waterskiing in 1956; Alfred Hitchcock; Clark Gable; Field-Marshal Lord Alexander, Earl of Tunis; Grace Kelly and her sister, snorkelling in 1954; Cole Porter; Rosalind Russell; Howard Hawks; Gloria Vanderbilt; Lee Remick; Charles Laughton; Truman Capote; Richard Widmark; Kirk Douglas; and many more. 'My old friend Jack Kennedy stayed with me for seven years at Round Hill and fucked all my maids. He'd fuck anybody he could lay his hands on,' said John Pringle.

Subsequently, after selling Round Hill in 1961, Pringle became minister of tourism in the first independent Jamaican government.

Today is a 'hot-fire day', in the words of the Round Hill beach barman. I pull on my swimming trunks and immerse myself up to my neck in the greeny-blue Caribbean soup of Round Hill Bay. Soon I find my back nuzzled and tickled by a translucent puffer fish, a sort of junior version of swimming with dolphins, I imagine; not only am I immersed in the ocean but also in great metaphysical depth.

But then the fish nips me surprisingly hard on my nipples. I jump, slightly disarmed. Is this a metaphor? I wonder, as I swim out to sea. In this sudden switch from the spiritual to the sensual, do we not see the essential paradox that is Jamaica?

My left hand brushes against a rock, and jarring pain shoots through my fingers as they are pierced by a sea urchin's spikes. Painfully I clamber out of the sea, my hand growing numb. I ask the beach barman if he has any remedies.

The barman looks at me as if I am an idiot. 'Piss on it, man!' he urges. 'Piss on it now!'

In Jamaica you should always expect the unexpected.

Insisting that it should no longer be trammelled by 'the season', the briskly efficient Josef Forstmaya, who in the 1980s restored the Trident to financial health, put Round Hill back into profit five years ago by operating a year-round policy. And it has changed hardly at all. In fact, the Jamaican high-end social scene is very much as it always was, with regular visits from Hollywood stars and supermodels. Once again the Jamaica Tourist Board is promoting the island as an upscale destination.

Jamaica remains one of the world's hidden treasures, and those who have discovered it keep coming back.

As he does his perky rounds of his guests, Forstmaya is wearing a striped polo-shirt, a tribute to Ralph Lauren, who redesigned Round Hill four years ago and is sitting on the headland in the sun this very moment. In front of him is the imposing sight of *Talitha*, Sir Paul and Victoria Getty's 300-foot yacht, which is anchored in the bay. Lord and Lady Rothermere arrive tomorrow: Jonathan and Claudia will be staying in Cottage Sixteen, formerly the property of Vere Rothermere and his wife Bubbles, who personally decorated the bedroom in a rather fruity style.

Whether they are staying in their own or rented cottages or in the hotel rooms, guests mingle at meals on the superb deep terrace. I note a kind of psychic exclusion zone around everyone that has grown out of the very nature of Round Hill – open and casual, but also very private. 'People can enjoy being recognized but not bothered: it provides the hotel with an interesting energy,' Forstmaya observes. That energy, however, can be sometimes a little uptight or prissy.

Cottage Three was the one that Noël Coward bought. A family from Philadelphia have recently sold it; when they come on the market the cottages go for around $1 million and rent for between $4600 and $11,000 a week (in summer there are two-weeks-for-one offers). The US publishing entrepreneurs Si and Donald Newhouse come and rent at Round Hill every year. In 1998 Bob Pitman, one of several people claimed to be the founder of MTV, and now the president of America Online, bought Cottage Six. Lady Dufferin, a featured star of

Noël Coward's diaries, had Cottage Twelve until she died, also in 1998. Like Goldie Hawn and Kurt Russell, Steven Spielberg always stays in the cottage owned by his fellow director Robert Zemeckis; Peter Rockefeller and his family are regularly in residence. Paul McCartney rents a cottage every Christmas, but, being cool, takes a boat every afternoon to a local beach a couple of bays along, hanging out at its couple of ramshackle rum bars and Rasta cook shacks. 'This is the only place in the world I can do that,' he told Josef Forstmaya.

To my surprise I find that Round Hill is low on the absolute peace scale. From early in the morning extraneous noises abound: toilets flush, waves lap, guests sneeze and cough, children hit each other, musical religious exhortations sail crashingly out from a loudspeaker van travelling along the coast road.

But the food is superb. A self-service buffet defeats the Jamaican 'soon come' problem with waiter service, and at the regular Friday 'Jamaica Night' I had what was quite possibly the best meal I have ever had on the island: enormous, succulent pieces of lobster; ackee with great chunks of saltfish; breadfruit dripping with butter. And, rather in the ironic way that Marco Pierre White might serve bread-and-butter pudding, one of the desserts was the peasant-ghetto dish of 'bun 'n' cheese': currant bread stuffed with processed cheese, a dietary staple of impoverished Jamaicans. The two blonde braided girls were ecstatic: here was yet more authenticity served up on a plate.

Although a stay at Round Hill does carry the danger that you might believe the rest of Jamaica is simply an extension of the hotel, anyone who has discovered Jamaica comes back for more. You can see the attraction: whatever the season, there is the tropical warmth tempered by a sea breeze, a beach seemingly composed of the purest sand, the reassuring, mysterious palm trees and the flashing colours of the flowers, as well as an extremely agreeable pace of life.

Its appeal was summed up by Ralph Lauren, who designed china and linen for Round Hill. He sees Jamaica, he told

Forstmaya, as an English-speaking African country in the Caribbean, one that allows him to enjoy all the emotional highs of that continent in a language he can understand. It is, he said, like a great cashmere sweater: it always fits, and it never goes out of style.

June 1998

In 1998, after over thirty years of effort, Jamaica at last achieved its ambition of reaching the final thirty-two teams at the FIFA football World Cup, in France in this instance. Jamaica was thereby the first English-speaking Caribbean island to progress so far. Would its footballers equal the exploits of such previous romantic underdogs as the Cameroons, eight years previously? In the eyes of the soccer-loving media Jamaica immediately acquired a similar mouse-that-roared status to the African nation: the cliché was coined of the island being 'everyone's favourite second team'.

The Jamaican national soccer team had come far from the days in 1974 when seventeen players were suspended for 'poor behaviour' during a fixture in Bermuda in the preliminary rounds of that year's World Cup. In France in 1998 Jamaica was able to present its most positive collective face since the reign of Bob Marley, himself a fanatical footballer: in fact, the Tuff Gong had wavered between a career in music and one as a soccer-player – his close friend, Alan 'Skill' Cole, was a star player for the national side, and for a time left the island to coach in Ethiopia.

It was back in 1966 that the precedents had been set for Jamaica's journey to France: Jorge Penna, a Brazilian coach, was taken on to shape the national team, in the vain hope that it would be ready in time to play at the World Cup being held in England that year. When the qualification for the 1998 competition came on 16 November 1997, after Jamaica's final qualifying match against El Salvador, it was again under a Brazilian – the team manager Rene Simoes, formerly in charge of the Brazilian Under-21 squad. 'The Jamaican team was unique in France,' he said. 'It qualified without money, without facilities, without professionalism. This is not just football: the Reggae Boyz is an idea and a dream.'

Social circumstances unique to the island had at first presented Simoes with special difficulties. 'Every footballing nation reflects its culture,' he told me over dinner at Kingston's Terra Nova hotel, three months after the competition.

African players have rhythm, so people think Jamaicans must have that. But these people also come from slavery. In slavery the strong people were split up. So at first I had eleven players and eleven teams. Also some Rasta players left because they were told they couldn't smoke marijuana: at the World Cup Jamaica was the only country tested for drugs. But all along I refused to accept the common belief that Jamaicans won't work, that they can't run their country properly, that they are lazy. And we proved that that is all nonsense.'

With a team that usefully employed a pack of players of Jamaican descent from the top two English divisions – Robbie Earle and Marcus Gayle from Wimbledon, Deon Burton from Derby, Fitzroy Simpson from Portsmouth – Jamaica had triumphed in the preliminary rounds over an opposition that included teams from El Salvador, Canada, Mexico, and the United States. The match in Mexico City had erupted into violence: several of the Jamaican side had dived into the crowd to physically express their disapproval of the barracking they were receiving. And the game in Washington D.C. was almost lost immediately after half-time when a penalty was awarded against Jamaica; it was for an infringement that television cameras showed to be a good two feet outside the box. Before conspiracy theorists could even express their beliefs that FIFA must surely be insisting on the USA playing in the final 32 nations, Deon Burton had sprinted to the other end of the pitch and equalised.

When Prime Minister P. J. Patterson's People's National Party made the snap announcement at the beginning of December 1997 that an election would be held before Christmas, no one doubted that their subsequent victory was partially due to the football team's achievement. (On the hugely popular phone-in radio show that Wally Perkins hosts you would hear ample proof. 'So what has the PNP done for us?' 'Well, there is the France thing . . .') No matter how disingenuous were the PNP's endeavours to co-opt the triumph of the football team, the success of the 'Reggae Boyz' – the sobriquet inevitably bestowed on them – brought a sense of unity to a Third World country riven by schism; that election was the most peaceful that Jamaica ever had experienced.

The games in France were preceded by matches in England, including one against London's Queens Park Rangers, who the Caribbean side beat 2–1. A Jamaican pastor travelled with the Reggae Boyz, doubling as counsellor, part of an approach by Simoes that he told me was 'on three levels – physical, psychological, and spiritual'. One of his main concerns, he said, lapsing into therapy-speak, was 'to create genuine self-esteem, instead of just ego – a common problem in Jamaica'.

When it came to the actual tournament in France, however, Jamaica proved unable to emulate the wily confidence and consummate agility of the Cameroons. Gone was the fluency and co-ordination shown in the earlier rounds of the tournament. Jamaica were unable to progress further than the first round: notwithstanding a spectacular bicycle kick goal from Robbie Earle at the beginning of the second half, they endured a 3–2 defeat by Croatia, who finished third in the tournament; then went down 5–0 to Argentina. Their only victory was the 1–0 win over Japan, again after a Robbie Earle goal.

What had gone wrong? And why? One thing in particular, said Simoes. In France, there had been a set of circumstances of which no one but the players was aware: the team, who were somewhat naïve about the cynical practices of some branches of the media, had been devastated by a condescending, tabloid-style documentary broadcast on British television the night before their first match, with Croatia. Watching the programme in their hotel in Lens, the Jamaica team saw a show centred on Portsmouth player Fitzroy Simpson, in which the full scale of what seemed his gargantuan ambitions portrayed him as a comprehensive fool. Yet the disparaging vision presented by the documentary was a consequence of selective editing, claimed Simoes: the irony behind much of Simpson's remarks was missed out. Plenty of positive footage had been shot by the crew. Why did they have to angle the editing the way they did? 'It destroyed the players,' said the manager. 'I spent the next morning from 8 a.m. to 1 p.m. talking to them, trying to rebuild their morale.'

'The TV show turned it round, causing us huge psychological problems,' confirmed Walter Boyd, Jamaica's super-star striker and midfield footballer. 'But Fitzroy is still my favourite player.'

Trumpeted as the 'bad boy' of the team (something of a compliment in Jamaica), Walter Boyd admitted to having gone through a steep learning curve. 'I know now that once you start working for something you can attain it. Also, I'd thought we were a powerful force, but realized how much better we can do.'

Walter 'The Pearl' Boyd lives at the tiny spotless house of his mother with Letitia, his two-year-old daughter, off Mountain View Road, in the shadow of the National Stadium, where Jamaica's games are played. Unbeknownst to Boyd, this is only a few hundred yards from the home of Skill Cole, in nearby Vineyard Town. Until Simoes arrived to drive Jamaica through its twenty qualifying matches to reach France, Boyd was the superstar of Jamaican football. The Argentine Diego Maradona was his hero, perhaps not the best role model. Boyd's chronically indisciplined timekeeping at first led to him being dropped from the national team: it was as though he was the personification of a celebrated national problem. 'My relationship with Rene was a nightmare,' he admits. 'At one point I was at the top of my country, and then the next moment at the bottom.'

When Jamaica went to play the USA in Washington D.C., Boyd was dropped from the side (Simoes received an anonymous death threat over this decision). The crisis seems to have brought him to his senses. Paying for his own fare, he travelled up to New York, to where the team were staying, prior to their match in the American capital. There he prostrated himself before Simoes, begging his forgiveness. As a consequence of so looking into himself, Walter Boyd played in all three of the French matches. What did he think to the complement of English players in the team? 'They were good guys. I wanted them there. But not if I was going to be left out. Fitzroy was my favourite. My room-mate. But that TV show turned it round for us all.'

Without dwelling on the disappointment ('For this first time in the World Cup we just went to see it and check it out'), Boyd could see the positive effects that the soccer team's success had brought his country: the previous week Boyd had been the star attraction in a football match between two rival ghettoes that for years had only competed with guns. 'The last election was the most peaceful, and I think football had a lot to do with it. Every kid has started juggling a ball – now everywhere is just football, football, football. Whole nation has gone mad about football.'

Although even in 1995, the players on Jamaica's national team -in a country that has no professional league – were being paid only $US100 a week. Simoes changed that, negotiating wages for his footballers of $US3500 a month. Now the twenty-six-year-old Walter Boyd can afford to drive to local matches in his Toyota Camry. More importantly, when he steps outside of his mother's home he can look up to the bluff jutting out high above him. There lies Beverley Hills, where he now owns a plot of land given to him – one was presented to all the national players – for his part in France '98. Boyd was looking for more than this, though: when I visited him at his mother's house, he was considering an offer from a Korean club. Eventually, he decided against it.

By autumn 1999, however, the name of Walter Boyd is celebrated any time I turn on Sky Sports and hear football reports about Third Division Swansea: he has become the leading goal-scorer of the Welsh side, a secret weapon that plays a large part in their winning of the Division and securing promotion.

No doubt he would have preferred playing with Manchester or Leeds United, but perhaps it is as Rene Simoes says of the Jamaica '98 team: 'What these players did, they will not get the benefit of entirely – but their children and grandchildren will.'

Mr Kill-One-Of-Them-Now, the character who asked me where the 'greenbacks' are, is standing on the landing onto which I am pushed. As I walk towards him, he suddenly makes as though to stab me with his knife. Reversing it with gunfighter-like sleight of hand, he slams the handle into my chest three times. I am surprised by this, and stagger as I am pushed through an open doorway into another bedroom, and am relieved to see Peter there, alive and unhurt. I am becoming exhausted.

Everyone in the house is now locked inside this room. Peter and I are pushed under a bed; I'm behind him, nearest the wall. 'Get in there, Chris. Keep away from these mad guys who want to hurt you,' says one of the reasonable ones.

I hear the door shut and the key turned. What are they going to do now? Set the house on fire?

No: they are tearing the place to pieces.

Then everything seems to be about to go off again. We once again seem in danger of death. Mr Psycho is back. 'You lied to us: you said there was no money here. Now mi find all this Chinese money.' I realize we are not dealing with a very bright chap. I find myself starting to say that this money has no value at all, it is only souvenir money. But I keep quiet; whatever I do may make things worse. Maybe if they believe the money has value, they will simply take it and go.

But Ducky pipes up. She is almost shouting at him about his stupidity: 'No, man, you can't spend that: it worthless.'

Other members of the gang begin castigating him. We hear snatches of a conversation. ''Im say 'im be here by twelve. 'Im late. It twelve fifteen now.'

After a few minutes it sounds as though perhaps they have left. But is this also a trick? Everyone suddenly starts talking and joking. I tell them to be quiet for a few more minutes.

245

Then someone finds a crowbar inside the room and the door is jemmied open. We emerge, looking round nervously. The house is empty.

August 1995–2000

Four days after the hold-up I am sitting on the verandah of my cottage at Strawberry Hill. It is around one o'clock in the afternoon. I am beginning to come down from the Port Antonio incident, and feel reassured by the presence of the Strawberry Hill security. I notice that it has suddenly begun to rain the customary fat tropical drops of water.

All of a sudden there is a violent crack of thunder, and a fork of lightning flashes down, almost on top of me. Exploding violently, it smashes into the hotel's satellite dish that is tucked about twenty yards below my new home. Sparks fly up into the sky and for a few seconds the underside of a tree branch is set alight, almost immediately extinguished by the downpour. I dive off the metal chair on which I have been sitting into my cottage, and lie on the floor against the wall, amazed, baffled, quite frightened, as the thunder crashes and lightning jags about; the rain smashes down like you've never seen it. Are the elements now conspiring against me as well? Or is this all part of some complex welcome that Jamaica has laid on for me? *Here's something for you to think about for the next few months!*

The gunmen have cut the telephone lines. The boy who jemmied open the door sets off on a bicycle into town to the police station. On the way he will find Peter's passport tossed in the middle of the road.

What have they taken? Travellers' cheques worth US$500 and a laptop computer from Peter, a cellular phone and a Walkman from me. Not very much for all that fuss, when shared between so many gang members. But plenty of robberies in Jamaica seem to yield even leaner hauls. I am very glad to be still in possession of my life: I hadn't really expected it.

We are all sitting at the bottom of the stairs, slumped and numb, when the police turn up about an hour later. There are two of them: one is one of life's sidekicks; the other is an apprentice superstar cop in his early thirties, part of the special crime-busting task force known as ACID (Anti-Crime Investigation Department). He is in plain clothes: baseball cap, sneakers, jeans, T-shirt, guns bulging out at various angles. Confident and intelligent, he asks a series of pertinent questions before sprinkling fingerprint dusting powder about, transmogrifying from Clint Eastwood to a Sherlock Holmes of the Caribbean.

Even as I'm driving to the police station the next morning, I'm still thinking what a fantastic place this town is, though I'm also scanning the sidewalks for faces I might recognize from last night.

The CID room at the police station in Port Antonio is a trip. Clumps of officers, in crisp Red Stripe uniforms and in motley plain clothes, are dotted about the place, resting on desks or standing with ramrod straightness, watching a cricket match on a state-of-the-art television set that is obviously recovered stolen property: it sits atop a pile of further TVs, ghetto-blasters, hi-fis and microwaves. Loud cheers occasionally erupt.

Peter and I are interrogated at opposite ends of the room. I draw the apprentice superstar cop. He says that they sound to be a gang that of late has operated in these parts. Then his cellular rings; he excuses himself and runs out of the room, checking the gun he openly wears today in a holster on his waist. When he returns, he tells me that the phone call was a tip-off that a notorious badman was out by Titchfield Point. But he was unable to find him. He takes very detailed notes about the robbery and says he feels there's a chance of catching the gang. However, I never hear anything more about it.

By contrast, Peter's interrogator, a very young detective,

scruffy in a suit and tie, seems to be of a staggering level of stupidity. While he laboriously writes down an answer that he has been given, Peter swivels round on his chair to watch the cricket. The detective thwacks him across the fingers with a pencil. 'Pay attention!' he snaps.

Eventually we find out that the gang had come in through the back door – they had got hold of Darcus, a young guy staying in one of the outhouses, held a gun to his head and ordered him to call out for Ducky to open the door and let him in to go to the bathroom.

'What do you think? Bunch of guys taking the piss?' asked Peter the next day. I don't really think so – but maybe … Aren't situations that end in mayhem often just the result of a few guys taking the piss? I know that some of them genuinely were motivated by having nothing. Peter thought he caught a vibe of their being police. But maybe it was more the sense of a professional bunch who'd done many jobs like this: I noted the way they moved swiftly and methodically through the house.

There are so many crickets that they roar at night. The rustling through the slats at Strawberry Hill – wind, small animals – makes me start. I'm the only person staying here tonight, kind of a romantic notion, very Graham Greene, really. It's edgy, this Jamaican world. I hope I've got the balance again: go with the flow, accept the inevitable but be cool and no harm will occur. And it didn't. But it's left its repercussions.

Because you think you are going to die, you live more intensely at those moments than you ever have in your life. I have talked to other people who have had similar experiences; Cedella Marley, for instance. It had happened to her the summer before at her home on Skyline Drive on Jack's Hill, a very upscale suburb overlooking Kingston, the first level ground up into the Blue Mountains on the road to Gordon Town. Five gunmen broke in, tied her up, ransacked the place for about an hour and left. 'No one who hasn't been through that knows what it's like,' she says to me, and she's right. She also had thought she was going to die,

249

largely because she knew the rules, as she would.

(A couple of years later, in the run-up to the 1997 election, a gateman was abducted from 56 Hope Road, causing the entire Marley family to leave the island within the next twenty-four hours. The gateman was never seen again.)

There are other people I've talked to: a friend who underwent a lengthy knifepoint rape; someone who was almost killed in a car smash. Both had thought that that was it: they weren't getting out of it. 'It changes your life for ever,' they both said, 'because you think you are going to die.' Because we have all had experiences from which we believed we were not coming back we feel a common bond. And as you get older, I suppose, you meet more people who've had that experience.

Does it change you for ever? After a while, you sort of forget about it and just get on with life, but it's only *sort of*. And it creates a new set of complexities. How would I react next time? I can't forget that I felt guided on that night. I did feel my prayers were answered; I did feel a presence come into me and guide me – no doubt about it at all. Think I'm a prat, if you like, but I know I felt the spirit of Bob Marley there, helping me through it. One of the gang said he knew I'd done work for Bob, and this seemed to stand me in good stead. I think it was after that that I first felt Bob. I told Cedella this and she said, 'Of course, man. I felt exactly the same thing. Bob was there with me, helping me through it.' This is Jamaica, after all. And it still didn't prevent me from suspecting it was unlikely we would survive. I tried to inject some calm into the scenario, to try to lead it without that being obvious. It seemed to be running out of control, the scent of panic was in the air: had some of them been doing coke or crack? This was worrying.

Six months later I was still having counselling, telling my therapist I was beginning to stop looking over my shoulder. I was just stumbling along that night. I nearly lost it. I was so numb I didn't even know I was numb.

Yet in some very odd way I feel as though I had longed for this for a long time. At that moment I came into my own. It was like something I'd been waiting all my life to do, some Very Big Test. Is this the reason men go and play paintball and video shoot-'em-up games? Was it some necessary rite of passage without which I wouldn't have felt I had grown to manhood, in these years in which Westerners are mainly protected from the vulgarity of human conflict?

For me, having grown up on a culture of cowboys and Indians – and thinking the Indians were the good guys – Jamaica's gunman culture had always held a certain fascination. But very quickly I had found it wasn't like listening to a Clash record; going to Tapper Zukie's place and seeing the guns had made me realize that. Moreover, I was so obviously white: was it at all possible not to be a stranger in a strange land?

I still didn't know what it was about. A simple hold-up, sure. But don't we create situations through our previous actions that we need to learn from? Had I been present at this robbery as a way of exorcising all the anger and bad situations around and inside me for so many months? Was it to make my war-hero dad proud of me? (Of course, not wanting my parents to be worried every time I went away, I never told him about it.) Did it enable me to comprehend something of the hell that many of my father's generation had gone through? And I wonder if there is any genetic predisposition in this. Hadn't my father insisted we always had our passports in order, in case we might suddenly have to split? As he had, of course. My dad, whose refugee status always made me associate and identify with outsiders. He had been a stateless person until 1956: I remember his joy and also his relief when he received his UK naturalisation papers.

I discover that the temptation to linger on a past terror successfully evaded is almost inescapable: but as it only succeeds in drawing up various potentially horrific alternative endings it is best avoided. Then I began to find out some of the background to the incident.

In the middle of the 1980s my English friend Peter finds some stunning virgin land on and behind the virtually unknown, quite fabulous Heaven Beach. He can't buy it, but it is very cheap to rent, US$200 a year. He arranges to give his friend Mike half-ownership in a house if Mike, who has certain Boy Scout-like abilities, will build it.

On the beach Mike meets a local youth, who is in his late teens. They talk. His name is Buju. Mike tells him of his plans to build a house there. At first sharing a tent on the beach together, Mike and Buju begin to build the house. Buju has never known a white man before. A true brotherhood grows between them that dilutes qualities in Mike that might otherwise give cause for concern: although very 'right-on' (itself a little worrying), he is somewhat colonial in manner, almost dangerous in his innocence. For his part Buju is the son of a thief, and at the age of five used to be lowered into homes through windows and told to go and open the door. His more recent character development seems to have been honest, however, and he has been a prized protégé of the local 'coster' (a sort of equivalent of a councillor).

Mike's judgement appears to be astute. On one occasion some local youth steals their wheelbarrow; Mike discovers who has done it, marches into town, confronts the thief, and makes him wheel it back from town along the road to the beach. This earns him great kudos and respect.

The house soon takes on a structure and they begin to live inside it. Mike has been on sabbatical from his job for an international charity. Now he goes back to his job in New York, flying all around the world, but returns to Jamaica as often as he can.

The charity has a mission in Moscow. In Red Square he meets Olga, a very beautiful, extremely sexy Czechoslovakian girl, who is an art student there. They hit it off – she plays bass in a Czech reggae group and is, of course, fascinated by his Jamaica connection. They fall in love and after ten days are married.

At parties in London he shows off his new bride, who is in the process of receiving all appropriate visas. Then he takes her back to Jamaica with him. There she makes no attempts to modify her behaviour to fit in with the requirements of the place. She goes out into town at night scantily clad, getting drunk, flirting with guys; once she causes Mike almost to have a fight over her with some guy. She doesn't do Mike's reputation any good.

Mike goes back to New York, leaving Olga in Jamaica. Not a good decision. She continues going out at night to the bars, flirting with inappropriate men. One night she meets one who doesn't take no for an answer. She walks home alone, along the abandoned railway track: he follows her, knocks her over the head with a rock and rapes her.

She calls Mike in New York. He flies back immediately. He discovers that everyone knows who has raped Olga. Incensed at this violation of his wife, he talks to Buju: does he know any hitmen in the area? Buju does – this is Jamaica, after all. Forty thousand Jamaican dollars (around £800) is handed over to a man called Slengteng, and the rapist is never seen again.

But after a time Slengteng comes to the house and demands more money. And then he keeps returning to the house, wanting more and more cash to keep quiet. They pay him off a few times and then tell him they have no more money. He threatens them. They take on a pair of security guards – men with sticks. To you or me it would perhaps seem time to relocate. Except that Olga doesn't want to leave, because she is finally in a 'proper' JA reggae group: she has turned the house into a studio and found a crew of musicians. 'I went round there and this girl had turned the living space into a rehearsal area,' someone told me.

The place was full of dread musicians, and she was dancing around in front of them, swinging her behind. The inevitable happened. Which caused huge problems for her husband, because the respect had gone as a result. She didn't seem to realize that there were unwritten codes of conduct that she should have adhered to. You could see what was coming. And just to add to this, Heaven has one of those tribes of relatives that on a British council estate would be known as a problem family.

Olga and Buju fall out over her bringing in all these people who he believes are going to cause Mike trouble. Buju moves to the end of the beach and sets up a little wooden shop and food shack. Then Mike and Buju fall out: Mike claims Olga finds Buju going through one of their suitcases. One night when Mike and Olga have gone into town, Slengteng comes round again, and shoots and cripples one of the security guards.

After this, Mike and Olga finally decide to leave Heaven.

That was a year or so before I had stayed at the house while writing the Bob Marley book – but no one had told me about it. And now there is a further irony. I have allowed Olga and Mike to stay in my house in London while I am in Jamaica: they are there at the very time the stick-up is taking place. Everyone keeps telling me that Mike is a really good guy, and he has agreed to decorate my house in return.

But when I have to go to London briefly, less than a month after the stick-up, I find that the attitudes that had caused the problems in Port Antonio have been imported to my home there. The person doing the decorating is a guy with whom Olga had been having an affair at the house in Heaven; she is clearly in the midst of another affair; and she has even made a pass at a woman friend who is also staying at my place. I'm all for freedom of expression, but I've already seen some of the results of this behaviour, and I can feel imminent problems. Besides, I'm pissed off with her and her husband: their frightening naivety came close to hastening my end, it seems to me. I ask them to leave, which seems to really surprise them.

Very shortly afterwards, Olga dumps her husband for good. He is devastated, although he later builds a better life.

Later I find they had consciously embarked on the difficult, dangerous road of an open marriage, but hadn't bothered to tell anyone around them that this was the case – if they had, it might have helped us to make sense of their actions (but in Jamaica?). When I ask him if he'd hired a gunman to get rid of the rapist, he denies it, of course. He attributes all sorts of venality to Buju, who has told me much of this. And, as we know, there are always at least a billion sides to every story.

Throughout the hold-up I never stopped praying: I thought I wasn't going to see my children again, or anyone else – my mum, my dad, the whole deal – this may well be it. There was a giant numinous sense of awe overhanging the house. The air was stark. My nose down in them, I could smell the strongly acrid wood of the insecticide on the boards (all the same, the floor was cleaner than it would have been at my own house!). The guy who tied me up hit me in the kidneys, which seemed a bit unnecessary. (Since then my kidneys have occasionally hurt.)

When they were ushering us to the back room, I was feeling close to losing it. Did the psycho read it in my eyes? By the time he stepped forward from the shadows, whipped out a giant knife . . . and smashed the butt of it against my chest three times, once on either side, once in the centre . . . by then, I was floating on a cushion of exhaustion and fear and a sort of curious exhilaration that I had made this next step. Everything seemed to be only in the present tense.

But, perhaps unsurprisingly, all my history there, in Jamaica and especially Heaven, came back to me. Had all my time in this place I loved simply been leading to this? Had it all been worked out to this moment? These were some of the things I thought about. It was a puzzle.

The fear lasted for about ten weeks. Then I went off somewhere and had a good time and largely forgot about it, although an edginess remained, a need to keep looking over my shoulder, an automatic locking of all the car doors as soon as I got inside it. Gradually that also went away.

It cannot be denied that this sort of earthquake-like situation does rather shift your perspective: thinking you're about to die has a certain focusing quality. On the other hand, for countless men and women in World Wars I and II such experiences have been commonplace. And all over the world – East Timor, Rwanda, the former Yugoslavia – such incidents are unsettlingly everyday. So who am I to go on about it? Do I simply now have a comprehension of the world-view and stance of people who have been in such terrifying situations? Was this what it was all about? To make me understand this?

Nine weeks after the stick-up I drive back to Heaven on an afternoon visit to show a friend the place. This is the first time I have been back. When we pull up at Buju's place, he greets me warmly. Then he whispers to me, so that no one can hear, 'Funny you come today. Only this morning Slengteng was sitting at that table, making calls on your cellular.'

The hold-up, I am told by Buju, was committed by a gang connected to Slengteng, market traders like himself, who came in from Kingston at the end of every week. From the bill that I got, the calls registered to my cellular phone after the theft were to numbers in Portmore, the Kingston overspill town.

When I go down to Heaven Beach for a swim in the sea, I tread on a sea urchin. It is momentarily paralysing. 'All I wanted was a peaceful swim,' I say to my companion, looking from out at sea at the house where I'd been in serious trouble.

Later in the evening I take Buju for a run in the car up the road so he can ask me what Peter's thoughts are about the house. (He didn't want to talk about the place in front of the other guys at his yard.) I tell him I don't know what Peter is thinking. I do a U-turn and run him down the road. Turn back here, he says, at the corner before his bar. But there's a motorcycle behind me and it's not easy to stop. I drive down to the bar. There's a scarlet pick-up truck parked with its nose sticking out onto the edge of the road, as though on starting blocks. 'Slengteng's,' Buju mutters to me. Is this a little overly dramatic? Or just Jamaica runnings? And should I wonder why Buju is so familiar with the hitman?

Some time later Peter returns to Heaven Beach with a friend and goes to check Buju. As they stand talking in his yard a pair of police squad-cars swoop up on them! Barechested, barefoot, Buju is off across the hard rockstone into the bush, police firing their guns after him. Some months later he is charged with possession of 'gunshots' and the rape of an elderly woman who is staying in the house – the charges are later dropped. Then there are rumours that his yard is where badmen stash their guns on the way into town. Who knows what happened?

The words of John Boorman, when he was publicizing his film *The General*, seem to explain why I still love Jamaica, though I am aware that the place is a double-edged sword. The film is about gang life in Ireland, but as we know, there are certain distinct Ireland–Jamaica parallels:

I think you're getting closer to what human nature is in those places. For better or worse, you recognize the truth of it. Psychologically and emotionally, we haven't really adjusted to the level of civilization that we've attained. That's the great conflict in human beings, between the savagery that remains with us and the civilization we aspire to. Most of us try to find ways of not resorting to violence. It's why nature is such a marvellous metaphor for the human condition. We can admire its majesty, but its violence is always present.

November 1998

Nine years ago Sir Nooshie became a gunman in Trench Town; he had just turned fourteen years old.

Thanks to the songs of Bob Marley, who grew up in that part of the Jamaican capital, the name of the Kingston ghetto of Trench Town is known across the world. Yet since the near civil war of the 1970s, it had become a murderous hellhole divided up by various gangs of killers, often no more than teenagers. Sir Nooshie never professed any political allegiance; how else than by taking up the gun, he had reasoned, could he survive in dirt-poor Trench Town?

Nooshie was good at his new job: stick-ups, protection rackets, the lethal despatch of rival gang members. So ruthless was his reign of terror that before he left his teens he had become one of the area's 'dons'. But when his closest friend was gunned down in front of him last year, Sir Nooshie finally woke up. 'If people see a man like me change, anybody can change,' he said. 'Now I never know life so sweet.'

Nooshie, intelligent and with movie-star good looks, is the greatest current success of Bobby Wilmott, a pastor whose mission is to save Trench Town from itself.

Wilmott's protégé tells his story while standing in the dusty, battered yard in front of the Joytown Remedial Centre, the Trench Town secondary school at which the one-time gunman now teaches full time. Even before Sir Nooshie finally gave up his former occupation, the fruits of which are evident in his crisp Tommy Hilfiger and Nike clothing, he used to teach maths and English at evening adult-education classes at the school. For the privilege of being taught by this articulate gunman don, students would pack his classes. Now Nooshie's message is clear. 'I don't have to tell you who I am,' he announced to his class. 'I have been a gunman. But I say to you, "Put down the guns. Don't take up the drugs." '

(For myself, a considerable blurring of reality takes place as Sir Nooshie tells me his story. The previous day I have visited the set of *Third World Cop*, a film I have co-written, the reason I came to Jamaica in 1995, when the hold-up took place. The shoot was in the ghetto of Standpipe, a few miles away. *Third World Cop* stars Paul Campbell, the moody actor who played the villain in *Dancehall Queen*. With almost the entire ghetto as his audience, he had chased badmen up and down alleyways, exuding his meanest Spaghetti Western postures. Meanwhile, local dons had extracted the maximum tax possible for allowing the filming to take place.)

Bobby Wilmott, who is thirty-eight years old, is a principal minister in the Jamaican Covenant Community Church, one of the many Baptist churches in the country. Baptists were vocal opponents of slavery, and the church's popularity has never waned. Wilmott exudes righteousness, his smiling eyes flashing with the fervour of his mission.

'Change Trench Town and you change Jamaica,' Bobby Wilmott decided when he began to hold services there in 1989; his first church was the shade of a large mango tree. Aware of the power of words, he whimsically renamed his parish of Trench Town as Joytown.

'Who yuh think yuh are to come to Trench Town?' local gunmen would ask him. Wilmott would stand tall while he gave his answer:

'I am also a badman, because of who I serve. I can fire gun like you. But I serve my God – he sent me here. Can you kill a dead man?'

'What yuh talk 'bout – a dead man is dead,' they'd say.

And I'd reply to that with the truth: 'The Bible tells me, You cannot kill a dead man, for I am dead to the world and alive in Christ.' Now I deal with respect. I have the full backing of the community.

Soon Wilmott saw that to effect real change in the area he should start with the future foundations of its society – its children. 'There were too many children not going to school. Because of expense, and also because there were not enough schools around, but mainly because it had often been dangerous to cross the area.'

In the shadow of the decayed shell of the Ambassador Theatre (where once Noël Coward watched Christmas pantomimes), Wilmott found a substantial abandoned building: a former Women's Institute, it still bears a cornerstone laid in 1947 by the wife of Sir Hugh Foot, the governor-general. Trench Town was a fashionable area until it went into decline in the 1950s. By the time Wilmott discovered the building in 1993, goats and chickens were wandering about its rubble-strewn floor. Because the building stood on a borderline between the territory of two gangs, it especially suited the pastor's purpose. 'We are into Jesus and Jesus came to break down the middle wall of partition,' he said, grinning knowingly.

With the help of his congregation, Bobby Wilmott restored the building. When local badmen would demand what he was doing, the preacher would tell them that he was starting a school. 'Do you want your children to grow up and fire gun like you?' he'd ask, and urge them to help him get the place into a usable condition. 'They wouldn't do that: they are big guys,' Wilmott said, with an ironic smile. 'When I first started working on the building, people would pass and say, "Yuh still dere?" I would tell them, "We are here to stay." '

Bobby Wilmott takes me the few hundred yards along a road running parallel with the Trench Town gully, past some dreads tending the land, creating a thriving market garden out of what used to be grim rubble, down to Second Street. At 19 Second Street, Bob Marley had lived with his mother Cedella. It was here that I had come to the cockfight with Valerie Cowan. 'Valerie may have been an uptown person, but she felt for all the ghetto,' says Bobby, who had known her well. Then he gives me a shock, confirming a rumour I'd once heard but had forgotten about: that Massive Dread, the 'singjay' for whom Valerie had been a mentor, had been gunned down at his home here on Second Street a couple of years after Valerie was killed. Although he wasn't certain, Bobby thought it was 'politics bisness'. Some men had apparently got into the building in which Massive was living, and gunned him down on the stairs.

This was the kind of thing that was on his mind in September 1994 when Wilmott opened the Joytown Learning Centre. His wife was headmistress, and the school had just twelve pupils. Today it teaches over a hundred children, with six teachers, all from surrounding streets, women of good education previously condemned to menial work or unemployment because of the address on their job applications – uptown Jamaicans dislike mixing with people from the ghetto.

All schools in Jamaica, where education is theoretically compulsory, now charge fees of some sort. But those for the Joytown Learning Centre are under a pound a week, and are often waived, such is the poverty. Sometimes Wilmott will come across mothers who deliberately don't pay their children's fees. But he realized he had won his spurs when local gunmen approached him about one such individual: 'Pastor, we understand someone dissed you. Do you want us to get rid of her?'

In order to prevent them from ever thinking along similar lines, the children's lessons are imbued with a rigorous morality; when the class of six-year-olds in unison recited their alphabet, it included the following definition: 'L is for labour for learning before you grow old, for learning is better than silver and gold. Silver and gold will vanish away, but a good education will never decay.' 'It is my intention,' said Bobby Wilmott, 'that the children will go home and quote such words to their parents.'

The children Sir Nooshie is teaching have not benefited from such a framework. In the Joytown Remedial Centre ('God's Advocates for the Disadvantaged') are around fifty pupils aged ten years and older with learning problems from their deeply dysfunctional environments and family backgrounds. 'Most of these children, 90 per cent of whom could not read or write, hardly ever had gone to school because it was too dangerous for them to venture into what was literally a war zone,' explained Lorna Stewart, a Jamaican returning resident, formerly a journalist in Palm Beach, who is the headmistress of the remedial centre.

Why did she come back to do this? 'I did it for the need. I saw children in terrible plight.'

Because they are consumed with anger, she said, many of the children fight each other with brutal compulsion. But the large task of saving their lives seems to be bearing fruit. Several children stood up in class and uttered similar words to those of Winston, who is twelve: 'When I first came to this school, I didn't even know when I was born. I could not read or know my ABC. And now I can and I am proud of myself.'

Bobby Wilmott looked on with optimistic pleasure. 'Correct the root of the problem,' he mused happily. 'Then you don't have to worry about the branches.'

Chris Salewicz has written about world popular culture for numerous publications, including the *Independent*, *Daily Telegraph* and *The Sunday Times*. He is the author of biographies of Jimi Hendrix, Paul McCartney, George Lucas, Oliver Stone, Noël Coward and Bob Marley. He has also worked in television and film, is co-screenwriter of *Third World Cop*, a Jamaican-set thriller.